INFINITE REGRESS

OCTOBER BOOKS

Rosalind Krauss, Annette Michelson, Yve-Alain Bois, Benjamin H. D. Buchloh, Hal Foster, Denis Hollier, and Silvia Kolbowski, editors

Broodthaers, edited by Benjamin H. D. Buchloh

AIDS: Cultural Analysis/Cultural Activism, edited by Douglas Crimp

Aberrations, by Jurgis Baltrušaitis

Against Architecture: The Writings of Georges Bataille, by Denis Hollier

Painting as Model, by Yve-Alain Bois

The Destruction of Tilted Arc: *Documents*, edited by Clara Weyergraf-Serra and Martha Buskirk

The Woman in Question, edited by Parveen Adams and Elizabeth Cowie

Techniques of the Observer: On Vision and Modernity in the Nineteenth Century, by Jonathan Crary

The Subjectivity Effect in Western Literary Tradition: Essays toward the Release of Shakespeare's Will, by Joel Fineman

Looking Awry: An Introduction to Jacques Lacan through Popular Culture, by Slavoj Žižek

Cinema, Censorship, and the State: The Writings of Nagisa Oshima, by Nagisa Oshima

The Optical Unconscious, by Rosalind E. Krauss

Gesture and Speech, by André Leroi-Gourhan

Compulsive Beauty, by Hal Foster

Continuous Project Altered Daily: The Writings of Robert Morris, by Robert Morris

Read My Desire: Lacan against the Historicists, by Joan Copjec

Fast Cars, Clean Bodies: Decolonization and the Reordering of French Culture, by Kristin Ross

Kant after Duchamp, by Thierry de Duve

The Duchamp Effect, edited by Martha Buskirk and Mignon Nixon

The Return of the Real: The Avant-Garde at the End of the Century, by Hal Foster

October: The Second Decade, 1986–1996, edited by Rosalind Krauss, Annette Michelson, Yve-Alain Bois, Benjamin H. D. Buchloh, Hal Foster, Denis Hollier, and Silvia Kolbowski

Infinite Regress: Marcel Duchamp 1910–1941, by David Joselit

Infinite Regress
Marcel Duchamp 1910–1941

David Joselit

An OCTOBER Book

The MIT Press
Cambridge, Massachusetts
London, England

This book was set in Bembo by Graphic Composition, Inc., Athens, Georgia.

Library of Congress Cataloging-in-Publication Data

Joselit, David.
Infinite regress : Marcel Duchamp 1910–1941 / David Joselit.
p. cm.
"An October book."
Includes bibliographical references and index.
ISBN 978-0-262-10067-0 (hc. : alk. paper) — 978-0-262-60038-5 (pb. : alk. paper)
1. Duchamp, Marcel, 1887–1968—Criticism and interpretation.
I. Title.
N6853.D8J67 1997
709'.2—dc21 97-28732
CIP

for Irvin Taube

in memory of Carl Insoft

Contents

Acknowledgments

I am fortunate in having had the guidance of an extraordinary community of scholars in writing the dissertation from which this book is drawn. The project was conceived while studying with Benjamin H. D. Buchloh at MIT. His rigorous understanding of Duchamp has continued to guide and stimulate me. I am enormously indebted to my primary adviser at Harvard, Yve-Alain Bois, whose close and provocative readings of this text have immeasurably improved it. His editorial advice has been matched by his sustained and good-humored assistance in bringing the project to publication. My far-ranging discussions with Norman Bryson have enriched not only this project but also my relationship to the changing definitions of the discipline of art history. Leila Kinney, in her grasp of theory and the opportunities and pitfalls of applying it to works of art, has been an important model. I owe a special debt of gratitude to Neil Levine, whose academic guidance and friendship have been invaluable to me for some twenty years.

My colleagues in the art history department at the University of California, Irvine have been very supportive of this project. I am particularly grateful to Jim Herbert, who took the time to read an early version of this text and to give me his rigorous and stimulating responses, many of which I have acted on. I have been the beneficiary of Dickran Tashjian's extensive knowledge of Duchamp and

New York dada, as well as his generosity in providing technical assistance. Sally Stein's lively and incisive reflections have long enriched my understanding of a wide range of art-historical issues. Jewel Wilson, our department manager, has been characteristically helpful and encouraging. I was drawn to Duchamp in large part through my curatorial work at The Institute of Contemporary Art in Boston between 1983 and 1989. To my former colleagues there, Elisabeth Sussman, Gillian Levine, Bob Riley, David Ross, Chriss Holderness, and Teil Silverstein I am grateful for many hours of stimulating discussion and debate. Naomi Sawelson-Gorse generously shared with me her vast knowledge of Duchamp and his patrons the Arensbergs and helped in acquiring photographs. Caroline Armacost at the Philadelphia Museum of Art was also particularly helpful in the course of photographic research, as were Jacqueline Matisse Monnier and Arturo Schwarz. André Burke graciously agreed to review my translations from French, and Dan Nadeau helped with design ideas. Many have supported me in this project through informal critical discussion. They include Roswell Angier, Margarita Crocker, Russell Ferguson, Paul Franklin, Susan Hawley, Karin Higa, Amelia Jones, Norman Kleeblatt, Ewa Lajer-Burcharth, Richard Meyer, Laurie Monahan, Steven Nelson, Pam Lee, David Román, Matthew Simms, Ann Temkin, Nancy Troy, Cécile Whiting, and Irene Winter. I am grateful to the Mellon Foundation for three dissertation research grants. Finally, this book is dedicated to two men: to my doctor and friend, Irvin Taube, with whom I had my first graduate education, and to the memory of my longtime companion Carl Insoft, who died just before I began writing the dissertation from which it is drawn. Although he is not present for the realization of this project, Carl's love and support have continued to sustain me.

Infinite Regress

Introduction

There is no single Marcel Duchamp but many. Even this apparently simple declaration must immediately be subdivided, for Duchamp's "plurality" refers equally to his artistic practice and his reception within art history. Strategies of self-multiplication—through the invention of discontinuous artistic styles and the adoption of an array of alter egos—are central to Duchamp's art. Not only did he explore several modernist idioms in quick succession, including fauvism, cubism, mechanomorphism, dadaism, and peripherally surrealism, he also invented several contradictory personae: artist and art dealer, conceptualist and craftsman, chess champion and dreamer, dandy and recluse. On different occasions he signed his works with aliases like R. Mutt or Rrose Sélavy or had himself photographed in women's clothing or with faunlike horns fashioned from shaving cream. This delirious play *of* and *with* identity within Duchamp's oeuvre is matched from the outside by the invention of a succession of "Duchamps" within the art-historical canon: Duchamp as alchemist, Duchamp as mathematician, Duchamp as critic of the institutions of art, and Duchamp as destabilizer of gender roles are among the most prominent.[1] This double plurality—both within and surrounding his oeuvre—is both dazzling and confounding for the commentator. Duchamp, as an author, and as a discursive field, is always on the verge of disappearing and reemerging elsewhere. This slippery nature of the object of study has led many of Duchamp's historians and critics in the post-war period emphatically to circumscribe the limits of their analysis to a single theme or body of works. In recent years this narrowing of focus has led to important localized insights about issues such as Duchamp's injection of carnality into vision through his optical researches of the twenties, the relationship between painting and the readymade, and the significance for gender theory of Duchamp's adoption of a feminine alter ego, Rrose Sélavy.[2] The drawback of this "spotlight effect" within Duchamp studies is that the artist's oeuvre is dismembered and its various limbs fetishized. We learn more about particular aspects of his career, but we are left with a nagging epistemological anxiety—"How do these parts add up?"

The ambition of *Infinite Regress* is to retain the plurality of identities and strategies within Duchamp's art between 1910 and 1941 while proposing a synthetic reading of his early and mid-career. I will argue that his work undergoes a series of transformations in this period—neither radical breaks nor simple continuities—between cubist painting in the early teens, his readymades and machine imagery of the mid-teens and early twenties, and the apparent disappearance of his art from the mid-twenties through the early forties. I will demonstrate that Duchamp's "plurality"—his array of seemingly discontinuous strategies—is organized around a consistent dynamic or interplay between materiality and its measure or the body and its (self-) identification. The title "Infinite Regress" refers to Duchamp's practice of establishing virtually limitless chains or spirals of identifications where one image, object, or self becomes simultaneously a thing to be measured and a standard of measurement. His fascination with the fourth dimension—which is too often read as a literal preoccupation with pseudo-science—is both a metaphor and a demonstration of the dynamic of transformation *en abyme* that characterizes his work: one-dimensional objects are seen as the diagram of a two-dimensional world; two-dimensional objects, as the projection of a three-dimensional world; and so on to infinity. What I have called Duchamp's plurality thus makes visible a transformative or transactual model of both the object world and the self wherein bodies, commodities, and identities are defined provisionally through various forms of measurement, inscription, or financial quantification. But in Duchamp's vertiginous universe, the form of measurement, inscription, or quantification always regresses to a mute materiality or carnality. The Duchamp that I want to bring to light, then, has invented a multilayered vision of exchange as the basis of representation: a vision that emerges at just that moment in the early twentieth century when capitalist structures of finance greatly expanded their powers of liquefying funds and reifying things. In developing this argument I have chosen to focus exclusively on Duchamp's art between 1910 and 1941 rather than on his subsequent critical reception. I am convinced that a broader and more synthetic analysis of Duchamp's various practices prior to World War II will be fundamental in reassessing his enormous artistic legacy in the postwar period. In the struggles to "possess" his art critically—whether as "Duchamp of the readymade" allegedly exposing the terms and ideologies of the art market or "Duchamp of Rrose Sélavy" who embodies the complexities of masquerade[3]—the only valid form of adjudication will emerge from a more sophisticated and nuanced understanding of Duchamp's complex production.

In the four chapters that follow I trace the development of Duchamp's transactual mode of representation from its earliest manifestation in his cubism to its "spatialization" in his virtually invisible readymade practices of the 1920s, '30s and '40s, such as the adoption of chess as an aesthetic model and his laborious projects of self-appropriation like the *Green Box* of 1934 and the early *Boîtes-en-Valise* of 1935–41, which reproduce his own notes or art objects as though they were discovered readymade. In chapter 1 I argue that in contradistinction to Picasso, whose cubism has been convincingly read as a dissolution of the body into a linguistic economy of signs,[4] Duchamp's cubism submits the apparently immensurable carnality of the female nude to a series of immanent and external forms of graphic measurement typically coded as masculine. Rather than demonstrating the transformation of the carnal into the scriptural, Duchamp establishes an aporia of measurement in which organic form is disciplined into a proto-geometry while endowing the supposedly weightless and universal terms of geometric measurement with the mass, volume, and even "volition" of bodies. This "infinite regress" of geometric quantification and organic immensurability is most vividly evoked in Duchamp's collagelike painting *Tu m'* of 1918 in which each visual component functions simultaneously as a thing-to-be-measured and a standard of measurement. In chapter 2 I demonstrate how Duchamp's readymade strategies of the teens transpose the terms of his cubist dialectic between immensurable carnality and geometric quantification to an opposition between commodities and the linguistic inscriptions that, in Duchamp's formulation, elevate manufactured objects to the status of art. This displacement of the body by the commodity, while central to Duchamp's move away from painting to the readymade, is not a simple allegory of reification. As my discussion of several under acknowledged readymades, textual works, and "simulated readymades"[5] of the teens and early twenties will show, Duchamp took pains to represent the commodity within the dynamic of exchange—caught in a perpetual cycle of emergence into form and regression into "liquidity." In works like *Tzanck Check* of 1919 or the *Monte Carlo Bond* of 1924, in which Duchamp reinvents the readymade as a financial instrument, he dramatizes the power of capitalism not simply to reify but also to dissolve, or deterritorialize, both objective form and subjective identity.

Chapter 3 concerns the metaphorical function of the machine. By situating Duchamp's *The Bride Stripped Bare by Her Bachelors, Even* or *Large Glass* of 1915–23 within a series of cultural redefinitions of industrial production and burgeoning consumption between 1885 and 1925, I argue that the Duchampian machine, and the dada machine more generally, operate as switching stations between the modern rationalization of the body and newly developing techniques of disciplining the mind—particularly through the colonization or commodification of desire. While the trope of the machine in modern art is often read as an optimistic celebration of the power of mechanization to reorder production by imposing new standards of efficiency on working bodies, Duchamp's malfunctioning and anachronistic apparatuses point equally to a mechanization of the "irrational" processes of the unconscious. I argue that the *Large Glass* signals a shift in Duchamp's oeuvre from a preoccupation with how the body and the commodity undergo "mensuration" or quantification to the mechanisms of the mind.

Chapter 4 explores what I would call Duchamp's spatialization of the unconscious through a renewed engagement with the readymade. I argue here that far from signaling his abandonment of art, Duchamp's pursuit of chess from the early twenties onward becomes a defining metaphor for a new topographical exploration of mental structures that encompasses both his optical devices of the twenties and his major acts of self-appropriation in the thirties, *The Green Box* and the *Boîte-en-Valise*. *Infinite Regress* thus traces one of the fundamental transformations in modern art. This book, like Duchamp, crosses the epistemological divide between cubism's profound effort—and heroic failure—to submit the modern body, or the "real," to representation and surrealism's invention of a "real" that resides not in flesh and blood but in desire and dream.

1

Mensuration *en abyme:* Marcel Duchamp's Cubism

> The *principal forms* of the bachelor machine are imperfect: rectangle, circle, parallelepiped, symmetrical handle, demi-sphere = i.e. they are mensurable (relation of their dimensions among themselves. and relation of these principal forms to their destination in the bachelor mach.) In the bride, the *principal forms* are *more or less large or* small, have no longer, in relation to their destination a mensurability: a sphere, in the bride will be of some radius or other (the radius given in the representation is fictitious and dotted.)
>
> Similarly and better in the Pendu femelle and the [wasp], parabolas hyperbolas (or volumes deriving from them) will lose all character of mensurable position. The actual representation will be but one *example* of each of these *principal freed forms.* (an example without representational value, but *permitting the more or less*).[1]

Marcel Duchamp's 1914 painting *Network of Stoppages* summarizes his cubist art. If we bracket Duchamp's 1916 version of the *Nude Descending a Staircase* executed in watercolor, ink, pencil, and pastel over a photographic reproduction as an "assisted readymade," then the *Network* is his penultimate painting. It also functions as a "last painting" of sorts, marking the beginning of a four-year period of

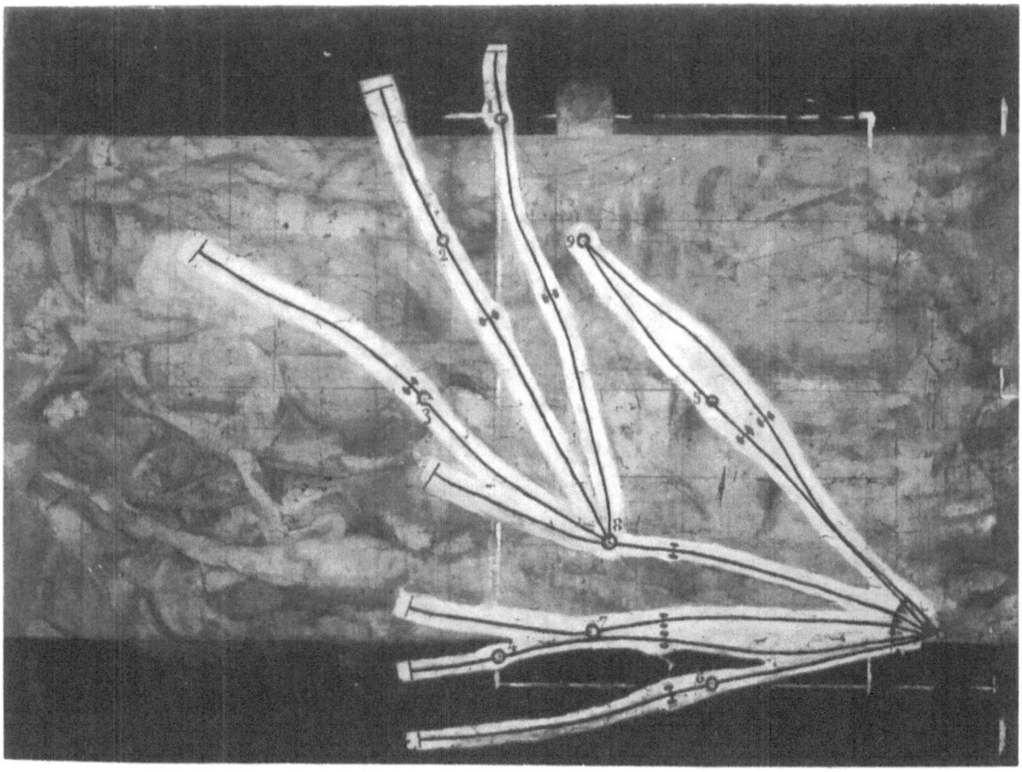

1.1 Marcel Duchamp. *Network of Stoppages* (*Réseaux des stoppages*). Paris, 1914. Oil and pencil on canvas, 58 ⅝″ × 77 ⅝″. The Museum of Modern Art, New York. Abby Aldrich Rockefeller Fund and gift of Mrs. William Sisler. Photograph © 1997 The Museum of Modern Art, New York. © 1997 Artists Rights Society (ARS), New York. ADAGP, Paris/Estate of Marcel Duchamp.

experimentation with language and the readymade—a period entirely without work on canvas until the execution of *Tu m',* his official last painting in 1918. But if the *Network,* like *Tu m',* has a valedictory dimension, it is also curiously regressive. By 1914 Duchamp had developed two sophisticated painterly idioms—a cubist vocabulary of fleshlike slabs of color and linear hinges and a precise and deadpan language of mechanical drawing. The *Network* does not belong to either of these idioms, at least not directly, and herein lies its mystery. Why, in 1914, after a short but productive period in which he developed a distinctive cubist practice, would Duchamp go back to a proto-cubist painting of 1911, *Young Man and Girl in Spring,* as the "ground"—both literally and figuratively—for a major work? Since Duchamp's cubism has often been considered a failed enterprise—little more than a phase preceding the more significant theoretical accomplishments of the readymade—this question calls for more than an art-historical solution to a vexing formal anomaly. Does the *Network of Stoppages* signify Duchamp's disavowal of cubism, or on the contrary does it function as a manifesto embodying a theoretical alternative to the inventions of Picasso and Braque?

Network of Stoppages is built from three superimposed visual systems: a version of the painting *Young Man and Girl in Spring* rotated 90 degrees and cropped by a black border at bottom and top; a half-scale layout sketch for Duchamp's canonical work on glass, *The Bride Stripped Bare by Her Bachelors, Even* or *Large Glass* of 1915–23,[2] and finally a view of nine capillary tubes, derived from the bachelors' region of the *Large Glass* and generated by Duchamp's aleatory deformation of the metric system, the *3 Standard Stoppages* of 1913–14. Like the *Glass,* which was conceived as an emphatically gendered, though failed, encounter between a bride, represented as a biomorphic abstraction in the upper half of the work on glass, and her bachelors whose machinic anatomies are projected in their own section below, *Network of Stoppages* suggests an eroticized struggle.[3] In this painting, an array of "capillary tubes," phallic organs that in the *Large Glass* are attached to the truncated torsos of the nine malic molds,[4] are locked in an optical embrace with a recumbant female form. For although *Young Man and Girl in Spring* nominally includes both a masculine and feminine figure, only the

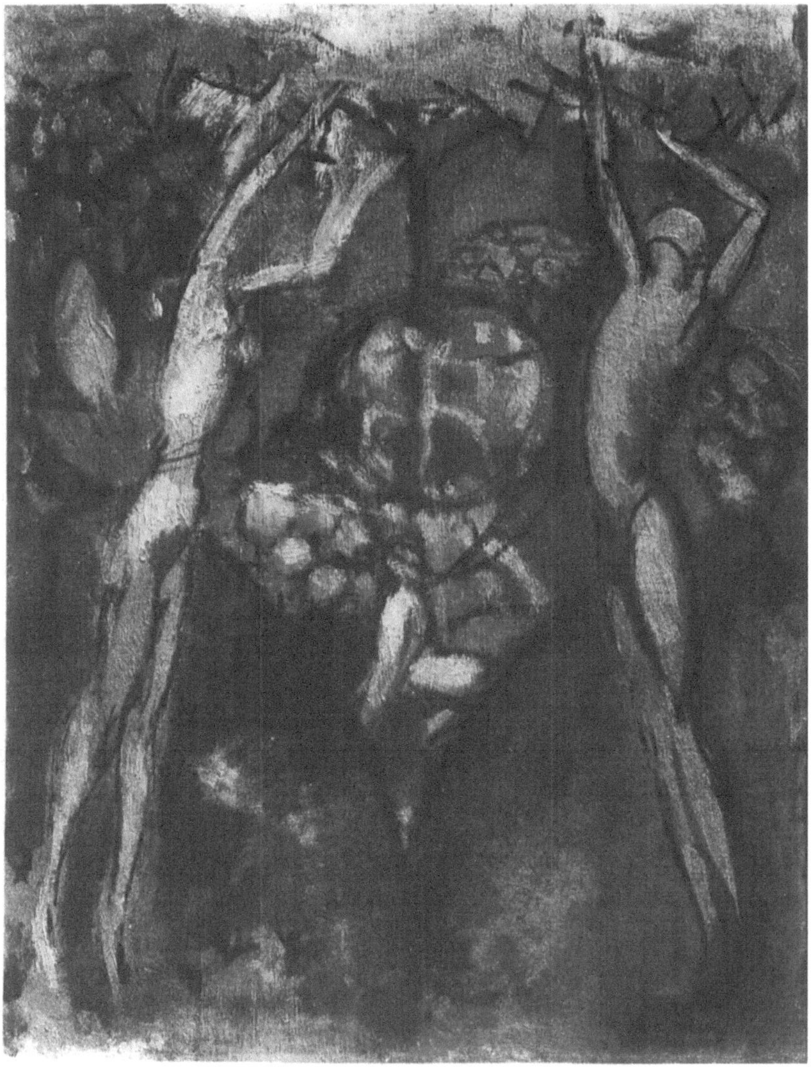

1.2 Marcel Duchamp. *Young Man and Girl in Spring.* Neuilly, 1911. Oil on canvas, 25 ⅞ × 19 ¾″. Arturo Schwarz Collection, Milan. © 1997 Artists Rights Society (ARS), New York/ADAGP, Paris/Estate of Marcel Duchamp.

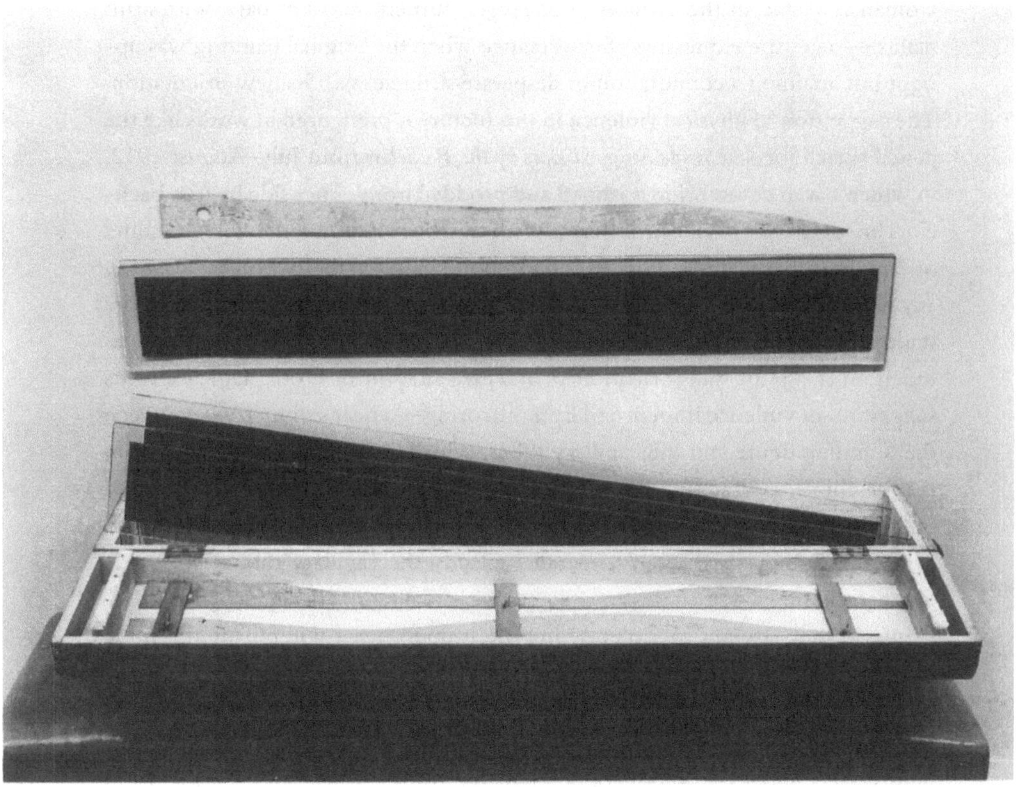

1.3 Marcel Duchamp. *3 Standard Stoppages* (*3 Stoppages Etalon*). 1913–14. Assemblage: three threads glued to three painted canvas strips, 5 ¼ × 47 ¼", each mounted on a glass panel, 7 ¼ × 49 ⅜ × ¼", three wood slats, 2 ½ × 43 × ⅛", 2 ½ × 47 × ⅛", 2 ½ × 43 ¼ × ⅛", shaped along one edge to match the curves of the threads the whole fitted into a wood box, 11 ⅛ × 50 ⅞ × 9". The Museum of Modern Art, New York. Katherine S. Dreier Bequest. Photograph © 1997 The Museum of Modern Art, New York. © 1997 Artists Rights Society (ARS), New York/ADAGP, Paris/Estate of Marcel Duchamp.

woman is visible in the *Network of Stoppages,* turned onto her back with arms flailing—a gesture expressive of exuberance when the original painting was upright but attaining a connotation of desperate struggle with its new orientation. The suggestion of physical violence in this picture is prefigured in works like the pencil sketch for *The Bride Stripped Bare by the Bachelors* from July–August 1912, in which a wan cubist bride is jabbed and prodded from either side by two bachelors bristling with phallic prostheses. With this work in mind, the spiky bouquet of capillary tubes seems aggressive and foreboding, but in the *Network of Stoppages* any physical threat is less potent than a *representational* violence deriving from the stark juxtaposition of two different systems of meaning. For *Network* may be as much an image of transformation as a representation of erotic aggression: its suggestion of violence is mediated by a mirroring—a near symmetry—between the feminine figure and the capillary tubes, which as we have seen derive from the masculine apparatuses of the *Large Glass.* Nowhere is this more clear than in the long, branchlike arms of the supine nude whose nearly regular width and gently bent disposition seem to parallel exactly the capillary tubes. The nude mirrors the tubes; she attains to their status as diagrammatic signs or measurements, as they attempt to violently impose it upon her. I will pursue this logic of violent opposition contained within symmetry—a logic of countervailing inversions—in my reading of this painting. To do so, I will make two excursions into Duchamp's oeuvre preceding the *Network:* first, a reading of his cubist paintings of 1911 and 1912; and second, an analysis of the *3 Standard Stoppages* from which the capillary tubes are generated.

If, as I have suggested, *Network of Stoppages* is structured as an agonistic and gendered drama of semiosis in which a feminine body is submitted to a masculine graph, then it might share what Rosalind Krauss and Yve-Alain Bois have identified as Picasso's attainment to a properly linguistic practice of representation in his *papiers collés* of 1912–13. Krauss and Bois argue that in these works Picasso developed a visual vocabulary premised on the rigorously arbitrary and differential character of the Saussurean sign. A fragment of cut-out newsprint, for instance, might read as the right side of a guitar, a tabletop, or an area of atmospheric shading, depending upon the elements with which it is combined. In a

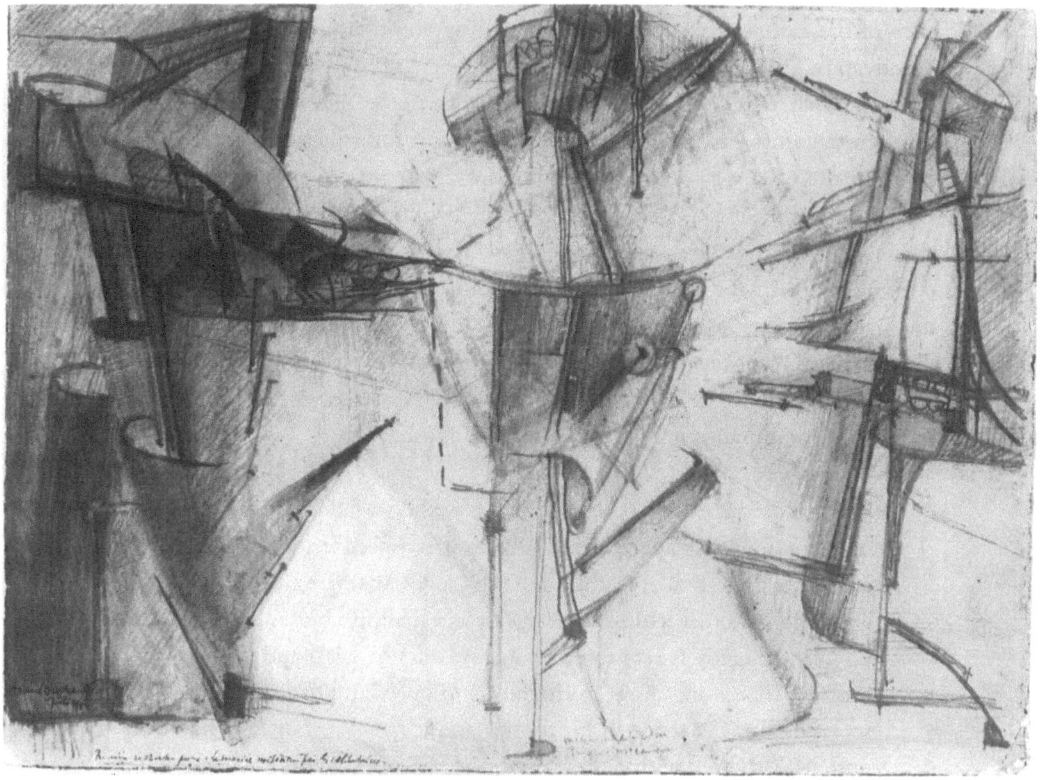

1.4 Marcel Duchamp. *The Bride Stripped Bare by the Bachelors* (*La Mariée mise à nu par les célibataires*). Munich, July–August 1912. Pencil and wash on paper, 9 ⅜ × 12 ⅝". Musée national d'art moderne, Paris. © 1997 Artists Right Society (ARS), New York/ADAGP, Paris/Estate of Marcel Duchamp.

recent essay, Krauss has linked this onset of semiosis in Picasso's art to a disappearance of the carnal or tactile quality within representation. She argues that the "motivation" for Picasso's invention of a proto-semiotic system within collage lies in what he perceived as a loss of the body to vision. This loss emerged both through the artist's own visual experience and, presumably without his knowledge, in the discovery among perceptual psychologists of the late nineteenth century that the flat retina could receive only flat impressions from the world. If vision is characterized by a relentless flatness, Krauss goes on to argue, then depth does not exist in the realm of the visual but may only be perceived through the memory of tactile experience in space. Picasso's response to this vertiginous discovery was to *signify* depth within the flatness of the picture plane rather than attempting to evoke it illusionistically. In short, Krauss theorizes an extraordinary transformation in cubism from the body to language:

> It seems . . . that this sense of a withdrawal of touch from the field of the visual was experienced by Picasso as a passionate relation to loss. That the carnal objecthood of the model was withdrawing progressively and that its loss was felt not as a triumph but as a kind of poignant tragedy is registered in Picasso's art of 1910 and 1911 by the way that work clings to the human figure, and to not just any set of figures but those of his friends and lovers. . . . For it to have gotten to the point that the carnal dimension—depth—is so unavailable to one of the most accomplished figure painters of his age that he must render his passion for a woman by *writing* it on his pictures is certainly one of the great ironies in the history of illusionist painting.[5]

Krauss is referring here to Picasso's inscription on his paintings of phrases like "Ma Jolie" or "Jolie Eva," but her argument also extends to the semiotic analysis of cubist collage elaborated by herself and Bois.[6]

Krauss's essay is premised on a starkly elegant economy: what is unavailable to vision must find its place in language. Picasso recuperated carnality at the

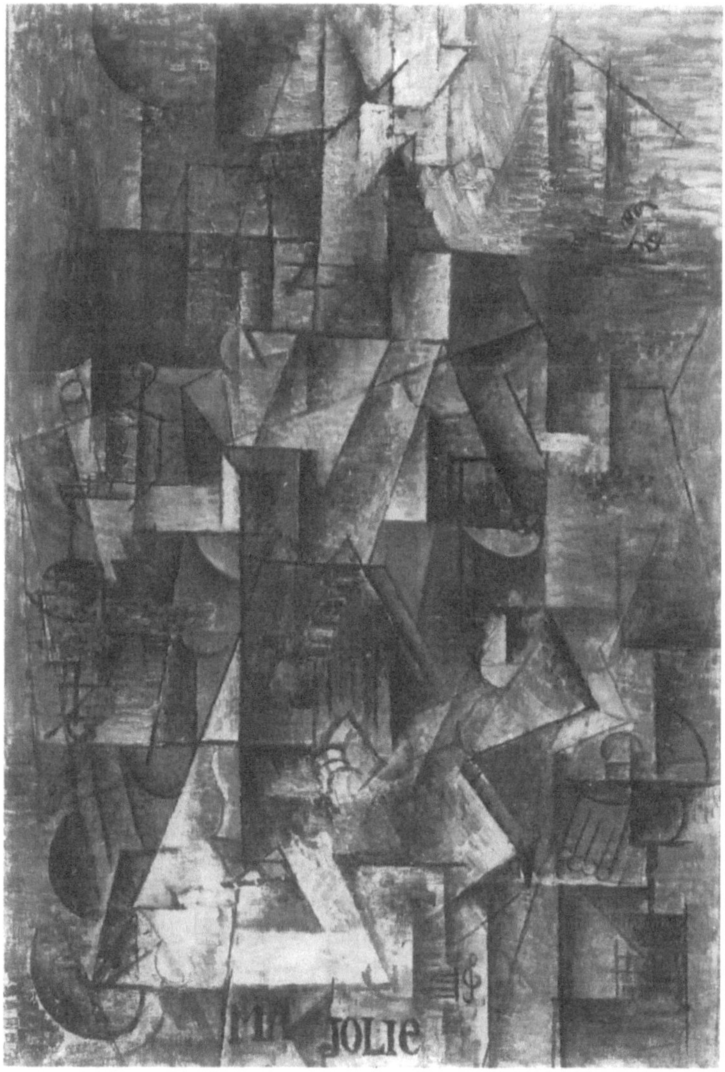

1.5 Pablo Picasso. *"Ma Jolie"* (*Woman with a Zither or Guitar*). Paris, Winter 1911–12. Oil on canvas, 39 ⅜ × 25 ¾″. The Museum of Modern Art, New York. Acquired through the Lillie P. Bliss Bequest. Photograph © 1997 The Museum of Modern Art, New York. © 1997 Estate of Pablo Picasso/Artists Rights Society (ARS), New York.

moment of its impossibility by creating a semiotic "script" through which it may be expressed. Her argument assumes, therefore, a transactional model in which the body of flesh is eclipsed by language: she accentuates the occlusion of carnality through semiosis rather than its reappearance as a new "body of the text." And indeed in the *papiers collés,* anatomies flicker in and out of legibility within an economy of everyday materials like newsprint, wallpaper, and charcoal. No one could mistake a column cut from a newspaper for the side of a head—and this arbitrary relationship to a signified meaning is precisely what qualifies Picasso's materials as signifiers. But if according to this argument Picasso was playing a zero-sum game in which the emergence of a semiotic economy of representation is inversely proportional to the visual experience of carnal plenitude, Duchamp's *Network of Stoppages* suggests a different model. For this painting envisions a *process* in which the body attains the status of sign while retaining a potent residue of its carnality.[7] Rather than focusing on the end points of the process—sign versus carnality—Duchamp positioned his work in the space *between,* where one is perpetually transforming and falling back into the other.

Such a vision of embodied semiosis appears in Jean-François Lyotard's *Libidinal Economy,* which elaborates a concept of signification in which the threshold between the real and the symbolic, or the body and language, is permeable rather than absolute. The sign emerges from carnality—it is literally carved from flesh—but it maintains a residue or "stain" of its original embodied state. Lyotard imagines the production of signs as a "disintensification" of organic pulsions: the semiotic emerges through an arrest rather than an eclipse of the body. What Lyotard calls the "tensor sign" holds carnality in suspension; it binds organic pulsions to the point of legibility without extinguishing them. According to this theory, the ground for signification and also for economic exchange is the body, or what Lyotard calls the "great ephemeral skin" or libidinal band. This "skin" is a pure site of intensity, an aleatory, unconscious field of surging pulsions. The band is a kind of acephalous body, split apart and spread out as a single surface. It is the material ground from which psychoanalytic, semiotic, or economic meaning is produced:

> All these zones are joined end to end in a band which has no back to it, a Moebius band which interests us not because it is closed, but because it is one-sided, a Moebian skin which, rather than being smooth, is on the contrary . . . covered with roughness, corners, creases, cavities which when it passes on the 'first' turn will be cavities, but perhaps on the 'second', lumps. . . . The interminable band with variable geometry . . . has not got two sides, but only one, and therefore neither exterior nor interior.[8]

Lyotard's tensor signs arise at points of distintensification on this moebius strip. His semiotic economy, like Saussure's, is premised on a network of differential meanings, but each sign also retains a *singularity* or residue of pulsional force form the libidinal band.

According to *Libidinal Economy* disintensification consists of a volumetric rigidification of the two-dimensional space of intensities: "The *dispositif* of confinement, that is to say of delimitation and conception, which will produce the exterior and the interior, which will enclose the extension of the concept, which will define *places* (of art, of culture, of production, of politics, of sexuality), this *dispositif* with its zero can only be engendered by disintensification."[9] There are several important notions in play in this passage. First, meaning is established, or the *dispositif* of language (as well as "of art, of culture, of production, of politics, [and] of sexuality") arises, through the inscription of an inside and an outside on the one-sided field of pulsional intensity. Meaning, in other words, is generated by piercing holes through the body of pure presence. Moreover, Lyotard, like Saussure, posits an absence at the core of semiotic meaning: a calm "zero" existing outside of the thumping rhythms of the body. However, Lyotard considers this absence, this zero, an ideal horizon, not an absolute condition: he speaks of *disintensification,* not of the near extinction of intensities. For Lyotard, the sign itself becomes an intensity—it never loses entirely, only by degrees, its rootedness in the pulsional mayhem of the great ephemeral skin.[10]

Lyotard's notion of the tensor sign casts light on the relationship that Duchamp posited between body and sign. To demonstrate the artist's fascination during this period with a body of pure intensity divested of firm boundaries, I will turn to one of his extensive commentaries or "notes" accompanying the *Large Glass*. These texts, largely published after completion of the work, though written during its generation, themselves occupy a middle ground, neither tools for explication of Duchamp's arcane imagery nor independent works of art. They are not translations of Duchamp's artistic vocabulary into words; rather they supplement or narrate visual tropes while retaining their own linguistic materiality and opacity. In a 1915 description of the "top inscription" that occurs within the "milky way," an outgrowth of the bride in the *Large Glass*, Duchamp wrote:

TOP INSCRIPTION

> obtained with the draft pistons. (indicate the way to "prepare" these pistons.).
>
> Then "place" them for a certain time. (2 to 3 months) and let them leave their imprint as 3 *nets* through which pass the commands of the pendu femelle (commands having their alphabet and terms governed by the orientation of the 3 nets [a sort of triple "*cipher*" through which the milky way supports and guides the said commands]
>
> Next remove them so that nothing remains but their firm imprint i.e. the *form* permitting all combinations of letters sent across this said triple form, commands, orders, authorizations, etc. which must join the shots and the splash
>
> Kind of milky way *flesh color* surrounding unevenly densely the 3 Pistons (i.e. there will be a transparent layer on the glass then the 3 Pistons then another layer of milky way) This flesh-like milky way to be used as a support for the inscription which is concerned with the cannon shots (at A)[11]

The draft pistons were to be generated by photographing the fluttering form of gauze curtains in front of an open window. Not only were they to be derived *from* a window, but they themselves function *as* windows in the milky way of the *Glass:* their warped rectangular contours define three openings of clear glass within the opaque cloud of the milky way. Within the fleshlike milky way—an analogue I would argue of Lyotard's great ephemeral skin—Duchamp opens up windows—(the very figure of transition between a "here" and a "there"), thus creating an inside and an outside and the concomitant possibility of signifiers: "Next remove them so that nothing remains but their firm imprint i.e. the *form* permitting all combinations of letters sent across this said triple form, commands, orders, authorizations, etc." Although Lyotard does not gender the window explicitly, for Duchamp it is consistently associated with a feminine form of inscription.[12] Through this gap, which breaks open the viscous pulsional surface of the milky way, language may enter in the form of alphabet, commands, authorizations, and so on.

Armed with Lyotard's and Duchamp's models of the relationship between the semiotic and the carnal, let's return to Duchamp's painting of 1911–12. It is clear that he, like Picasso, was preoccupied with the loss of the body to vision. A work like *Apropos of Little Sister* of 1911 performs a profoundly unsettling disarticulation of its subject. However, unlike Picasso's analytic paintings, where carnality is dispersed across a shimmering, tightly woven surface, Duchamp's figure falls apart into larger melon slices of flesh—almost as though her limbs have been pulled apart and splayed out like the articulated body of an insect. In this and other paintings like *Sonata,* also of 1911, Duchamp developed a two-pronged painterly vocabulary: thickly painted passages of "flesh" tones deposited across the surface but only partly disciplined into the contours of a recognizable anatomy through a series of thin, skeletal lines in dark brown or black. In *Apropos of Little Sister,* the body seems to have been drained of its fullness—its flesh running out onto the surrounding field of the painting—leaving a residue of desiccated "rinds." Such an idiom of immensurable agglomerations of what appears to be the material of the body, attenuated or rigidified into long skeletal rods,

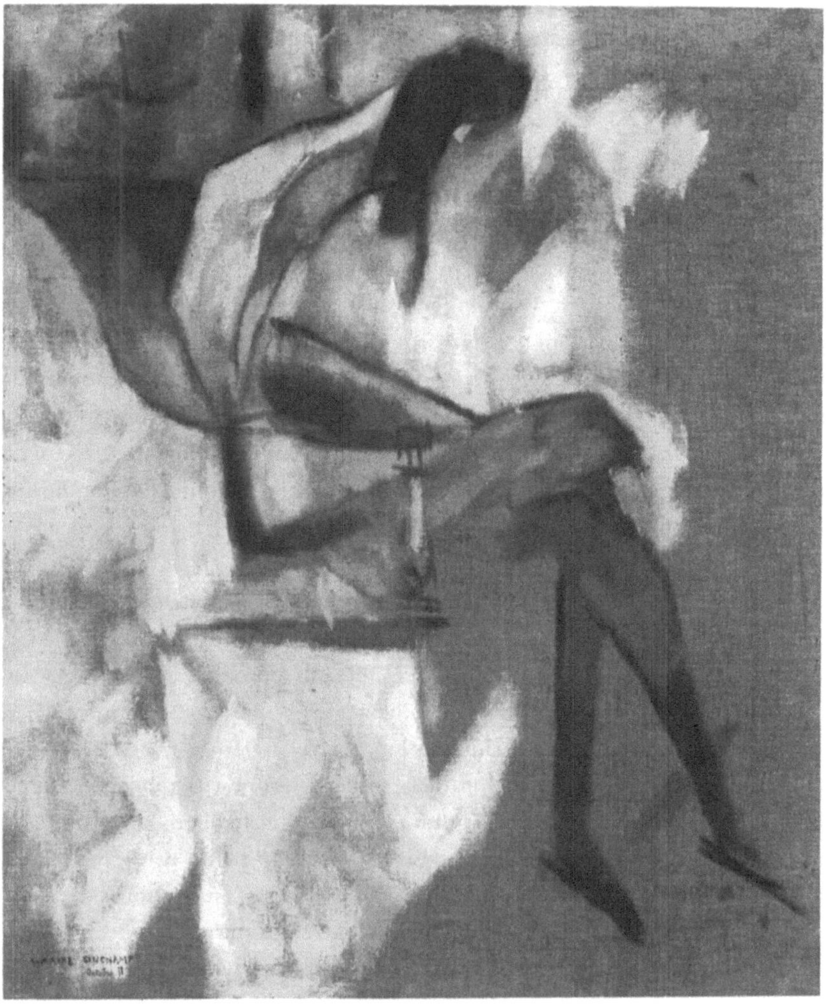

1.6 Marcel Duchamp. *Apropos of Little Sister.* October 1911. Oil on canvas, 28 ¾ × 23 ⅝″. Solomon R. Guggenheim Museum, New York. Photograph © The Solomon R. Guggenheim Foundation, New York. © 1997 Artists Rights Society (ARS), New York/ADAGP, Paris/Estate of Marcel Duchamp.

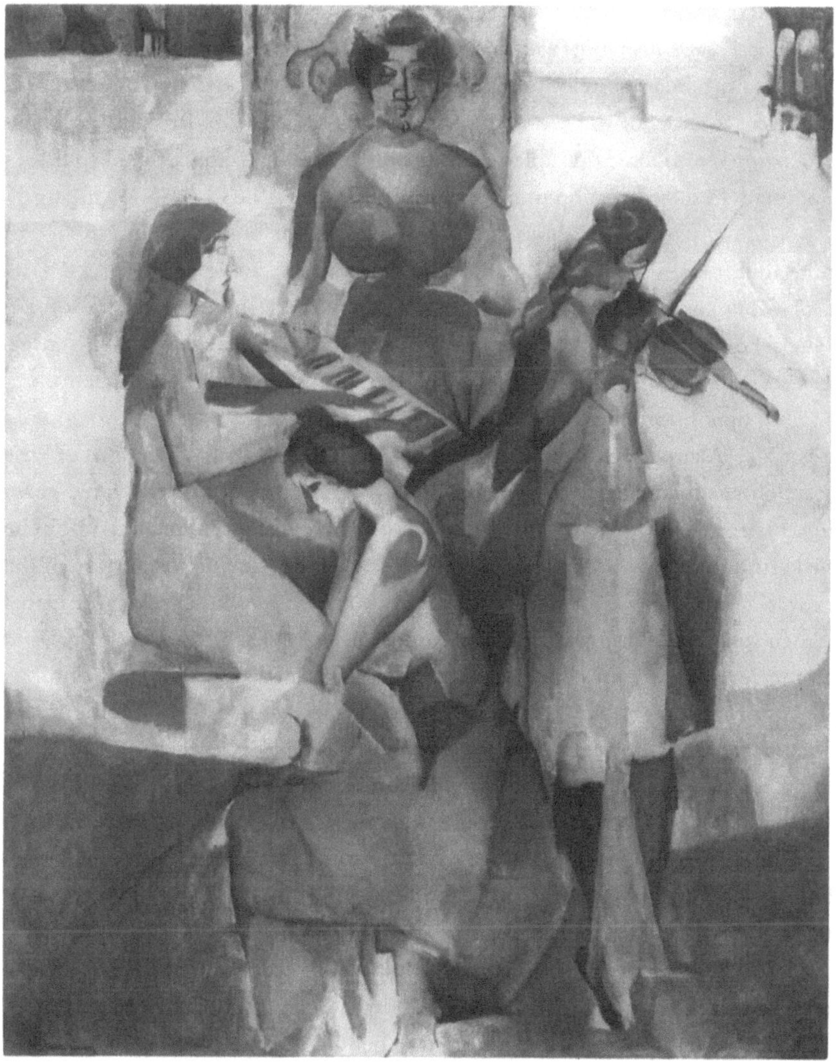

1.7 Marcel Duchamp. *Sonata.* 1911. Oil on canvas, 57 ⅛ × 44 ⅝". Philadelphia Museum of Art: The Louise and Walter Arensberg Collection. Photo by Graydon Wood, 1994. © 1997 Artists Rights Society (ARS), New York/ADAGP, Paris/Estate of Marcel Duchamp.

attains to a state of pure abstraction in Duchamp's great works of 1912, the *Bride* and *The Passage from Virgin to Bride.* But, as Duchamp himself remarked with regard to the *Bride,* abstraction was perhaps only a side effect: "It isn't abstract in the narrow sense of the word. It's visceral, so to speak."[13] In these paintings Duchamp represented the collapse of the body into a field of indefinable pulsions no longer localized around individual subjects or even clearly defined organs.[14]

The visual field in *Bride* and *The Passage* is not organized as a surface of pure, unbroken flatness. Compared to a work like Picasso's *"Ma Jolie" (Woman with a Zither or Guitar)* of 1911–12, the *Bride* and the virgin in transition of *The Passage* are shot full of holes. Deep caverns of space split apart or erode the tangle of viscera, creating a curious effect of vertigo suggesting but not quite delivering a stable opposition between figure and ground.[15] In *"Ma Jolie,"* Picasso entered what Yve-Alain Bois has called the second semiological phase of cubism or "the search for a unitary mode of notation"; as well as the third, or hieroglyphic phase in which "any information, in a quasi-hieroglyphic form, can be hung upon the flickering pattern [which the grid and chiaroscuro] define on the surface of the canvas."[16] In other words, Picasso has replaced the three-dimensional, or carnal dimension of his virgin-bride with a graphic script that is both indexical and iconic, leaving only a residue—a flickering—of chiaroscuro as the now obsolete means of evoking a volumetric body. Duchamp's paintings on the other hand occupy a semiotic moment preceding that of *"Ma Jolie":* they attempt to signify the emergence of language from the pulsional field of the body *without sacrificing the visceral residue of the sign.* He accomplished this in two ways. First, as in Picasso's analytic cubism, the move toward a unitary form of notation, a vocabulary of bulbs and stems, or swellings and attenuations, that reorganize the elements of the body into a semi-regular skein reminiscent of networks of nerves or telegraphic wires. But perhaps more originally, Duchamp evoked the claustrophobia of the libidinal band—which appears later in the *Large Glass* as the milky way—and then vertiginously opened an expanse behind it, instituting an "outside" to the body that makes language possible. Duchamp juggled two apparently contradictory themes: the immensurability of the body set free from its anatomy and its reterritorialization through a proto-semiotic system. If we define the cubist

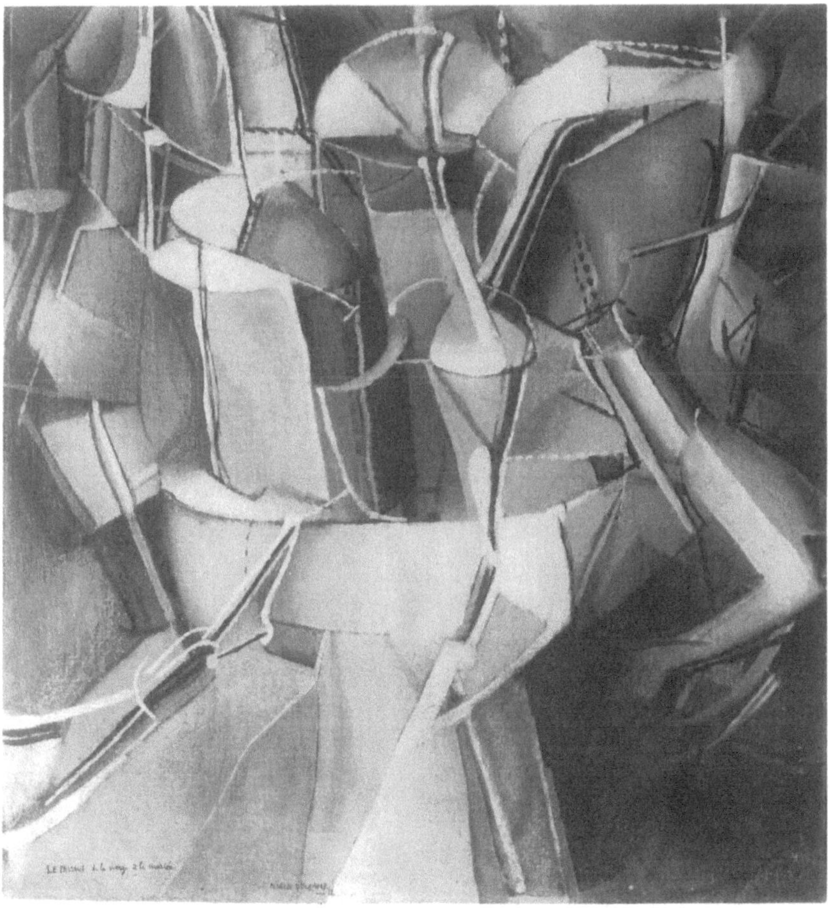

1.8 Marcel Duchamp. *The Passage from Virgin to Bride.* Munich, July–August 1912. Oil on canvas, 23 ⅜ × 21 ¼″. The Museum of Modern Art, New York. Purchase. Photograph © 1997 The Museum of Modern Art, New York. © 1997 Artists Rights Society (ARS), New York/ADAGP, Paris/Estate of Marcel Duchamp.

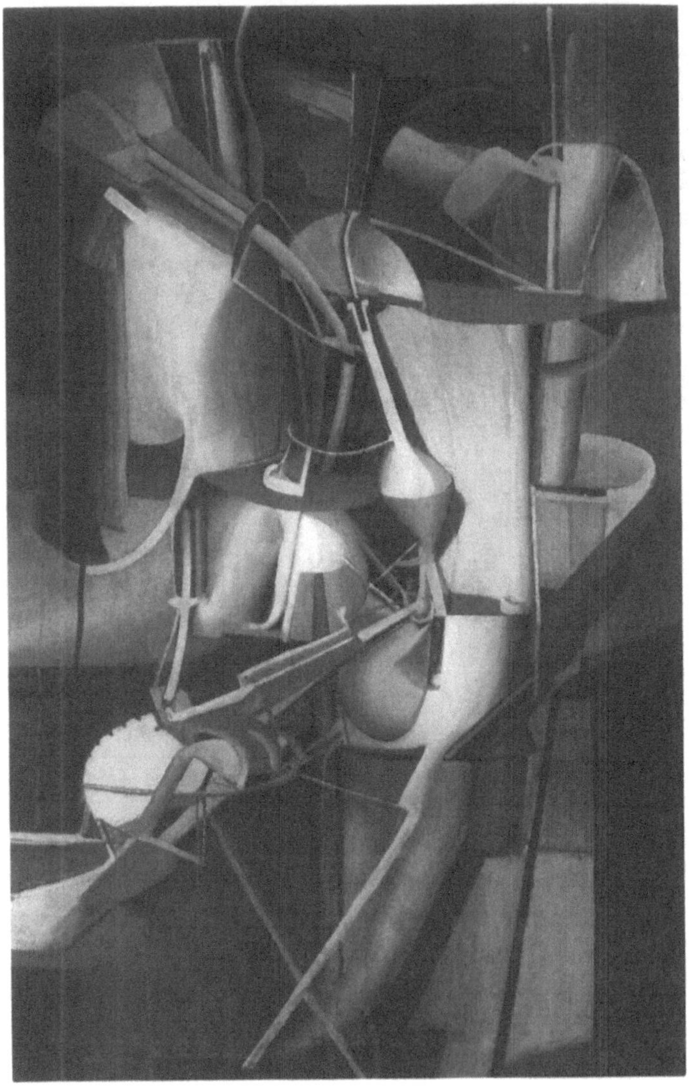

1.9 Marcel Duchamp. *Bride.* 1912. Oil on canvas, 35 ¼ × 21 ⅞". Philadelphia Museum of Art: The Louise and Walter Arensberg Collection.

project as a transformation of the body into script, then Duchamp must be credited with a contribution that challenges and redefines Picasso's classic and central definition of the paradigm. Duchamp's approach toward cubist semiotics was *embodied* in 1911 and 1912 in a way that Picasso's was not in those years. With Picasso, cubism led temporarily to the suppression of carnality; with Duchamp it led back to the virtually primordial point where language and the body cross. If Picasso's analytic cubism attests to a loss of the body to vision and its consequent entry into language, Duchamp's paintings of 1911–12 might be described as machines for producing language from the tangled labyrinth of the pulsional body.

This move toward a semiotic state within Duchamp's cubism, in which the immanence of the body is disciplined as a field of signs, would seem to cast light on the "contest" established in *Network of Stoppages* between a feminine body and a menacing constellation of lines. Yet we must still investigate the converse dynamic in the *Network:* the way in which the nude's masculine "twin" and "adversary," the bouquet of capillary tubes, collapses back into the pulsional chaos of the body. The capillary tubes derive from Duchamp's *3 Standard Stoppages* of 1913–14, a set of templates that the artist generated by dropping a meter length of sewing thread from the height of one meter onto a piece of canvas and then fixing it. This operation was performed three times, and templates made from the resulting curves. Duchamp himself accounted for the process in the following manner:

The Idea of the Fabrication

> —If a straight horizontal thread one meter long falls from a height of one meter onto a horizontal plane distorting itself *as it pleases* and creates a new shape of the measure of length.—
>
> —3 patterns obtained in more or less similar conditions: *considered in their relation to one another* they are an *approximate reconstitution* of the measure of length.
>
> The *3 standard stoppages* are the meter diminished.[17]

If dramatizing the impossibility of carnality in painting is one of the central stakes in cubism, then it would seem that choosing to represent a standard of measurement like the meter would be a perfect statement of the "end" of illusionistic painting—one contemporary with the readymade's analogous gesture of displacing the work of art with mass-produced commodities. Strictly speaking, the meter, as a unit of measurement, can have no body of its own but only acquires form contingently through the mediation of a template or, importing Duchamp's terminology, a "mold." The standard meter, then, is as purely conventional and abstract as the letters of an alphabet. In fact, Duchamp envisioned the standard stoppages as the building blocks of his own utopian language:

Conditions of a Language:

> The search for *"prime words"* ("divisible" only by themselves and by unity).
>
> Take a Larousse dict. and copy all the so-called "abstract" words. i.e., those which have no concrete reference.
>
> Compose a schematic sign designating each of these words. (this sign can be composed with the standard stops)
>
> These signs must be thought of as the letters of the new alphabet.[18]

The standard stops therefore collapse two sets of abstract conventions—measurement and language—onto a single graphic figure. They establish a mode of inscription very different from the "window" opened up in the milky way by its draft pistons or the interplay between visceral surface and vertiginous void in the *Bride* and *The Passage*. This difference lies, I believe in the gendered opposition between mensurability and immensurability elaborated by Duchamp in the passage quoted at the outset of this chapter. In this text he associated mensurability with the masculine machinic forms of the bachelor machine and immensurability with the bride, whose flesh seeps away from its skeletal container to form an amorphous libidinal band. Note that the quality of mensurability—the containment of form—*is in no way necessary to the capacity for inscription.* In other words, both the immensurable feminine and the mensurable masculine have their own forms of inscription: the window and the meter/alphabet, respectively.

These stark, simple oppositions are seductive, and in fact are largely legitimate. But, as always with Duchamp, each term tends to generate its paradoxical opposite. For if the meter, as a conventional standard of measurement, is the negation of carnality, the *3 Standard Stoppages* endow it precisely with the qualities of a body and even a will. By allowing gravity to pull the length of string that represents a meter into a gentle curve, Duchamp invested it with weight and mass—he *embodied* it. Moreover Duchamp anthropomorphized the string, furnishing it with a kind of volition by stipulating that it will "[distort] itself *as it pleases*." Jean Clair has noted Duchamp's similar metaphoric metamorphosis of the illuminating gas in the *Large Glass,* which travels through the capillary tubes at one point in its journey:

> All of these metamorphoses of the properties of a chemical substance are thus treated as metaphors borrowed from the domain of psychology. Just as one "fatigues" a metal in the manner of an organism, here as well the gas passes through different states, sublimation, liquefaction, crystallization, which appear as states of mind, a veritable "natural history" of the principle of gas, an initiation ritual in the course of which it must lose its "soul," its knowledge, its individuality, only to regain them at the end of the journey![19]

Clair's insight here—that Duchamp psychologizes and anthropomorphizes inorganic materials like the illuminating gas—may be applied productively to several of the artist's pseudo-scientific themes and images, including the "falling meter" of the *3 Standard Stoppages.* For if Duchamp was drawn to a standard of measurement on account of its pure abstractness and complete lack of carnality, he seized this image only to invest it paradoxically with weight, mass, and volition—the very qualities that a meter lacks but a body possesses.

We are now equipped, I think, to reconsider the *Network of Stoppages* as an allegory of the chiasmatic relationship between mensurability and immensurability theorized in Duchamp's notes. The painting ostensibly presents the violent juxtaposition of a woman's body and a system of measurement. As in *Apropos of Little Sister,* this feminine body is attenuated: its arms extend in crudely defined branches; its face, hair, and breasts lack specificity; and it is literally truncated, cut off at the hips. Its anatomy remains recognizable but caught in a process of dissolution. By comparison, the capillary tubes seem to possess the scientific precision of a malignant graph as they spread across the surface of the canvas. But, as we have seen, Duchamp complicated this simple opposition between the measurable and the unmeasurable. The apparently weightless abstraction of the standard stops is ballasted by the opacity of the body, as well as its presumed volition, and the supine woman makes herself available to language—and thus measurement—through the semioticization of her collapsed body, particularly her arms. It is impossible not to see these two improbably long limbs, joined together unnaturally at a point in the figure's neck, as a repetition of the several pairs of lines forming acute angles within the branch of capillary tubes. This uncanny repetition of the geometric or alphabetic form—itself distorted by gravity—within the dissolving body of the woman generates the haunting paradox at the core of this painting: the standard of measurement falls into carnality as the libidinal field is disciplined into form. This is why Duchamp used *Young Man and Girl in Spring* in the *Network,* instead of the more abstract vocabulary of *Bride* or *The Passage from Virgin to Bride*. The gap between the "masculine" figure of measurability and the immensurable feminine body had to be wide enough so that their collapse would be dramatic and meaningful: the abstract vocabulary of the 1912 paintings was too close to the embodied geometry of the capillary tubes for Duchamp to make his point powerfully. This need for a disjunction of artistic vocabularies—vocabularies that ultimately and paradoxically show themselves to be analogous—probably also explains Duchamp's invention of a masculine machinic idiom to be paired with the abstracted viscera of the bride in the *Large Glass*.

Indeed, the various bachelor machines of the *Glass* seem to be generated through rigidifying the "freed forms" of the feminine, immensurable body. This is particularly evident in two sketches for the "uniforms" of malic molds on recto and verso of a page dating from 1913–14. In these drawings the kinds of scalloped, cylindrical, and wedge-shaped forms that in the *Bride* and *The Passage* are unhinged from any recognizable anatomy and recombined in indeterminate webs have been isolated and "frozen" into single objects in order to produce the nine bachelors. Such isolation and stiffening of form is equally dramatic in the *Chocolate Grinder No. 1* of 1913. The creamy reddish- and beige-brown rollers of the grinder describe warped volumes that, divested of their machinic girding, could belong to the virgin and bride paintings of 1912. In fact the same kind of visual rhyming as occurs in the *Network of Stoppages* between the arms of the nude and the branches of the capillary tubes suffuses the *Large Glass*. Not only Duchamp's painting, therefore, but also his canonical work of 1915–23 reveal a pervasive interplay between the mensurable and immensurable, the masculine and feminine. On the one hand freed form attains the status of the sign, and on the other a mechanized geometric order falls back into the carnal flows of gas or chocolate. As I have argued, this opposition of genders may constitute a representational violence, which in the *Network of Stoppages* I have characterized as an eroticized form of aggression. Klaus Theweleit's assertion that male revulsion to feminine immensurability provokes a compensatory rigidifying of the masculine body may help to theorize Duchamp's particular conjunction of gender and form. *Male Fantasies,* Theweleit's study of interwar fascist literature in Germany, establishes the problematic in the following terms:

> In chapter 1 I described the way in which soldier males freeze up, become icicles in the fact of erotic femininity. We saw that it isn't enough simply to view this as a defense against the threat of castration; by reacting in that way, in fact, the man holds himself together as an entity, a body with fixed boundaries. Contact with erotic women would make him cease to exist in that form. Now, when

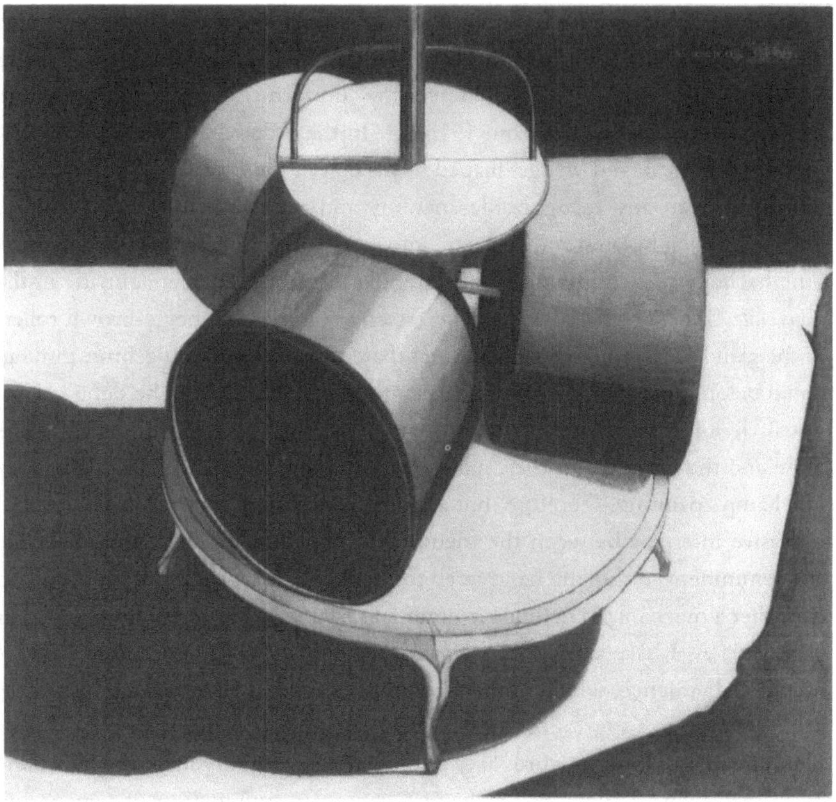

1.10 Marcel Duchamp. *The Chocolate Grinder (No. 1).* 1913. Oil on canvas, 24 ⅜ × 25 ⅜″. Philadelphia Museum of Art: The Louise and Walter Arensberg Collection. Photo by Graydon Wood, 1994. © 1997 Artists Rights Society (ARS), New York/ADAGP, Paris/Estate of Marcel Duchamp.

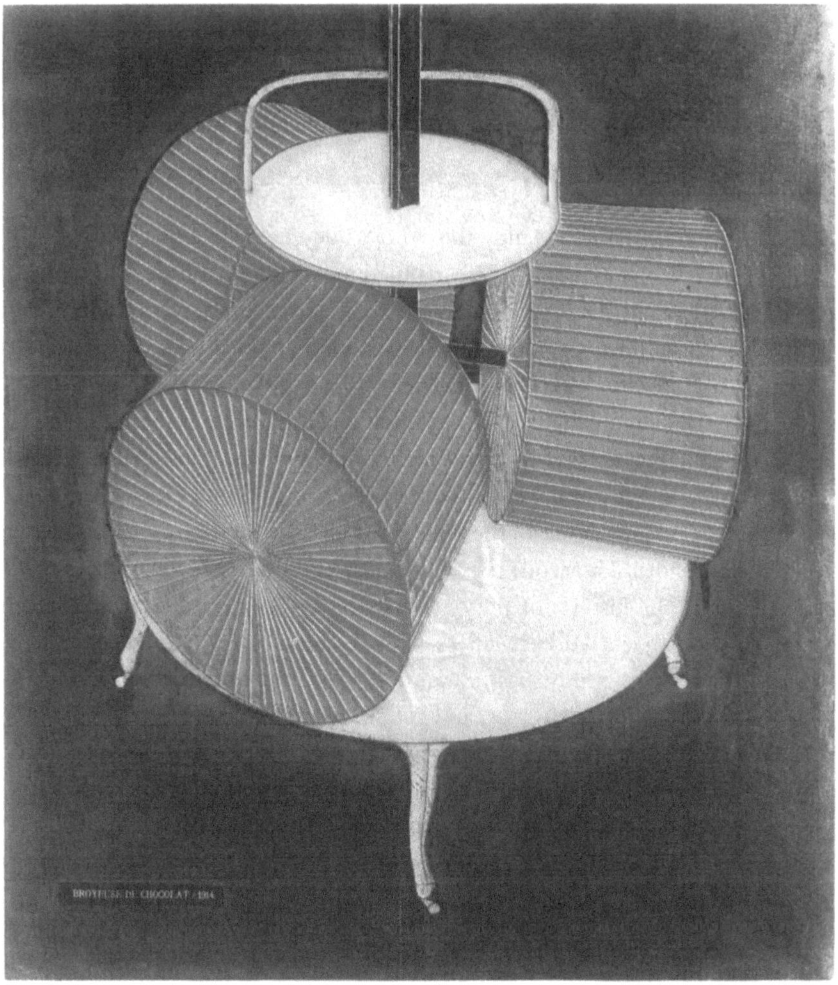

1.11 Marcel Duchamp. *The Chocolate Grinder (No. 2).* 1914. Oil, graphite, and thread on canvas, 25 ¾ × 21 ⅜″. Philadelphia Museum of Art: The Louise and Walter Arensberg Collection. © 1997 Artists Rights Society (ARS), New York/ADAGP, Paris/Estate of Marcel Duchamp.

> we ask how that man keeps the threat of the Red flood of revolution away from his body, we find the same movement of stiffening, of closing himself off to form a "discrete entity." He defends himself with a kind of sustained erection of his whole body, of whole cities, of whole troop units.[20]

Duchamp demonstrated not only this whole-body erection but also its prehistory *for men as well as women* in a visceral medium of libidinal flow. The *Network of Stoppages,* like the *Large Glass,* performs an eternal cycle of rigidifying and liquefying whose progress is enmeshed with the perpetual generation and degeneration of semiotic meaning from the medium of the body.

If we accept that Duchamp, like Picasso and other painters of this moment, was participating in a project called cubism whose practice transforms the carnal into the semiotic, what can we say about the meaning of such a metamorphosis? How does the disappearance of the body into language, or measurement, belong to a broader historical horizon? In order to answer such a question, we must take a fresh look at the history, or the discourse, of the female nude from 1863 to 1924, a period bracketed by Manet's *Olympia* and Man Ray's *Violon d'Ingres. Olympia* initiates a properly *modern* tradition in painting in which the body dissolves into a marketplace of signs, and cubism occupies a particularly tense moment of equilibrium—signified by its tendency to abstraction—in this history. I use the term *marketplace* deliberately, for I want to expand the working definition of "semiotic" to incorporate at least three interrelated levels of *exchange:* the linguistic, the economic, and the erotic. Such a triple homology is clearly demonstrated by the parallel notions of "value" held by Saussure and Marx. Fundamental to Saussure's semiotics is his concept that language operates as a differential economy of words. A sign is invested with meaning through its distinctness from every other sign, and this meaning varies with systemic fluctuations or transformations. Saussure's famous comparison of the word *mouton* in French with *sheep* in English is often invoked to demonstrate this concept. Although they seem to be synonymous, *mouton* and *sheep* have different values:

the French word signifies both the animal and its meat while the English word encompasses only the animal, another word—mutton—designating its meat. *Mouton* and sheep, associated as they are with unequal units of signification, are therefore invested with different values by their different languages: they are ultimately untranslatable to one another. Less familiar is the extensive analogy that Saussure established between language and money. He returned to such a metaphor twice in the course of his chapter on value. First, with regard to its conceptual aspects:

> Values always involve:
>
> (1)something *dissimilar* which can be exchanged for the
> item whose value is under consideration, and
> (2)*similar* things which can be *compared* with the item
> whose value is under consideration.
>
> These two features are necessary for the existence of any value. To determine the value of a five-franc coin, for instance, what must be known is: (1) that the coin can be exchanged for a certain quantity of something different, e.g. bread, and (2) that its value can be compared with another value in the same system, e.g. that of a one-franc coin, or of a coin belonging to another system (e.g. a dollar).[21]

And with regard to the material aspects of value: "It is not the metal in a coin which determines its value. A crown piece nominally worth five francs contains only half that sum in silver. Its value varies somewhat according to the effigy it bears. It is worth rather more or rather less on different sides of a political frontier. Considerations of the same order are even more pertinent to linguistic signals."[22] According to Saussure, then, the coin is an exact analogue of the word: they are both forms of currency whose conventions are arbitrary and whose value is determined through a marketplace where differentiation and exchange occur in tandem.

Just as for Saussure the material of language is transformed into an abstract currency upon its entry into a differential system, for Marx an object loses its purchase on the "real" when it becomes a commodity:

> Yet, for all that, the table continues to be that common, every-day thing, wood. But, so soon as it steps forth as a commodity, it is changed into something transcendent. It not only stands with its feet on the ground, but, in relation to all other commodities, it stands on its head, and evolves out of its wooden brain grotesque ideas, far more wonderful than "table-turning" ever was.[23]

This passage, drawn from Marx's seminal discussion of commodity fetishism, highlights the vertiginous aspect of an object's passage from the fairly stable realm of use value to the deliriously differential market of exchange value, where the contortions of a thing are "more wonderful than 'table-turning' ever was." Not surprisingly, Marx's concept of exchange is significantly darker than Saussure's. More startling is the violence with which he gendered its "promiscuity": "What chiefly distinguishes a commodity from its owner is the fact, that it looks upon every other commodity as but the form of appearance of its own value. A born leveller and a cynic, it is always ready to exchange not only soul, but body, with any and every other commodity, be the same more repulsive than Maritornes herself."[24]

In this extraordinarily potent and nuanced passage Marx anthropomorphized the commodity:[25] exchange becomes a relay of identifications, in which the commodity sees itself reflected in an infinite number of other commodities, resulting in an intersubjective and psychoanalytic concept of value significantly more sophisticated than Saussure's later formulation. Even more striking however, is Marx's association of the commodity with Maritornes, the notorious prostitute of *Don Quixote:* in this vicious metaphor, exchange elides with sexual transaction. The German sociologist Georg Simmel identified prostitution and the money system more evenhandedly, but perhaps for that very reason, his analysis even more effectively annihilates both desire and the figure of the prostitute:

> Since in prostitution the relationship between the sexes is quite specifically confined to the sexual act, it is reduced to its purely generic content. It consists of what any member of the species can perform and experience. It is a relationship in which the most contrasting personalities are equal and individual differences are eliminated. Thus, the economic counterpart of this kind of relationship is money, which also, transcending all individual distinctions, stands for the species-type of economic values, the representation of which is common to all individual values. Conversely, we experience in the nature of money itself something of the essence of prostitution. The indifference as to its use, the lack of attachment to any individual because it is unrelated to any of them, the objectivity inherent in money as a mere means which excludes any emotional relationship—all this produces an ominous analogy between money and prostitution.[26]

The central insight of this passage, as in Marx's, is not the obvious fact that prostitution occurs *through* a money transaction but rather that genital exchange is itself a *form of currency* homologous to money. While it is hard to accept Simmel's naive presumption that an anonymous sexual encounter is drained of any desire, that its brevity precludes phantasmatic attachment, his argument that both money and prostitution are initiated through a radical alienation from the real is profoundly important.

I am arguing then, for a use of the term *semiotic* that can expand and contract to incorporate three dimensions of exchange: the linguistic, the economic, and the sexual. Structurally, the exchange of signs, of commodities, and of women tend toward isomorphism, but practically (within a specific social instance) they are seldom completely reducible to one another. Here, in the friction between semiotic dimensions, in the changing registers of superimposition particular to a historical moment, the modern translation of the body into a semiotic field of exchange takes place. Manet's *Olympia* initiates this tradition through its uncanny elision between the body of money and a woman's body.

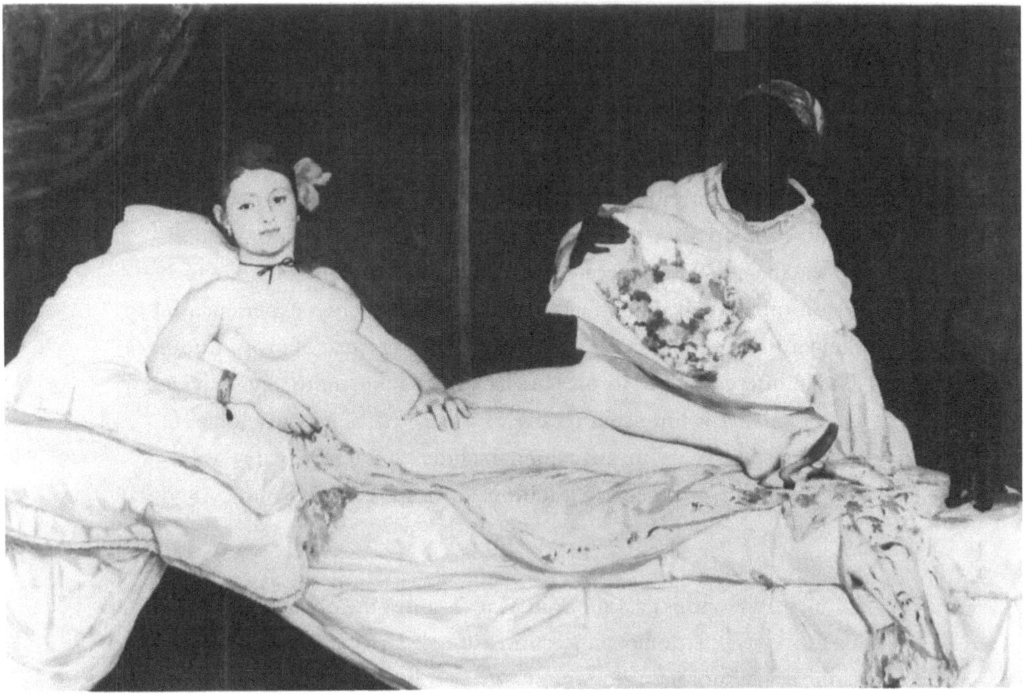

1.12 Edouard Manet. *Olympia*. 1863. Oil on canvas, 51 ½ × 74 ¾". Musée d'Orsay, Paris. © Photo Réunion des musées nationaux–Gérard Blot.

T. J. Clark in his famous discussion of *Olympia* asserts that the really offensive crime of this scandalous work is its inscription of class within the nakedness of the prostitute. There was nothing wrong with representing prostitution in the mid-1860s, as long as its nature as currency was suppressed within a masquerade of classical references and idealized formal tropes. For Clark, the difference between *Olympia* and the salacious academic representations of voluptuous women produced by the likes of William Bougereau and Alexandre Cabanel lies in the difference between the *naked* and the *nude:*

> If class could be shown to *belong* to that body; if it could be seen to remake the basic categories of nudity and nakedness; if it became a matter of the body's whole address and arrangement, something read *on* the body . . . then the circuit would be broken, and the category *courtisane* replaced by others less absolute and comforting. The body and money would not be unmediated terms any longer, intersecting in the abstract.[27]

Building on two of Clark's insights, I would like to draw slightly different conclusions about the nature of *Olympia*'s scandal. First, he notes that one of the most uncomfortable aspects of the picture is its straightforward *combination* of sexuality and money: "When the two intersect there is an uneasy feeling that something in the nature of capitalism is at stake, or at least not properly hidden."[28] Second, Clark is particularly sensitive to the degeneration of form that contemporary critics noted in the painting and that still strikes the viewer today. In the following passage he catalogues some of the terms that were applied to the work:

> *Olympia* was "informe," "inconcevable," "inqualifiable," "indéchiffrable"; the picture "ne s'explique pas." "The least handsome of women has bones, muscles, skin, form, and some kind of colour," whereas Olympia had none; she was "neither true nor living nor beautiful." The negatives multiplied: "she does not have a human form," and therefore "I can say nothing about her in truth, and do not know if the dictionary of French aesthetics contains expressions to characterize her."[29]

Could it be that Olympia's transformation into a type of currency—her promiscuous embodiment of *money*—causes a compensatory disarticulation of her biological body that dissolves into near monochromy on the one hand and is trussed up in a diagrammatic idiom of crude outlines on the other?[30] Olympia, lying on her bed, notoriously appears as a kind of afterimage, almost a "milky way"[31] of sallow, undifferentiated flesh. Within the logic of exchange, which in this painting is localized around Olympia's blatant, but unknowable stare, there is no longer any need for an individualized body—as Simmel paradoxically argued, the genital transaction of the prostitute is one in which "the most contrasting personalities are equal and individual differences are eliminated." The scandal of *Olympia* is not only that class is inscribed upon her nakedness but that the body is eroded, made elastic through its transformation into currency.

The female nude was not a favored subject among avant-garde artists after Manet's *Olympia*. Baudelaire's physiognomic and sartorial codification of modern femininity in "The Painter of Modern Life," which ranged from the woman of fashion to the most abject streetwalker,[32] signals a shift among impressionist painters from the comparatively unmarked, undressed body to the highly coded social creatures who populate the paintings of Manet, Edgar Degas, Berthe Morisot, and Mary Cassatt. In the late 1880s and '90s, however, two new models for representing the nude emerged in the work of Georges Seurat and Paul Gauguin. Seurat's *Les Poseuses* of 1888 represents three figures of an artist's model—or a single model passing through three stages of undressing, posing, and dressing—standing in the corner of his studio. Visible behind the model(s) and introducing a fourth life-size female figure is the right end of Seurat's masterpiece *A Sunday Afternoon on the Island of La Grande Jatte*. It is possible—at least theoretically—that *Les Poseuses* represents the same person four times: a single artist's model, posing and painted, "before and after." Whether this is literally true is however irrelevant: in the absence of individualizing features the model(s) and the clothed figure are indistinguishable. In them, the nude is reduced to a bland, desexualized automaton and then multiplied—even "cloned." By contrast to *Olympia*'s brazen stare at a presumed client, the central *poseuse* looks disconsolately at the artist, and the others look away: the place of monetary transaction has been deflated and displaced from genitality to representation. If Olympia is paid to have sex, and consequently lends herself to semioticization as currency, the figures in *Les Poseuses* are employed by the artist as *models* who submit their bodies to representation directly. Manet's painting is organized around an exchange of glances that initiates the prostitute's financial and genital transaction;

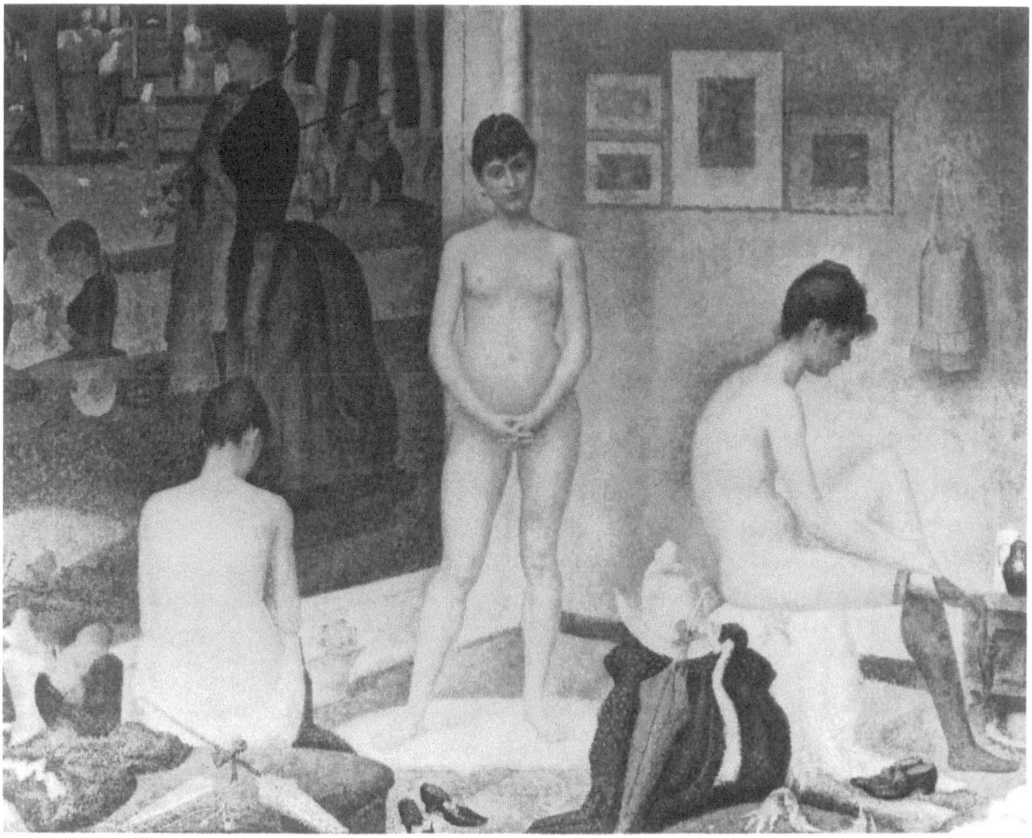

1.13 Georges Seurat, *Les Poseuses*. 1888. Oil on canvas, 79 × 98″. The Barnes Foundation, Merion Pennsylvania. Photograph © 1997 by the Barnes Foundation, all rights reserved.

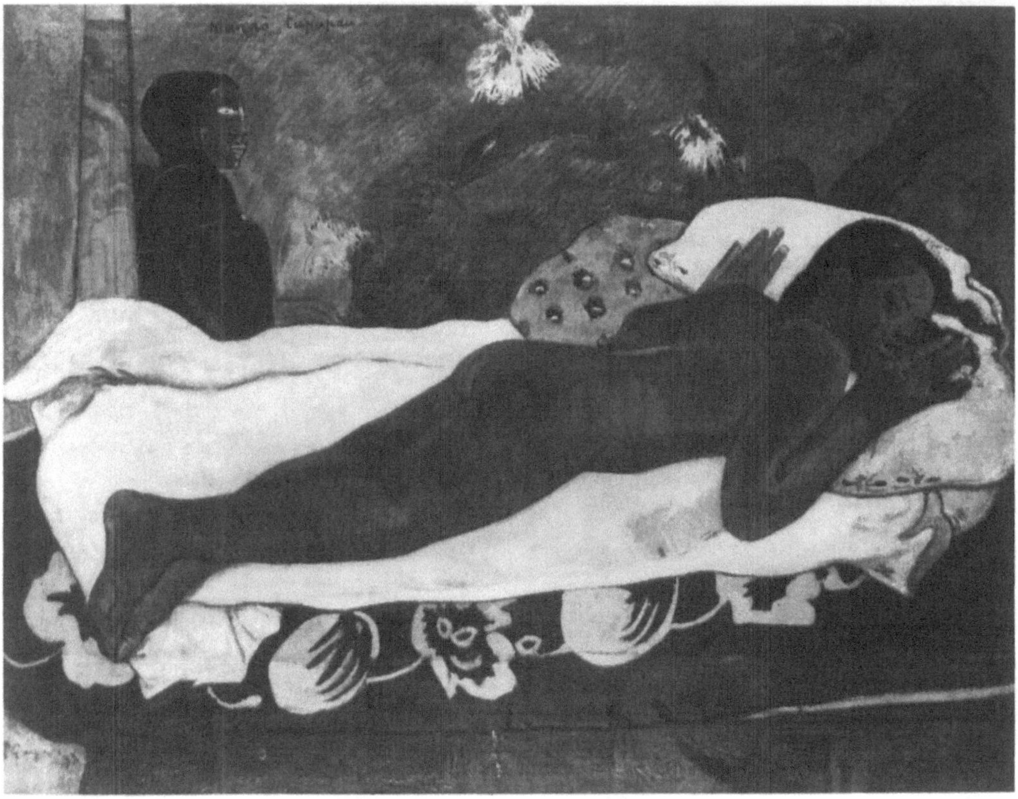

1.14 Paul Gauguin. *Spirit of the Dead Watching*. 1892. Oil on burlap mounted on canvas, 28 ½ × 36 ⅜". Albright-Knox Art Gallery, Buffalo, New York. A. Conger Goodyear Collection, 1965.

Seurat's work centers exclusively on the visual nature of such interchange—a woman is paid to become an image. The sullen moment of erotic encounter is refigured as the rendezvous of artist and model. In this transaction Seurat's *poseuses* further dissolve into the "currency" of vision: their bodies are reorganized as constellations of identically formed colored dots, presumed to be the building blocks of sight. This rationalized pointillist system itself participates in a logic of exchange by exploiting the managerial strategies of industrial production: analysis, standardization, and repetition. Seurat's insistence that painting a nude, like procuring a prostitute, is premised on an unidealized moment of exchange suggests the impossibility among avant-garde artists in 1888 of representing the female nude as anything but a form of currency.[33] To solve this insoluble problem—to endow the female body with plenitude—Gauguin found it necessary to desert the metropolitan West and to seek out, or to *invent,* the realm of the "primitive" in Tahiti. Gauguin's dependence on a French way of life and the support of French colonial officials in the South Pacific has recently been unveiled,[34] but this only highlights the pathetic poignancy of his search for women untouched by the capitalist system. In *Spirit of the Dead Watching* of 1892, Gauguin balanced the place of a masculine "client" or intruder—the presumed space of the viewer—with the figure of a god whose "look" is directed toward a young woman lying face down on a bed. The vulnerable female figure stares, half-demurely but also invitingly out at her visitor, as she herself is gazed upon by the god: she exists at the intersection of these male looks, establishing an axis from the sacred to the profane. The exchange of women is therefore resituated in the realm of the gift, of the sacred, and putatively extracted from the money economy of Manet and Seurat.[35]

This contradictory discourse of the nude at the end of the nineteenth century, characterized on the one hand by its abstraction into currency and on the other by a search for plenitude within the primitive, comes to a violent climax in Picasso's *Les Demoiselles d'Avignon.* It hardly bears repeating but is nevertheless fundamental that this painting represents a brothel scene and that the trauma experienced before it amplifies the scandal of *Olympia* to nearly intolerable levels for many male viewers. In order to revivify the automaton body of exchange—the doll-like figures of the prostitutes—Picasso invested them with a violence borrowed in part from the "primitive" iconography of African masks and medieval sculpture. The painting is torn apart in a terrible earthquake of representation that initiates an extraordinary crisis in Picasso's subsequent depictions of the nude. In the few years following the *Demoiselles,* a dramatic transformation occurs from images like the hunkering giantess slouching toward the viewer in *The Dryad* of the spring–autumn of 1908 to the dispersed, drained figure of *Seated*

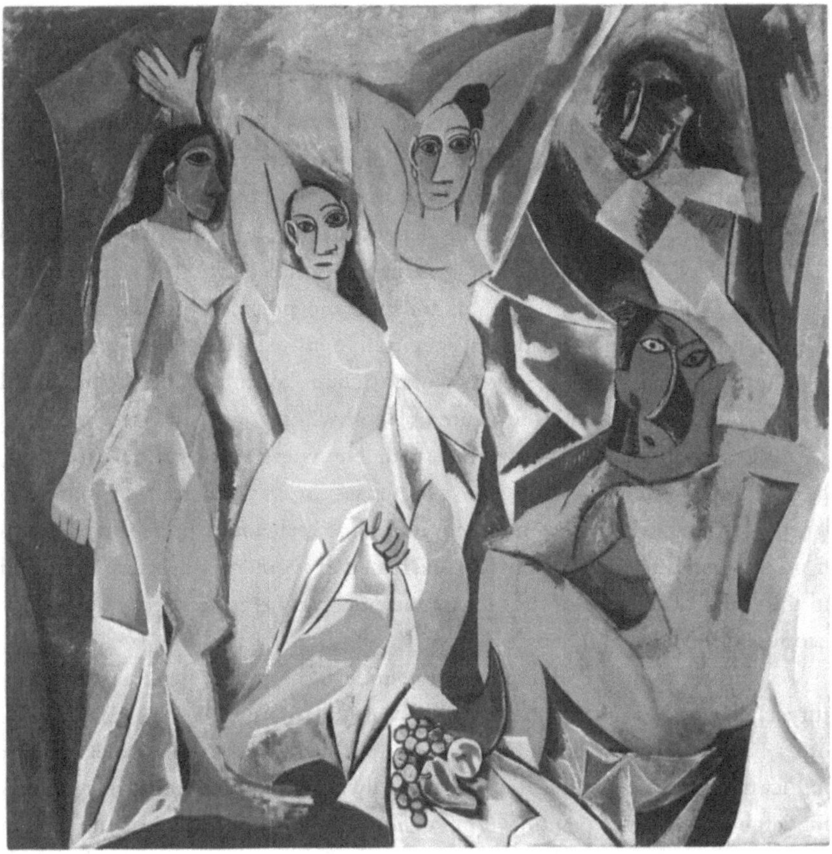

1.15 Pablo Picasso. *Les Demoiselles d'Avignon*. Paris, June–July 1907. Oil on canvas, 96 × 92″. The Museum of Modern Art, New York. Acquired through the Lillie P. Bliss Bequest. Photograph © 1997 The Museum of Modern Art, New York. © 1997 Estate of Pablo Picasso/Artists Rights Society (ARS), New York.

Woman of the summer of 1909 and the completely dissolved *Woman in an Armchair* of the spring of 1910. Here we return to the problematic identified by Krauss as Picasso's tragic and anxious confrontation with the loss of the body to vision. In paintings like *The Dryad* he pushed the body to its breaking point: he inflated it, filled it with sculptural mass and volume—as Matisse had done in his *Blue Nude* of 1907—until finally anatomy collapsed under its own weight into the dispersed field of cubism. Because Picasso tried harder than any painter since Courbet to depict the feminine body as a site of plenitude, he came to recognize the impossibility of this venture and to reject it outright in favor of semiosis. As Krauss is at pains to point out, acknowledging the loss of the body in his art was not easy for Picasso, and he quickly returned to it after World War I, never to lose his hold again. The palpable relief and pleasure that he felt in his "return to order" is itself a dramatic gauge of how *necessary* cubism's gesture of liquidation must have felt to Picasso in 1910.

As I have argued, the epistemological transformation of the biological body into a semiotic marketplace did not begin with cubism but was initiated fifty years earlier in the *informe* of *Olympia.* Manet submitted the nude to an anatomical distortion and dissolution culminating in two great paintings of 1907: Matisse's *Blue Nude*[36] and Picasso's *Les Demoiselles d'Avignon.* Cubism responded to this moment of enormous aesthetic tension by establishing an equilibrium between the body and the sign. It marks the crossing point of two countervailing tendencies in the nineteenth century: the slipping away of the carnal body and the emergence of a full-scale semiotic marketplace. With *Olympia,* the body was eroded by the semiotic—by money—but remained the dominant ground of inscription. In the course of the nineteenth century the nude became ever more attenuated, always more impossible to represent until, in cubism, body and sign were made equivalent through an abstract and indeterminate field of embodied signifiers. This moment, however, was both delicate and historically limited. The nude—or perhaps its simulacrum—returned after World War I, but only from *the other direction,* through the semiotic matrix of the commodity. No longer was the feminine figure inscribed by the sign; the sign itself was inscribed by the body. Man Ray's *Violon d'Ingres* of 1924 performed such an inversion. *Violon d'Ingres* is a manipulated photograph representing a nude woman from behind,

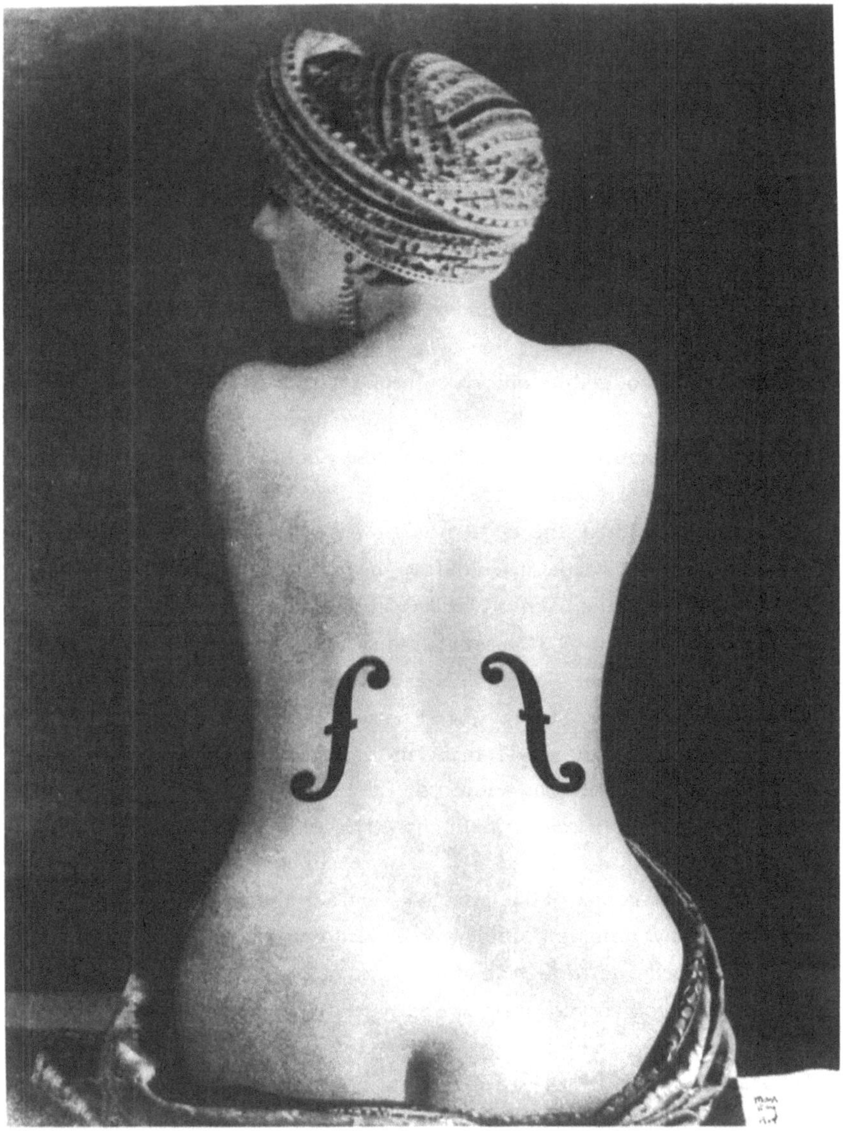

1.16 Man Ray. *Le Violon d'Ingres.* 1924. Photograph, 15 ¾ × 11 ¾". Photo Telimage. © 1997 Artists Rights Society (ARS), New York/ADAGP/Man Ray Trust, Paris.

posed and turbanned like a bather from Ingres's *Bain turc*. Unlike its art-historical precedent, the back of Man Ray's figure is "pierced" by two black "f-holes," causing an uncanny metamorphosis of woman into violin. This transformation accomplished a witty and economical resolution of the historical dilemma posed by cubism: instead of transposing the nude into a violin, as Picasso had done in painting and sculpture, Man Ray held in suspension both the fullness of the body and its objectified or semioticized transformation into an object: a violin. His image does not recognize the choice *between* the carnal and the semiotic that Picasso faced because, I believe, by the moment of the mid-1920s any remaining hope for a body unmediated by the semiotic marketplace had been foreclosed. The experience of World War I and the multitude of shattered bodies it produced[37] called for a simulation of biological wholeness, but more importantly, the proliferation of visual forms of advertising in the 1920s had relentlessly represented the intact body *as a commodity already*. The nude reappeared for Man Ray—as well as for Picasso during the 1920s—because there was no longer anything at stake: it had already been semiotically colonized and was therefore not only *like* a violin, it *was* a violin.

In a treatise on cubism published in 1913 Apollinaire polemically proclaimed, "The fact is not without importance—that Duchamp is the only painter of the modern school who today (autumn 1912) concerns himself with the nude."[38] I have suggested that it was difficult to paint the female nude in 1912: Picasso had already given it up for collage, but Duchamp continued to explore and expand its significance within the semiotic marketplace. Duchamp's exact knowledge of cubism as defined by Picasso and Braque remains in question. He told Pierre Cabanne that he had taken cubism very seriously in 1911 after occasionally visiting Daniel-Henry Kahnweiler's gallery and that he was in Braque's studio toward 1910 or 1911 but that he had hardly any relationship with Picasso at this moment and was much more aware of Gleizes's and Metzinger's theories than Picasso's.[39] Whether he was responding directly to Picasso's move away from the subject or not, it seems that Duchamp was aware of his own idiosyncracy in painting the nude, at least in retrospect. In discussing the 1911 painting *Dulcinea*, he told Cabanne: "The repetition of the same person four or five times, nude, dressed, and in the shape of a bouquet in 'Dulcinea,' was primarily intended, at that time, to 'detheorize' Cubism in order to give it a freer interpretation."[40] And further, "I don't know how it happened but, after 'Dulcinea,' I felt the need to do still another small canvas, called 'Yvonne and Magdeleine Torn Up in Tatters.' In this case, it's more tearing than it is movement. This tearing was fundamentally an interpretation of Cubist dislocation."[41] Through these seemingly offhand remarks, Duchamp indicated a significant challenge to cubism as defined by Picasso and Braque. To "detheorize" its practice, he would literalize its program: instead of making the body "disappear" into a veil of contradictory signifiers as Picasso had done in his analytic paintings, Duchamp put the nude through two complementary transformations of multiplication and fragmentation. The model for *Dulcinea* was a woman whom Duchamp met casually in the street but never came to know: "'Dulcinea' is a woman I met on the Avenue de Neuilly, whom I saw from time to time going to lunch, but to whom I never spoke. It wasn't even a matter of being able to speak to her. She walked her dog, and she lived in the neighborhood, that's all."[42] But as he himself noted, there is no attempt at a futurist evocation of motion in this painting,[43] which might indicate the ephemeral nature of his sightings of "Dulcinea." On the contrary, the feet of the compound figure are bound together into a "bouquet" prefiguring the branchlike graph of capillary tubes inscribed on the *Network of Stoppages.* Not only does Duchamp choose to commemorate an anonymous experience of "cruising" in the street—a specifically modern type of urban encounter familiar in nineteenth-century avant-garde painting from Manet to Gustave Caillebotte—he chooses to *replicate* the figure. This, I think, is the significance of the bouquet composition: it highlights the fact that this is a single woman and not a crowd. In the manner of Seurat's *Poseuses,* the boundaries of Dulcinea's person blur through multiplication at the same time as the definition of her several bodies is distorted through the painterly idiom of indeterminate and dissolving flesh noted above in *Apropos of Little Sister* of the same year. Duchamp responded to Picasso and Braque's cubism[44] not with the vulgar notion of representing the same figure from several points of view but with the much more

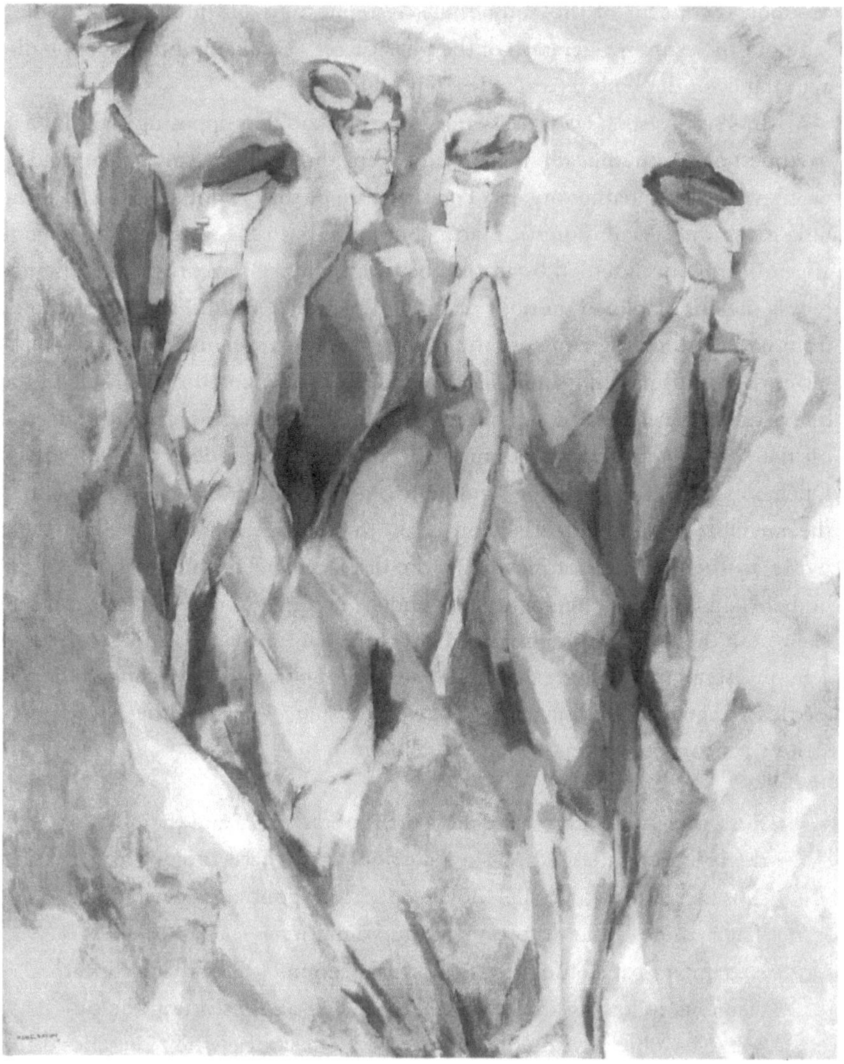

1.17 Marcel Duchamp. *Dulcinea.* 1911. Oil on canvas, 57 ⅝ × 44 ⅞″. Philadelphia Museum of Art: The Louise and Walter Arensberg Collection. Photo by Graydon Wood, 1994. © 1997 Artists Rights Society (ARS), New York/ADAGP, Paris/Estate of Marcel Duchamp.

productive concept of the body endlessly replicating and multiplying itself: a kind of cancerous proliferation of the physical self. Duchamp imagined the disappearance of the body as its endless reproduction.

In *Yvonne and Magdeleine Torn in Tatters* he took an opposing tack: instead of undergoing multiplication, the body is fractured into a collagelike field of profiles and free-floating organs. The structure of this painting, while allowing little recession into illusionistic space, confounds both the scale and the boundaries of form: an unsettled oscillation between physical proximity and distance recalls the undisciplined pulsions of Lyotard's libidinal band. Fragments emerge from within other fragments as though they constituted mental images of themselves. Both this painting and *Dulcinea* radically challenged the plenitude of the body: on the one hand, its uniqueness was destroyed through replication, and on the other its integrity as a bounded whole was exploded. Unlike Picasso, Duchamp did not disperse the figure into a graphic script but rather disciplined the medium of the body itself into a proto-language, characterized in these works by the dual axes of metaphor (the displacement of one fragment of the body by another) and metonymy (the endless linking of bodies in to an infinite chain).[45] If these two paintings from 1911 represent Duchamp's effort to develop a graphic script *from the body itself,* his *Nude Descending a Staircase* began to rationalize this "language." In discussing *Sad Young Man on a Train* and the *Nude* he described his concept of "elementary parallelism":

> First, there's the idea of the movement of the train, and then that of the sad young man who is in a corridor and who is moving about; thus there are two parallel movements corresponding to each other. Then, there is the distortion of the young man—I had called this elementary parallelism. It was a formal decomposition; that is, linear elements following each other like parallels and distorting the object. The object is completely stretched out, as if elastic. The lines follow each other in parallels, while changing subtly to form the movement, or the form of the young man in question. I also used this procedure in the "Nude Descending a Staircase."[46]

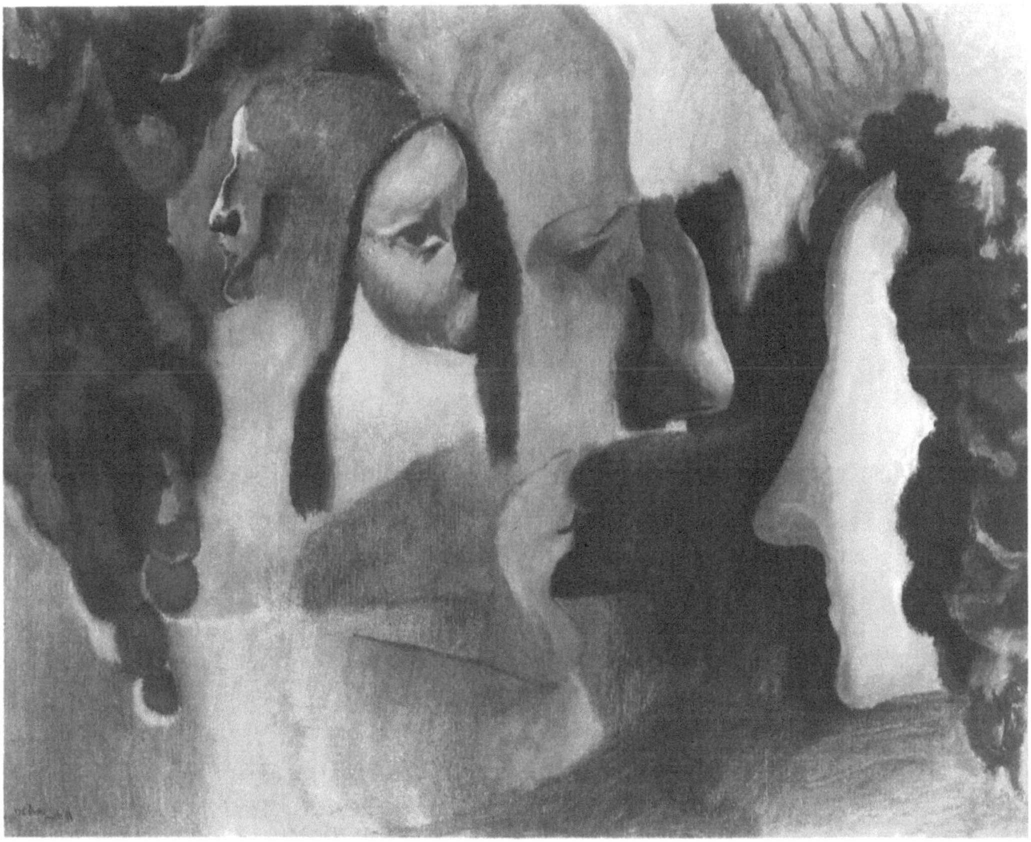

1.18 Marcel Duchamp. *Yvonne and Magdeleine Torn in Tatters.* 1911. Oil on canvas, 23 ¾ × 28 ⅞". Philadelphia Museum of Art: The Louise and Walter Arensberg Collection. © 1997 Artists Rights Society (ARS)/ADAGP, Paris/Estate of Marcel Duchamp.

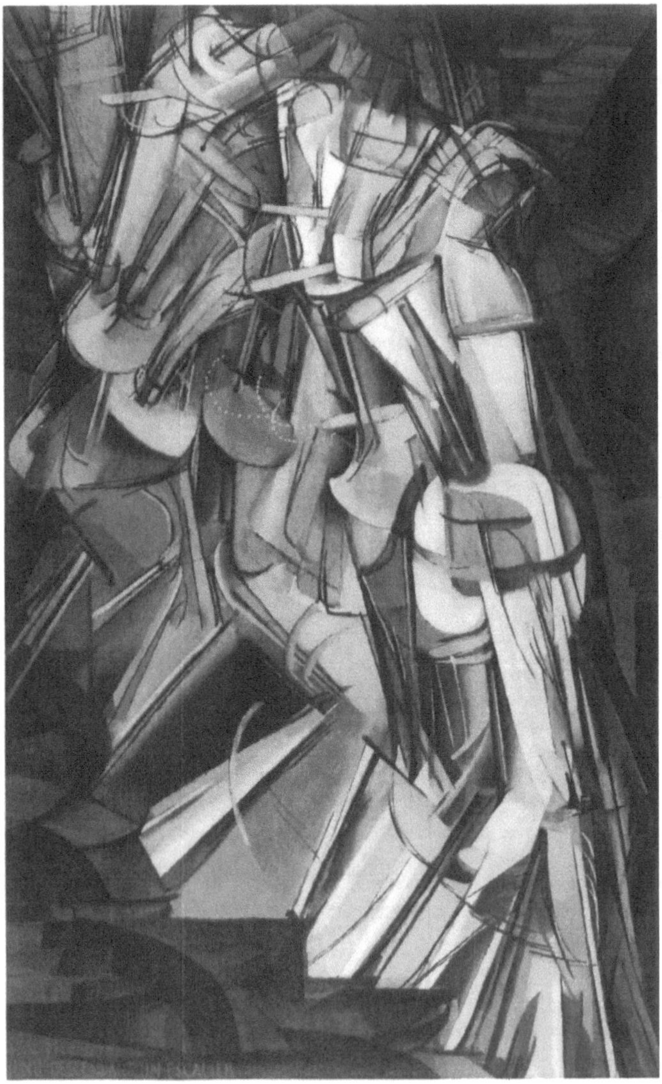

1.19 Marcel Duchamp. *Nude Descending a Staircase, No. 2.* 1912. Oil on canvas, 57 ⅞ × 35 ⅛″. Philadelphia Museum of Art: The Louise and Walter Arensberg Collection. Photo by Graydon Wood, 1994. © 1997 Artists Rights Society (ARS), New York/ADAGP, Paris/Estate of Marcel Duchamp.

The "elementary parallelism" of these two paintings established a relay between an "elastic" body and a geometric system. Such an opposition not only anticipated but perhaps initiated the countervailing idioms of the supine nude and the capillary tubes that appeared two years later in *Network of Stoppages*. As in the later painting, the term of measurement in the *Nude Descending a Staircase*—the field of parallel lines—is distorted or warped by the mass and volume of a body: it attains a new, non-Euclidean and *embodied* geometry. This is the significance of Duchamp's much-cited indebtedness to the French scientist-photographer Etienne-Jules Marey. As Duchamp told Cabanne:

> In one of Marey's books, I saw an illustration of how he indicated people who fence, or horses galloping, with a system of dots delineating different movements. That's how he explained the idea of elementary parallelism. As a formula it seems very pretentious but it's amusing.
>
> That's what gave me the idea for the execution of the "Nude Descending a Staircase." I used this method a little in the sketch, but especially in the final form of the picture. That must have happened between December and January 1912.
>
> At the same time, I retained a lot of Cubism, at least in color harmony. From things I had seen at Braque's or Picasso's. But I was trying to apply a slightly different formula.[47]

This passage offers several important insights. First, Duchamp explicitly described his invention of "elementary parallelism" as a self-conscious response to Picasso and Braque's cubism. He underlined this by telling Cabanne a moment later that the anatomy of the *Nude Descending a Staircase* was "a sort of distortion other than that of Cubism" and "a Cubist interpretation of a Futurist formula."[48] In spite of this unambiguous testimony as well as his frequent and equally direct disavowals of any serious interest in futurism, critics and historians have typically interpreted Duchamp's interest in Marey's chronophotography as a preoccupation with the depiction of movement and speed. This constitutes a misreading both of Marey's photographic project and Duchamp's painterly one: neither man was interested in evoking the sensation of movement, but both attempted to create a static representation—a kind of graph—of the body's internal and external motion.

Born in 1830, Marey was a French physician whose passionate interest in engineering led him to develop a graphic method for describing the "human machine."[49] Although he is best known for his photographs of animal and human locomotion—those which Duchamp mentioned to Cabanne—this work took place in the context of Marey's lifelong search for a rational mode of analyzing bodily motion. Early in his career he concentrated on internal fluxes like the circulation of blood, but later he focused on the external animal or human movements of walking, running, galloping, and flying. Marey was profoundly skeptical of both human perception and experimentation as scientific tools, believing that the senses of the doctor or scientist were too imprecise to record complex physiological data and that conventional language was inadequate to express even what s/he perceived directly.[50] As a result, he invented several generations of apparatuses for inscribing movement in which an animal or human was transformed into a kind of writing machine. Connected to these machines, the movement of Marey's subjects—the muscle contractions of a frog or the walk of a man—were transformed into the pure lines of a graph, which the doctor could then analyze and interpret. His objective was literally to extract a language of the body: "The graphic system translates all of these changes in the action of forces into a striking figure that one could call the language of phenomena themselves, in that it is superior to all other modes of expression."[51] Marey's goal was to capture "the language of phenomena themselves," by disciplining the apparently aleatory and irrational realm of locomotion into an abstract idiom of the graph that could be deciphered like "inscriptions written in an unknown language."[52] Deeply distrustful of linguistic signs, Marey sought to coax a graphic language directly from living things. François Dagognet has argued that this project is structurally related to photography, which would eventually become Marey's primary tool: "What was important throughout was eliminating the human intermediary, a screen that complicated, distorted and prevented access to reality. . . . Wasn't this also the goal of photography—letting the sun do its writing—to dispense with the intermediary of the painter and interpreter?"[53] Unlike Eadweard Muybridge's motion photography, which broke up a particular movement into a series of discrete moments, Marey's chronophotography, like his inscription machines, sought to show an entire trajectory—a kind of graph or graphic language—of an instance of locomotion. To enhance the linear effect Marey sometimes had subjects dress entirely in black uniforms marked with white lines and points along the legs and arms, so that their movements were those of stick figures—images that clearly prefigure the formal idiom of Duchamp's *Nude Descending a Staircase*.

There is reason to believe that Duchamp's acquaintance with Marey's work was more than casual. Dagognet tells us: "It is known that Duchamp had read Marey, whom he quotes, and that he also knew his work through his brother, Raymond Duchamp-Villon, a medical student working under Marey's assistant and follower, Albert Londe, a radiologist and clinical photographer at Salpêtrière."[54] This evidence combined with Duchamp's explicit rejection of any interest in the sequential movement associated with futurism allows us to see Marey's impact in a new light. For both Duchamp and Marey, I believe, were interested in developing a "language of phenomena themselves." What the artist saw in the doctor's work was not merely a mode of capturing movement but a way of representing the body through a graphic system immanent to it. The *Nude Descending a Staircase* rationalized Duchamp's cubist idiom of 1911, the slabs of flesh and linear rinds of *Apropos of Little Sister, Dulcinea,* and *Sonata.* There is nothing here but passages of flesh-toned paint and spiky constellations of straight lines that introduce more economically than the earlier paintings an interplay of the mensurable and the immensurable—the carnal and the geometric. What was accomplished analytically in the *Nude,* its superimposition of line and flesh, would be synthesized in the two major paintings that follow, the *Bride* and the *Passage from the Virgin to the Bride.* In these two works lines swell into organic growths, or fleshy agglomerations are attenuated into lines: there is no way, as in the *Nude,* to extract one vocabulary from the other. Duchamp was well aware of this accomplishment. Not only did he distinguish between these paintings and his more explicitly cubist works of 1911–12, he described their character positively as a "juxtaposition of mechanical elements and visceral forms."[55]

As I have argued, Duchamp's cubism is premised on a logic of rigidifying and liquefying form that, in the *Network of Stoppages,* is explicitly gendered as an agonistic encounter between a feminine body and a masculine system of measurement. But even in the *Network,* and especially in his works of 1912, Duchamp's painting, like Marey's chronophotography, sought to produce an immanent graphic language for the body extracted from deep within its biological architecture. This perpetual oscillation between mensurability and immensurability is however only one dimension of Duchamp's accomplishment—he invested the formal process of liquidation in his paintings with a *social* significance through explicit reference to the exchange of women through marriage. The *Bride Stripped Bare by Her Bachelors, Even* is preceded by cubist works like *The Passage from Virgin to Bride* and *Bride* that, through their titles, situate the nude, as Manet's *Olympia* had, in a marketplace of erotic exchange. Indeed, the trade in virgins and brides is not always easy to distinguish from prostitution: Simmel, in trying to differentiate the courtesan and the wife, continually returns to the indefinite overlap between them.[56] Within structural anthropology, and particularly in the work of Claude Lévi-Strauss, the relationship between marriage and currency becomes clear. Lévi-Strauss claims that the incest prohibition is the "fundamental step because of which, by which, but above all in which, the transition from nature to culture is accomplished."[57] The incest prohibition occupies this position because it makes the exchange of wives possible: "As soon as I am forbidden a woman, she thereby becomes available to another man, and somewhere else a man renounces a woman who thereby becomes available to me. The content of the prohibition is not exhausted by the fact of the prohibition: the latter is instituted only in order to guarantee and establish, directly or indirectly, immediately or mediately, an exchange."[58]

The purpose of the exchange of wives, then, is to knit together communities of men; to link them positively, and to forestall wars between them. It is also a form of exchange that encompasses each of the semiotic dimensions I have noted: the linguistic, the economic, and the sexual. Lévi-Strauss enriches the semiotic discourse of Marx and Saussure by exploring commodity and linguistic exchange in light of the exchange of women: the bride becomes a figure of both the commodity and language. In Lévi-Strauss's analysis, women are not *like* commodities, they *are* commodities, just as Simmel argued that the prostitute was literally a form of currency: "It would then be false to say that one exchanges or gives gifts at the same time that one exchanges or gives women. For the woman herself is nothing other than one of these gifts, the supreme gift among those that can only be obtained in the form of reciprocal gifts."[59] Not only is the exchange of women isomorphic with the exchange of goods, it is also structurally parallel to language: "Indeed, from this point of view, 'exogamy and language . . . have fundamentally the same function—communication and integration with others.' . . . The incest prohibition is universal like language."[60] Lévi-Strauss is careful, however to distinguish between linguistic signs that tend toward abstraction and universal transparency of meaning and women, who retain a "residue" of subjectivity and therefore may resist their complete transformation into semiotic currency: "Woman could never become just a sign and nothing more, since even in a man's world she is still a person, and since in so far as she is defined as a sign she must be recognized as a generator of signs. . . . In contrast to words, which have wholly become signs, woman has remained at once a sign and a value."[61]

The "value" that women retain in this economy is not simply exchange value but the capacity to produce children, which as Lévi-Strauss demonstrates is also a form of semiotic reproduction. This paradoxical positioning of "woman" as sign and generator of signs has motivated feminist theorists and historians to reveal the contradictions inherent in feminine semioticization. Luce Irigaray has particularly emphasized what she calls the hom(m)o-sexual monopoly inherent in the exchange of women as theorized by Lévi-Strauss. Women in their status as commodities enable relations between men to occur while they themselves disappear. In terms highly suggestive with regard to Duchamp, Irigaray argues that only in her *passage* from one man to another, one state to another, can a woman's value be perceived:

> The value of a woman always escapes: black continent, hole in the symbolic, breach in discourse. . . . It is only in the operation of exchange among women that something of this—something enigmatic, to be sure—can be felt. *Woman thus has value only in that she*

> *can be exchanged*. In the passage from one to the other, something else finally exists beside the possible utility of the "coarseness" of her body. But this value is not found, is not recaptured, in her. It is only her measurement against a third term that remains external to her, and that makes it possible to compare her with another woman, that permits her to have a relation to another commodity in terms of an equivalence that remains foreign to both.[62]

According to Irigaray women are measured "against a third term" that is none other than that commodity "whose use value becomes, from that point on, a standard of value"[63]—simply, financial currency or money. A woman's *passage* between men is the moment of her measurement within the marketplace, the moment of her emergence into semiotic legibility. The virgin embodies this exchange: "*The virginal woman . . . is pure exchange value*. She is nothing but the possibility, the place, the sign of relations among men."[64] Irigaray helps us to understand the role of Duchamp's virgins passing into brides as a literal performance of mensuration through exchange, just as the parallel lines in *Nude Descending a Staircase* or the capillary tubes in *Network of Stoppages* impose a kind of geometry onto the dissolving body of the nude. Duchamp contains the historically disappearing body of woman within the socially originary institution of marriage: an institution founded on the exchange and measurement of women.

An idiosyncratic passage in the article "Buddha of the Bathroom," whose nominal author was Louise Norton but which was probably heavily influenced by Duchamp himself,[65] elaborates an analogous concept of marriage. Written in defense of Duchamp's *Fountain* (1917), an inverted urinal that he submitted to the Society of Independent Artists under the pseudonym R. Mutt, this article meditates on the relationship between marriage and polysemy:

> At least one charming thing about our human institution is that although a man marry he can never be *only* a husband. Besides being a moneymaking device and the *one* man that *one* woman can sleep with in legal purity without sin he may even be as well some other

> woman's very personification of her abstract idea. Sin, while to his employees he is nothing but their "Boss," to his children only their "Father," and to himself certainly something more complex.
>
> But with objects and ideas it is different. Recently we have had a chance to observe their meticulous monogamy.
>
> When the jurors of *The Society of Independent Artists* fairly rushed to remove the bit of sculpture called the *Fountain* sent in by Richard Mutt, because the object was irrevocably associated in their atavistic minds with a certain natural function of a secretive sort.[66]

Marriage is discussed in a strikingly figurative manner in this passage. It is imagined as a means of stabilizing categories in two distinct but related ways: first, it interpellates a man, whose possible identities are infinite, as a *husband,* and second, through "monogamy" it ties a single object, or signifier, to a single idea, or signified. In spite of her irony, Norton represents marriage as a means of founding a stable self from a field of multiple selves and of making meaning possible by linking signifier to signified. Needless to say, the article, in deriding "monogamous" relationships among people and objects, intends to condemn such unilateral connections. After all, the point of a readymade like *Fountain* is to replace the lawful marriage of object and idea—urinal with urination—with a promiscuity of the commodity in which any manufactured thing can enter into many different "liaisons" with an infinity of ideas.[67] Moreover, this text demonstrates the kind of paradoxical inversions that I have noted in *Network of Stoppages.* As men are transformed into machines—moneymaking devices—objects and ideas are anthropomorphized; they engage in the human institution of marriage or "monogamy." "Buddha of the Bathroom" is important because it indicates that Duchamp's use of virginity and marriage as metaphors in the titles of his paintings was both self-conscious and highly nuanced. For him, the passage from virgin to bride meant not only sexual initiation but the entry of the body into the marketplaces of language and the commodity. What began with the distortion of Olympia's body through its entry into a money economy therefore finds logical conclusion in Duchamp's brides, whose completely collapsed physiques submit to the marriage contract—a figure of exchange in all of its dimensions.

I have used two models of semiotic analysis in discussing Duchamp's cubism: Lyotard's notion of the tensor sign extracted from a libidinal field and Saussure's concept of linguistic value as an economic marketplace. This theoretical dualism leads not, however, to contradiction but rather to a means of distinguishing how Duchamp undertook the cubist project of transforming the carnal into the semiotic differently from Picasso. Duchamp, like Marey, sought to transpose the nude into a language immanent to it, whereas in his analytic cubism Picasso liquidated the nude into an arbitrary economy of graphic signifiers composed of elements alien or external to it. As Krauss argues, for Picasso the body in cubism must disappear, whereas for Duchamp, as Apollinaire understood, the nude persists. The difference between Lyotard's tensor sign and Saussure's arbitrary signifier is that the tensor, which can only emerge when a part of the libidinal band is isolated and disciplined into form, retains a greater residue of the matter from which it is extracted, whereas Saussure's concept of value presumes a drastic minimizing of what he calls "substance" in the production of form.[68] Thus the two semiotic theories line up along a temporal axis, rather than canceling each other out synchronically. Duchamp's cubism, like Lyotard's semiotics, focuses on the body as a point of transfer between libidinal flux and signification, whereas Picasso's cubism is premised on a subsequent moment in which the body drains away only to reemerge as language. Duchamp's painting of 1910–14 evokes a visceral field—an acephalous body exploding the bounds of its anatomy and collapsing back onto itself—which, as Roland Barthes might have said, is "carved up" into a proto-linguistic system and disciplined to lesser and greater degrees along the axes of metaphor and metonymy. Fundamentally, however, Duchamp's concept of language centers on an unresolved or suspended opposition between mensurability and immensurability, where *measurement* is conceived as an act of exchange in one or all of its three dimensions. For Barthes, such an act of measurement makes language possible: "It is in fact the very definition of the syntagm, to be made of *a substance which must be carved up.* The syntagm, when it takes the form of *speech,* appears as a 'text without end': how can one spot, in this text without end, the significant units, that is, the limits of the signs which constitute it?"[69] If we replace *syntagm* with *body* (with which it shares the quality of a "text without end") we have an accurate description of Duchamp's cubist project: his attempt to divide the body into signifying units, to chart its unruly topography. What gives his effort to invent a "language of phenomena themselves" piquancy is Duchamp's acknowledgement of its ultimate, paradoxical impossibility. Such is the lesson of *Network of Stoppages*. In this work the body is subjected to a standard of measurement, but one that collapses back into the carnal. Even as the nude is carved up into semiotic units, it retains the irreducible opacity of the body and never loses its tendency to fall back into the pure intensity of the libidinal field. For Duchamp the signifier was neither completely arbitrary nor completely transparent to its signified. It *performs* the endless cycle of being cut from the body and falling back into the presemiotic "noise" of its unconscious, aleatory flows.

Tu m', Duchamp's true "last painting" of 1918, pushes such a cycle of semiotic mensurability and immensurability to its logical extreme. Whereas the *Network of Stoppages* instituted an unstable but nonetheless dichotomous opposition between the body and a standard of measure, *Tu m'* initiates an infinite regress of measurement. Whether or not he fully understood its mathematical foundations, Duchamp's rhetoric of the fourth dimension established a powerful metaphor for a world in which any object is the measure of another: "Each ordinary 3-dim'l body, inkpot, house, captive balloon is *the* perspective projected by *numerous* 4-dim'l bodies upon the 3-dim'l medium. There are 3-dim'l bodies which correspond to fewer perspective projections (in the 4 to 3-dim'l region) than others."[70] In other words, a series is established in which any thing of n dimensions may be represented—may be measured—by something of $n-1$ dimensions: two nondimensional points establish a one-dimensional line; two lines determine a two-dimensional plane; two planes evoke a third dimension; and the intersection of two three-dimensional spaces will establish a four-dimensional continuum. Just as in *Network of Stoppages* a feminine body approaches the form of the standard stoppages while the unit of measurement is endowed with weight and volition, *Tu m'* represents a reality in which every

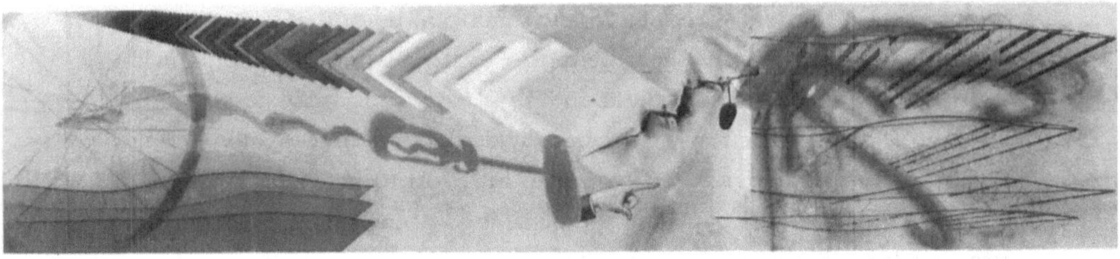

1.20 Marcel Duchamp. *Tu m'*. 1918. Oil on canvas with bottle brush, three safety pins, and one bolt, 27 ¼ × 123". Yale University Art Gallery; Gift from the Estate of Katherine S. Dreier. Photo by Joseph Szaszfai. © 1997 Artists Rights Society (ARS), New York/ADAGP, Paris/Estate of Marcel Duchamp.

thing is both an object to be measured and a standard of measurement.[71] In the infinite anamorphosis of this painting every element becomes the figure of something else. Jean Clair has pointed to such a dynamic between the painting and a commodity in his striking analysis of the bottle brush that protrudes through an illusionistic tear in the central portion of the canvas. When the painting is viewed from the front, the brush tends to be foreshortened into a single point within the painted field, whereas from the side, the painting disappears into a line as the brush emerges in profile:

> If one places oneself in the same plane as the painting, it is reduced to no more than a line; inversely, the bottle brush appears in all its incongruity as an object piercing the canvas. . . . There where painting disappears, the ready-made emerges. Painting (the art of painting) is a matter of point of view—"It is the spectator who makes the painting"—once subjected to anamorphosis, it gives way to the manufactured object (anti-painting, anti-art, etc).[72]

Such dramatic instances of anamorphosis as the transformation of a point into a bottle brush or a painted field into a line suffuse each aspect of *Tu m'*: each of its constituent parts is both an object and a standard of measurement.

Commissioned by Katherine Dreier to fit above a bookcase in her library, *Tu m'* is long and narrow like a frieze. It includes, in addition to the protruding bottle brush, a series of distorted shadows of readymades projected across its surface. On the lower left of the painting are the contours of templates made from the three standard stoppages stacked one behind the other while a long perspective of color chips emerges from the upper left corner into the center. On the right side of the painting is a series of colored lines generated by the standard stoppages, from which recede several straight lines divided into segments of different colors and intersected by series of superimposed circles. A text from the *Green Box* suggests an early plan for *Tu m':*

> shadow cast by 2, 3, 4, Readymades. *"brought together"*
>
> (Perhaps use an enlargement of that so as to extract from it a figure formed by an equal [length] (for ex.) taken in each Readymade and becoming by the projection a part of the cast shadow
>
> for ex. 10 cm in the first Rdymade
> 10 cm " " 2nd "
> etc.
>
> each of these 10 cm. having become a part of the cast shadow
>
> Take. these "having become" and from them make a tracing without of course changing their position in relation to each other in the original projection.[73]

In this formulation several shadows of readymades—already the traces or indexical signs in two dimensions of a three-dimensional object—are transformed into the uniform segments of a "ruler." Duchamp imagined a work in which ordinary objects (readymades) are disciplined into standards of measurement. Although this particular operation was not performed on the shadows in *Tu m'*, the painting does exhibit an analogous dynamic of measurement and inscription. The templates of the standard stoppages appear in the same work—the *same space*—as a series of lines generated from them: their coexistence sets in motion a cycle leading from object to template to linear measure that places measurement *en abyme*. In a text titled "Cast Shadows," which pertains more directly to *Tu m'*, Duchamp demonstrated his preoccupation with multiplying the terms of mutual mensuration:

> *probably to relate to the notes on 4-dim'l perspective.*
>
> after the bride. . . .
> make a picture. of *shadows cast*
> by objects 1st on a plane.
> 2nd on a surface of
> such (or such) curvature
> 3rd on several transparent surfaces
> thus one can obtain a hypophysical
> analysis of the successive transformations
> of objects. (in their form-outline—)[74]

This text accurately reflects the infinite regression of measurement—from the first through the fourth dimension or from a plane to a curvature to transparency—that organizes *Tu m'*. The object—any readymade object—is lost within a "hypophysical analysis of [its] successive transformations" within the rhetoric of measurement.

In *Tu m'* virtually every image in the visual field sets such a destabilizing process in motion. Its clashing perspectives and discontinuous imagery have often been noted, as have its trompe-l'oeil illusions such as the painted rip in the middle of the canvas secured by real safety pins and the pointing finger executed by the professional sign painter A. Klang. These details are the surface effects of an even more fundamental freeing of form: in *Tu m'* the familiar object world is overcome by a contradictory profusion of dimensions and measures. Color itself, often considered the most "intuitive" quality in painting, is rationalized—and commodified—through the series of color samples that Duchamp had copied from a catalogue of oil paints.[75] In a text from *A l'Infinitif* he called for a means of ordering color: "As in geographic maps, as in architects' drawings or diagrams with color wash, need of a color key: *substantive meaning* of each color used—(e.g. for certain metals, for wood, etc., determine the *conventional color* used."[76]

Such an effort to discipline color into a map or architect's plan transforms it from an expressive tool into a means of specification or measurement. Similarly, in his text on language and the readymade, Duchamp associated color with grammar:

> Take a Larousse dict. and copy all the so-called "abstract" words. i.e., those which have no concrete reference.
>
> Compose a schematic sign designating each of these words. (this sign can be composed with the standard stops)
>
> These signs must be thought of as the letters of the new alphabet.
>
> A grouping of several signs will determine
>
> (utilize colors—in order to differentiate what would correspond in this [literature] to the substantive, verb, adverb declensions, conjugations etc.)[77]

If the emotional or expressive characteristics of color are forced into service as a language, map, or diagram, the line—ostensibly painting's most rational and geometrically inclined tool—is destabilized in an oscillation between one, two, three, and four dimensions. This I think is the meaning of the strange constellation of lines on the right side of the painting. The tracings from the templates of the standard stoppages appear to exist in one dimension. However, the segments receding from them—divided into colored units like the array of color samples on the opposite side of the canvas—individually imply an extension into a second dimension as planes while collectively producing an illusion of three-dimensionality through perspectival recession.[78] Several of Duchamp's cryptic statements on the transition from the space of everyday life to the four-dimensional continuum suggest that the series of overlapping circles superimposed upon these segments indicate entry into a fourth dimension. For Duchamp, the circle was a figure of dimensional collapse. In a text from *The Green Box* he demonstrated this conviction by describing the rotation of a horizontal dividing line, G, that intersects a vertical axis. This vertical line suggests a division into a left plane and a right, which are occupied by points A and B. Duchamp attempted to demonstrate the collapse of such a "left" and "right" by asserting that the dividing line G may rotate in three dimensions either to the left toward A or the right toward B, but in either case the continuous path of circular rotation—in which one end meets the other—destroys left and right, displacing them by two isomorphic but directionally opposite continuums:

> And *on the other hand:* the vertical axis considered separately turning on itself, a generating line at a right angle e.g., will always determine a circle in the 2 cases 1st turning in the direction A, 2nd direction B.—
>
> Thus, *if it* were still possible, in the case of the vertical axis at rest., to consider *2 contrary directions* for the generating line G., the figure engendered (*whatever it may be*), can no longer be called left or right of the axis—
>
> As there is gradually less differentiation from axis to axis., i.e. as all the axes gradually disappear in a fading verticality the front and the back, the reverse and the obverse acquire a circular significance: the right and the left which are the 4 arms of the front and back. melt. *along the* verticals.
>
> the interior and exterior (in a fourth dimension) can receive a similar identification. but the axis is no longer vertical and has no longer a *one*-dimensional appearance[79]

The collapse of interior and exterior, left and right, represented by the circle, indicates entry into a four-dimensional continuum. Duchamp's description of "four-dimensional lines" gives further evidence for reading the chains of circles along these segments in *Tu m'* as an image of dimensional transfer: "The *4-dim'l straight line* is defined by *the whole set of successive spheres with larger and larger radii* starting from point 0. . . . This straight 4-dim' line = 3-dim'l space and does not get out of that space."[80] Although the radii of all of the circles attached to a single multicolored segment in *Tu m'* are equal, the circles vary in radius from segment to segment, as does the spacing between them. Whereas the text specifies a line composed of successive spheres, *Tu m'* contains chains of circles. Nevertheless the resemblance between the "four-dimensional line" as theorized in Duchamp's writing and the segments covered in linked circles in the painting is sufficiently striking to suggest an identity between them.

The case is strengthened by considering one of Duchamp's typical acts of conceptual metamorphosis in which a comb (like the one he inscribed as a readymade in 1916) is understood as a unit of measurement or a "generator of space." He developed this metaphorical association in a series of texts not directly related to *Tu m':*

> with a kind of comb, by using the space between 2 teeth as a unit, determine the relations between the 2 ends of the comb and some intermediary points (by the broken teeth).
>
> Use, as a proportional control, this comb with broken teeth, on another object made up, also of smaller elements.[81]

This initial transformation into a ruler is succeeded by another. The comb may become, as Duchamp told Arturo Schwarz in an interview, a "generator of space":

> D[uchamp].—Well, the Rattle is a toy for children that makes noise when you turn it, and the comb becomes a generator of space, space generated by the teeth.
>
> S[chwarz].—Like the handle of the *Coffee Mill.*

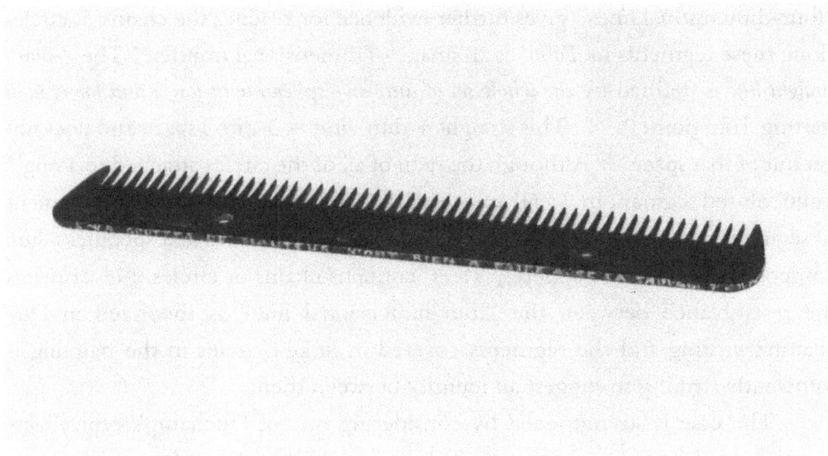

1.21 Marcel Duchamp. *Comb.* New York, February 1916. Steel comb, 6 ½ × 1 ¼". Philadelphia Museum of Art: The Louise and Walter Arensberg Collection. Photo by Graydon Wood, 1994. © 1997 Artists Rights Society (ARS), New York/ADAGP, Paris/Estate of Marcel Duchamp.

> D[uchamp].—Yes, but more than that, because the axis would be at the edge of the comb on the other side from the teeth, and the teeth would describe a series of circles which would be nothing at all in fact but a comb with different curves. It would no longer be a flat comb, but rather a curved comb. All these things never went further than the remark I made here in writing. But there is a possibility, as I said, of generating space from a flat surface. You can do it with any surface.[82]

It seems then, that the curious lines of *Tu m',* which consist of a sequence of circles emanating from a line, bear a distinct resemblance to the rotated comb that Duchamp described to Schwarz. Whether we imagine them as spanning the first through the fourth dimensions or only the first through the third, these lines are undoubtedly meant to function as "generators of space": taking any surface and reinventing it as a volume. Just as color is reordered into a graphic language in both the chips and the segments of *Tu m',* line is subjected to an infinite regression, putting stable dimensionality *en abyme.*

Duchamp said that *Tu m'* was "a kind of inventory of all my preceding works, rather than a painting in itself."[83] His use of the term *inventory* is no accident, nor is the painting's destination in a library over a bookcase irrelevant to its meaning. For *Tu m'* assiduously avoids any form of synthesis: it performs the disappearance of the object world into its own multiple and unstable representations in what the artist called a "hypophysical analysis of the successive transformations of objects." Every image in *Tu m'* is both an object and a representation or measure of another object—a shadow, a ruler, a sign, etc. Such a transfer—a kind of mutual mensuration—accounts for Duchamp's interest in the fourth dimension. The dichotomy between geometric line and immensurable body initiated in the cubist works of 1910–14 has been infinitely multiplied in this painting, to the point of transforming signification into aporia. Moreover, the subject of the nude, which had preoccupied Duchamp long after Picasso and Braque had abandoned it finally disappears within this maelstrom of relative meanings. With the exception of the completely reified pointing finger of the sign, there is no longer any trace of the body—or not quite. For as is so typical of Duchamp, the title of the work introduces a set of themes marginalized by the images within the canvas. Schwarz asserts that "tu m'" refers specifically to "a polite contraction for the French colloquialism *tu m'emmerdes* (you bore me)."[84] Despite this particular connotation these speech particles—like each of the visual elements in the painting—introduce a dynamic of specification and despecification. Pronouns mark persons only within the unique syntactic context of a particular utterance. The word *he* may signify an individual at one moment only because it also may stand for any other male subject at any other time. Moreover, the fragment, *Tu m'* retains an openended reflexivity. In this title the personal pronoun for "you" is pressed against the reflexive pronoun for "me," establishing an infinite regress of two bodies in language that begins outside the self and comes toward it (*tu* m').[85] By endlessly multiplying the dichotomous opposition between body and diagram that *Network of Stoppages* polemically established in 1914, *Tu m'* pushes Duchamp's cubist dynamic of mensurability and immensurability to its breaking point. As I shall argue in chapter 2, it was the readymade that brought painting to this impossible juncture.

2

Between Reification and Regression: Readymades and Words

Specifications for "Readymades"

by planning for a moment to come (on such a day, such a date such a minute), "*to inscribe* a readymade"—The readymade can later be looked for.—(with all kinds of delays)

The important thing then is just this matter of timing, this snapshot effect, like a speech delivered on no matter what occasion but *at such and such an hour.* It is a kind of rendezvous.

—Naturally inscribe that date, hour, minute, on the readymade as *information.*[1]

In Duchamp's cubism a distinctive graphic language seizes upon the painted nude. His major paintings of 1912—*Nude Descending a Staircase, The Passage from Virgin to Bride,* and *Bride*—are characterized by a poetics of "mensuration" in which "immensurable" flesh is captured by a diagrammatic armature drawn from deep within the body's architecture. In most critical accounts Duchamp's readymades are thought to eclipse this cubist painting. By seeming to elide the practice of art with the consumption of mass-produced commodities, the self-reflexive allegory of reification that the readymade performs is credited with making painting obsolete.[2] Yet in Duchamp's formulation reification is not understood as an irreversible move from painting to commodity. Indeed the readymades manifest a dynamic of immensurability and mensuration already well established in his canvases of 1912. In them the terms of Duchamp's cubism are not occluded but transposed: the diagram returns as the inscription, and carnality is established not by the nude but in the material bodies of commodities like a snow shovel or a urinal. For Duchamp the readymade was not simply a thing but a "rendez-vous," a fleeting encounter between subject and object that can only emerge into representation through an act of inscription. The transformation of commodity into artwork is therefore an effect of writing. But language held no metacritical authority for Duchamp: words are vulnerable to the same process of displacement and desublimation to which he submitted things. In a now-familiar logic of infinite regress the instrument of measurement—in this case, an inscription—itself falls into immensurability.

Accounts of Duchamp's readymade strategy in the teens typically center on now-canonical works such as *Bicycle Wheel* (1913), *In Advance of the Broken Arm* (1915), *Comb* (1916), and *Fountain* (1917), each of which stripped a utilitarian object of its function by situating it within the discourses of art. In the preponderance of art-historical and critical analysis, readymades are believed to initiate a double critique, of the capitalist field of exchange on the one hand, and its subset, the art market, on the other. In such readings, what Duchamp calls the "inscription" of the readymade is either ignored or aligned with the artist's presumably knowing and transcendent gesture of social criticism.[3] Yet alongside the object-oriented readymades of the mid-teens, Duchamp produced an underappreciated series of works in which language is submitted to analogous acts of desublimation.[4] If as Duchamp's definition suggests, the readymade is conceived not simply as a displaced commodity but as a dynamic of linguistic specification, these textual projects must be essential to understanding the significance of the readymade. In them language doubles back *in order to inscribe itself,* calling into question the neutrality or transparency of words. As a consequence the capacity—or intention—of the readymade to *unveil* the mechanics of exchange from some rational or transcendent position collapses as soon as it arises.

One of the fundamental concepts through which Duchamp theorized the linguistic readymade is his notion of the "prime word," described in a note from *The Green Box:*

> The search for *"prime words"* ("divisible" only by themselves and by unity).
>
> Take a Larousse dict. and copy all the so-called "abstract" words. i.e., those which have no concrete reference.
>
> Compose a schematic sign designating each of these words. (this sign can be composed with the standard stops)
>
> These signs must be thought of as the letters of the new alphabet.
>
> A grouping of several signs will determine
>
> (utilize colors—in order to differentiate what would correspond in this [literature] to the substantive, verb, adverb declensions, conjugations etc.)[5]

In this note Duchamp suggested a two-part process: taking words from the dictionary that have no concrete referents and then transposing these words into the elements of a new alphabet. As in *Tu m'* where measurement is put *en abyme* the word here undergoes an infinite regress. An already arbitrary signifier—what Duchamp called an "'abstract' word"—is displaced from the differential semiotic economy of language (whose locus is the dictionary) to the equally arbitrary vocabulary of painting: "(utilize colors—in order to differentiate what would correspond in this [literature] to the substantive, verb, adverb declensions, conjugations etc.)." Duchamp thus established a bilateral relay of identification between the arbitrary signifiers of language and their equally differential counterparts in painting. The result is the "prime word," which, stripped of its function as a means of signification, regresses into pure materiality.

Two textual works of 1915 and early 1916 respectively, *"The"* and *Rendezvous of Sunday, February 6, 1916,* actualize Duchamp's search for "prime words." The purpose of both texts was to invent grammatically correct sentences that were nevertheless completely incoherent. *"The"*[6] was written in English, soon after Duchamp's arrival in New York, while he was still mastering the language. Wherever the article *the* would have appeared in the handwritten manuscript, Duchamp inserted an asterisk. The text was lighthearted and completely incomprehensible; its first sentence is typical: "If you come into ⋆ linen, your time is thirsty because ⋆ ink saw some wood intelligent enough to get giddiness from a sister." *Rendezvous of Sunday, February 6, 1916* is a typewritten text in French on four postcards taped together to form a windowlike grid. Although they are linked in this way, the sentences are not continuous from one card to the next. Duchamp explained his concept for the work to Arturo Schwarz:

> There would be a verb, a subject, a complement, adverbs and everything perfectly correct, as such, as words, but meaning in these sentences was a thing that I had to avoid . . . the verb was meant to be an abstract word acting on a subject that is a material object; in this way the verb would make the sentence look abstract. The construction was very painful in a way, because the minute I *did* think of a verb to add to the subject, I would very often see a meaning and immediately I saw a meaning I would cross out the verb and change it, until, working it out for quite a number of hours, the text finally read without any echo of the physical world. . . . That was the main point in it.[7]

Duchamp's project here is extraordinary and quite different from the puns he devised in the 1920s, which established two or more countervailing meanings within a single sentence. These later textual works operate along a linguistic fault line where a displaced or fragmentary parallelism in words provokes a convulsive contradiction.[8] For instance, the English text "My niece is cold because my knees are cold" is tautological but grammatically incorrect on the level of pro-

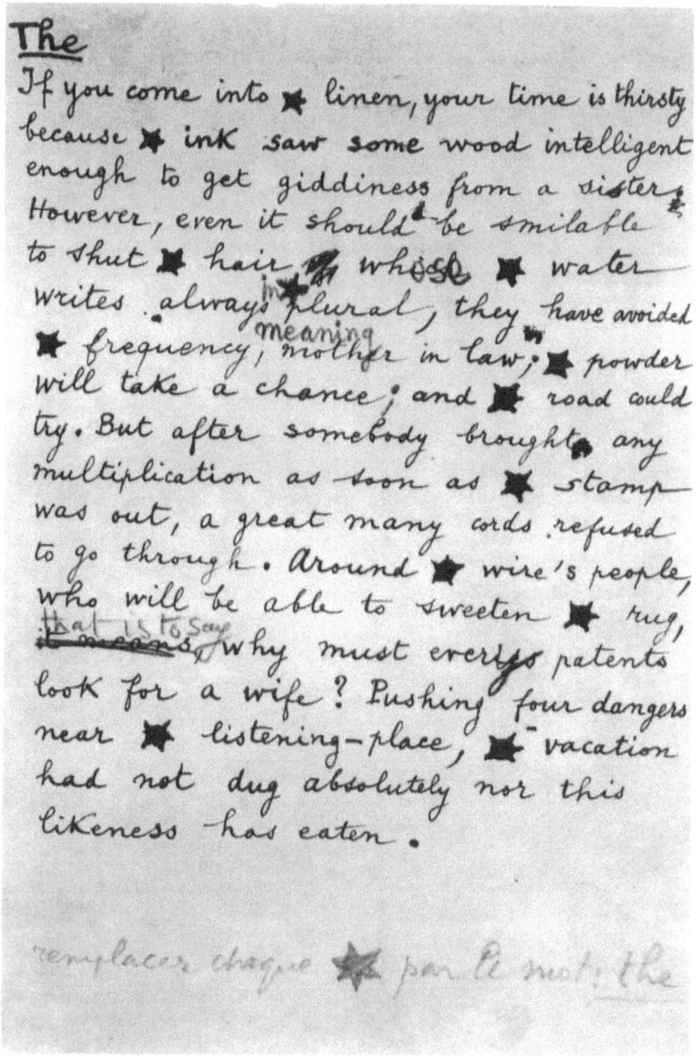
The
If you come into ★ linen, your time is thirsty
because ★ ink saw some wood intelligent
enough to get giddiness from a sister.
However, even it should be smilable
to shut ★ hair whose ★ water
writes always in plural, they have avoided
★ frequency, meaning mother in law; ★ powder
will take a chance; and ★ road could
try. But after somebody brought any
multiplication as soon as ★ stamp
was out, a great many cords refused
to go through. Around ★ wire's people,
who will be able to sweeten ★ rug,
that is to say ~~means~~, why must every patents
look for a wife? Pushing four dangers
near ★ listening-place, ★ vacation
had not dug absolutely nor this
likeness has eaten.

remplacer chaque ★ par le mot: the

2.1 Marcel Duchamp. *"The"*. 1915. India ink and pencil manuscript, 8 ¾ × 5 ⅝". Philadelphia Museum of Art: The Louise and Walter Arensberg Collection. © 1997 Artists Rights Society (ARS), New York/ADAGP, Paris/Estate of Marcel Duchamp.

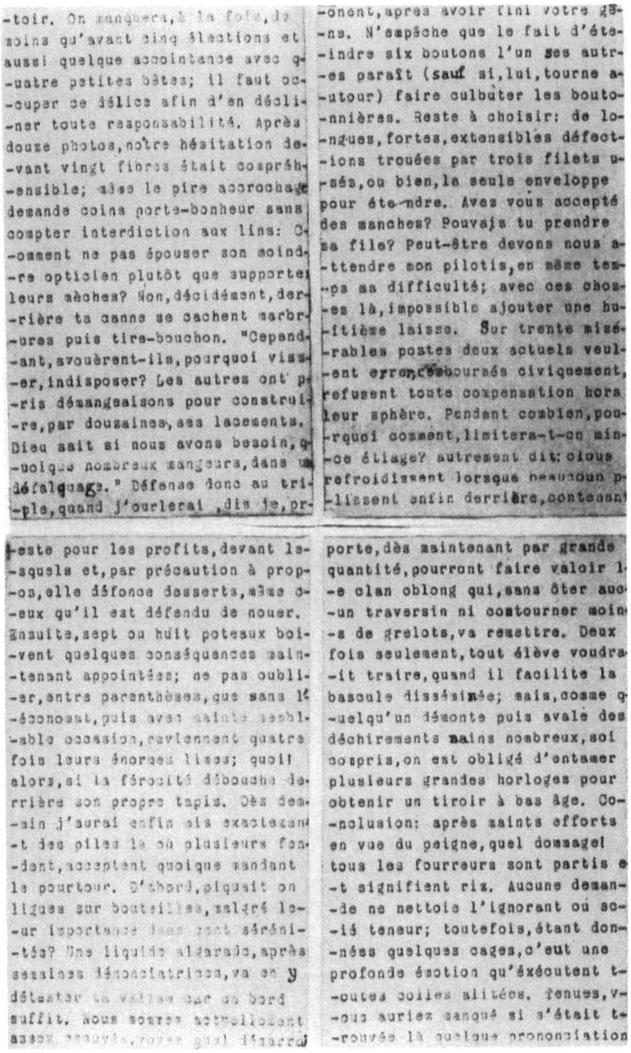
-toir. On manquera, à la foie, de
moins qu'avant cinq élections et
aussi quelque accointance avec q-
-uatre petites bêtes; il faut oc-
-cuper ce délice afin d'en décli-
-ner toute responsabilité. Après
douze photos, notre hésitation de-
-vant vingt fibres était compréh-
-ensible; même le pire accrochage
demande coins porte-bonheur sans
compter interdiction aux lins: C-
-omment ne pas épouser son moind-
-re opticien plutôt que supporter
leurs mèches? Non, décidément, der-
-rière ta canne se cachent marbr-
-ures puis tire-bouchon. "Cepend-
-ant, avouèrent-ils, pourquoi viss-
-er, indisposer? Les autres ont p-
-ris démangeaisons pour construi-
-re, par douzaines, ses lacements.
Dieu sait si nous avons besoin, q-
-uoique nombreux mangeurs, dans un
défalquage." Défense donc au tri-
-ple, quand j'ourlerai, dis je, pr-

-ônent, après avoir fini votre ga-
-ne. N'empêche que le fait d'éte-
-indre six boutons l'un ses autr-
-es paraît (sauf si, lui, tourne a-
-utour) faire culbuter les bouto-
-nnières. Reste à choisir: de lo-
-ngues, fortes, extensibles défect-
-ions trouées par trois filets u-
-sés, ou bien, la seule enveloppe
pour éte-ndre. Avez vous accepté
des manches? Pouvais tu prendre
sa file? Peut-être devons nous a-
-ttendre mon pilotis, en même tem-
-ps ma difficulté; avec ces chos-
-es là, impossible ajouter une hu-
-itième laisse. Sur trente misé-
-rables postes deux actuels veul-
-ent errer, remboursés civiquement,
refusent toute compensation hors
leur sphère. Pendant combien, pou-
-rquoi comment, limitera-t-on min-
-ce étiage? autrement dit: clous
refroidissent lorsque beaucoup p-
-lissent enfin derrière, contenant

-este pour les profits, devant le-
-squels et, par précaution à prop-
-os, elle défonce desserts, même c-
-eux qu'il est défendu de nouer.
Ensuite, sept ou huit poteaux boi-
-vent quelques conséquences main-
-tenant appointées; ne pas oubli-
-er, entre parenthèses, que sans le
-économat, puis avec mainte semb-
-able occasion, reviennent quatre
fois leurs énormes lises; quoi!
alors, si la férocité débouche de-
rrière son propre tapis. Dès dem-
-ain j'aurai enfin mis exactement
-t des piles là où plusieurs fon-
-dent, acceptent quoique mendant
le pourtour. D'abord, piquait on
ligues sur bouteilles, malgré le-
-ur importance dans sont séréni-
-tés? Une liquide algarade, après
semaines dénonciatrices, va en y
détester la valise car un bord
suffit. Nous sommes actuellement
assez ennuyés, voyez quel désarroi

porte, dès maintenant par grande
quantité, pourront faire valoir l-
-e clan oblong qui, sans ôter auc-
-un traversin ni contourner moin-
-s de grelots, va remettre. Deux
fois seulement, tout élève voudra-
-it traire, quand il facilite la
bascule dissimulée; mais, comme q-
-uelqu'un démonte puis avale des
déchirements mains nombreux, soi
compris, on est obligé d'entamer
plusieurs grandes horloges pour
obtenir un tiroir à bas âge. Co-
-nclusion: après maints efforts
en vue du peigne, quel dommage!
tous les fourreurs sont partis e-
-t signifient riz. Aucune deman-
-de ne nettoie l'ignorant ou sc-
-ié teneur; toutefois, étant don-
-nées quelques cages, c'eut une
profonde émotion qu'exécutent t-
-outes colles alitées. Tenues, v-
-ous auriez manqué si s'était t-
-rouvée là quelque prononciation

2.2 Marcel Duchamp. *Rendezvous of Sunday, February 6, 1916 (Rendez-vous du Dimanche 6 Février 1916)*. 1916. Typewriter and ink on four postcards, with tape, 11 ¼ × 6 ½″. Philadelphia Museum of Art: The Louise and Walter Arensberg Collection. Photo by Lynn Rosenthal, 1992. © Artists Rights Society (ARS), New York/ADAGP, Paris/Estate of Marcel Duchamp.

nunciation (either "my knees is cold because my knees are cold" or "my niece is cold because my niece are cold"), but within this bland repetition of congruent sounds a transgressive incestuous attachment explodes ("my niece is cold [frigid] because she won't sit on my lap"). In this short text, a linguistic doubling stands in for, as it represents, a forbidden libidinal "doubling": the incestuous encounter. The only trace of the disturbance, appropriately enough, is a change in tense from singular to plural—from "is" to "are."

If the puns of the twenties establish a bilateral relay in which one metaphor rebounds from another, *"The"* and *Rendezvous* sought to pulverize the logic of metaphor altogether. While the metonymic axis of language remains intact in these texts—grammatical structure is respected and rigorously correct—the metaphoric axis, that dimension of language in which one word may be substituted for another, is completely disrupted. The fact that Duchamp found the process of producing such disruption "very painful" suggests how close the exercise must have felt to pathology, to a type of aphasia defined by Roman Jakobson as "similarity disorder": the inability to find or identify synonyms, circumlocutions, or heteronyms. Jakobson's account of the experience of one such aphasic subject might serve as a description of the experience of reading *"The"* or *Rendezvous:*

> As long as he does not regard another's speech as a message addressed to him in his own verbal pattern, he feels, as a patient of Hemphil and Stengel expressed it: "I can hear you dead plain but I cannot get what you say . . . I hear your voice but not the words . . . It does not pronounce itself." He considers the other's utterance to be either gibberish or at least in an unknown language.[9]

By simulating aphasia, Duchamp was able to insist upon the materiality of language. Like gibberish or an "unknown" language, words are drained of their significance, falling back into a sensuous medium of sound.

According to the interview with Schwarz, Duchamp wanted to exorcise from his text "any echo of the physical world," which is consistent with his desire to invent "prime words" characterized by a second-order abstraction. Certainly *"The"* and *Rendezvous* accomplish this goal, but they also serve a more specific function. Duchamp hinted at his objective to Schwarz: "The verb was meant to be an abstract word acting on a subject that is a material object; in this way the verb would make the sentence look abstract." In these textual exercises, an abstract verb *inscribes* "a subject which is a material object" in order to make it, too, appear abstract—to displace it from its accustomed place, just as in 1915 the inscription "In Advance of the Broken Arm" made a snow shovel an *abstract(ed)* artwork. Setting free the axis of equivalent "material objects" in language is directly analogous to setting actual commodities free from their intended functions.[10] *"The"* and *Rendezvous* are thus narrative performances of the same process of inscription that produces readymades: in these textual works a "material" noun allegorizes the commodity and the "abstract" verb, its inscription. In *"The"* the asterisk replacing the article *the* highlights the "material objects"—nouns—that inevitably follow, just as their lack of coherent sense in the context of the sentence throws each into relief. Such an analogy between text and readymade is made explicit in the title of *Rendezvous of Sunday, February 6, 1916,* which cites one of the latter's qualities as specified in Duchamp's definition: "It is a kind of rendezvous." In *Rendezvous* each of the four postcards—themselves commodities[11]—unites to form a new object. The "inscription"—or text—is therefore carried by a commodity, just as, in the mass-produced readymade, the commodity is imprinted with an inscription. A text fragment from *The Green Box* confirms the analogy between the commodity and words set free from their conventional meanings:

> Identifying
>
> *To lose the possibility of recognizing 2 similar objects*—2 colors, 2 laces, 2 hats, 2 forms whatsoever to reach the Impossibility of sufficient *visual* memory, to transfer from one like object to another the *memory* imprint.
>
> —Same possibility with sounds; with brain facts[12]

This statement transposes the delirious vertigo of Jakobson's similarity disorder—and its absurdist transposition in *"The"* and *Rendezvous*—to the realm of objects. For Duchamp, displacing a word from the marketplace of language or a product from the economic market releases an explosive and annihilating power—an ecstatic incapacity to differentiate that may dissolve "any echo of the physical world."

These parallel crises of identification of words and objects are explicitly linked in an "assisted readymade" of 1916, *With Hidden Noise*. Duchamp described the work as follows:

> *With Hidden Noise* is the title for this assisted readymade: a ball of twine between two brass plates joined by four long screws. Inside the ball of twine Walter Arensberg added secretly a small object that makes a noise when you shake it. And to this day I don't know what it is, nor, I imagine does anyone else.
>
> On the brass plaques I wrote three short sentences in which letters were occasionally missing like in a neon sign when one letter is not lit and makes the word unintelligible.[13]

The "plaques," like two disembodied nameplates hugging a ball of twine, suggest an official public discourse: the language of bourgeois office buildings or apartment houses. The *object* is therefore built of *words;* even the ball of twine is no more than a single "line" that doubles back on itself, just like Duchamp's own linguistic acrobatics or the bits of string that he dropped to generate the three standard stoppages.[14] But the phrases inscribed with white paint on the two plaques of *With Hidden Noise* are anything but coherent. Each plate includes a text of three lines, with some letters replaced by periods, and a fourth line of instructions. The bottom plaque reads, ".IR. CAR.É LONGSEA→ / F.NE, HEA., O.SQUE→ / TE.U S.ARP BAR.AIN→ / *Remplacer chaque point par une lettre*," and the top one: "P.G. .ÉCIDES DÉBARRASSE. / LE. D.SERT. F.URNIS. ENT / AS HOW.V.R COR.ESPONDS / *Convenablement choisie*

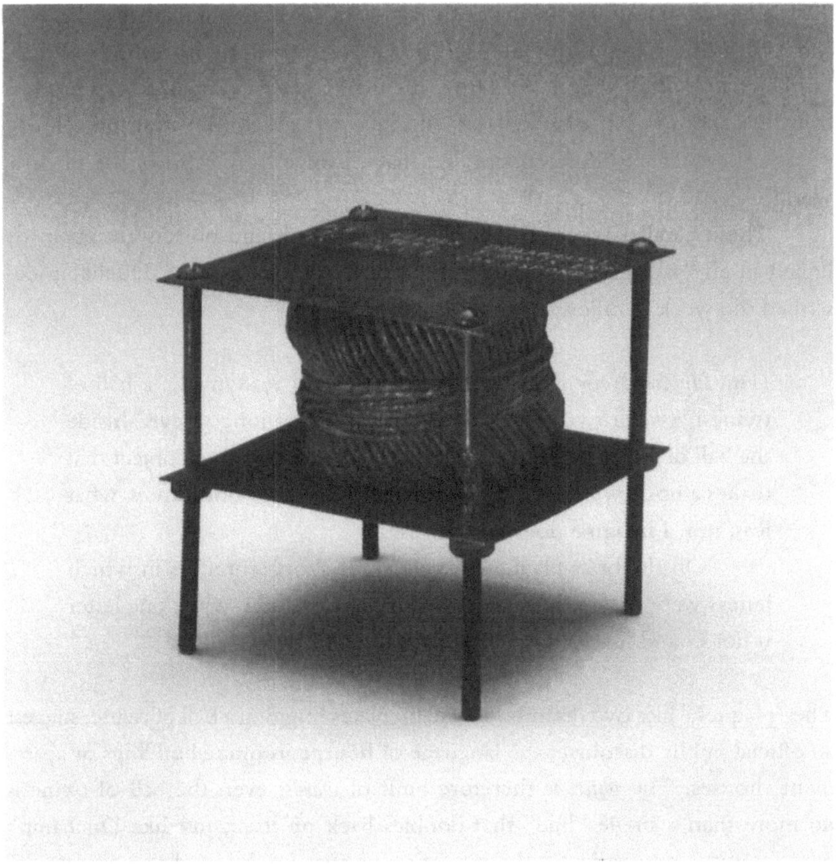

2.3 Marcel Duchamp. *With Hidden Noise.* 1916. Assisted readymade: ball of twine between two brass plates, joined by four long screws, containing a small unknown object added by Walter Arensberg, 5 × 5 × 5 ⅛". Philadelphia Museum of Art: The Louise and Walter Arensberg Collection. © 1997 Artists Rights Society (ARS), New York/ADAGP, Paris/Estate of Marcel Duchamp.

dans la même colonne." In a letter to Arturo Schwarz, Duchamp explained how the words were meant to function:

> [They were] an exercise in comparative orthography (English-French). The periods must be replaced (with one exception: débarrassé[e] by one of the two letters of the other two lines, but in the same vertical as the period—French and English are mixed and make no "sense." The three arrows indicate the continuity of the line from the lower plate to the other [upper] still without meaning.[15]

With Hidden Noise spatializes language not only through the volume produced by the bolted brass rectangles[16] but in three other ways. First, within the planes of the plaques, a series of vertical "semiotic" axes is established from the position of each missing letter—indicated by a period—to the letters above and below that may replace it. Second, Duchamp explicitly suggested through the arrow at the end of each line of text on the bottom plaque of the work that one is meant to turn it over in order to continue reading on the top. Following Duchamp's fascination with dimensional transfer,[17] The line of text—presumed to exist within the two-dimensional grid of the page—bends into a sphere leading from the plaque below to the one above, precisely echoing the winding length of twine compressed between them. These geometric and volumetric spatializations are amplified by an additional geographical and cultural displacement, that between the language of France and of America, jumbled together in an incoherent heap.

With Hidden Noise therefore summarizes—and completes—the themes of *"The"* and *Rendezvous* both by materializing or objectifying language as a readymade and by unloosening the material signifier from its conceptual signified. But Duchamp went one step further. These materialized signifiers—"prime words" set free from the burden of carrying signifieds—form themselves into a physical envelope, an *object,* but their purpose is to conceal yet another object that itself *cannot be known*. As Duchamp said of what Arensberg placed inside the

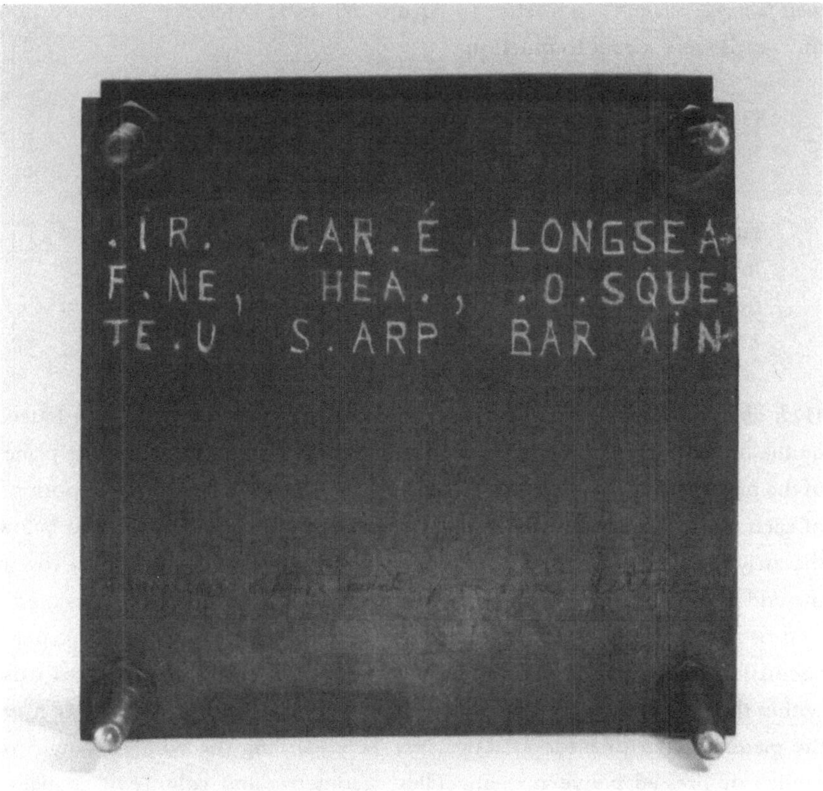

2.4 Marcel Duchamp. *With Hidden Noise* (detail of bottom plaque). Philadelphia Museum of Art: The Louise and Walter Arensberg Collection. Photo by Lynn Rosenthal, 1995. © 1997 Artists Rights Society (ARS), New York/ADAGP, Paris/Estate of Marcel Duchamp.

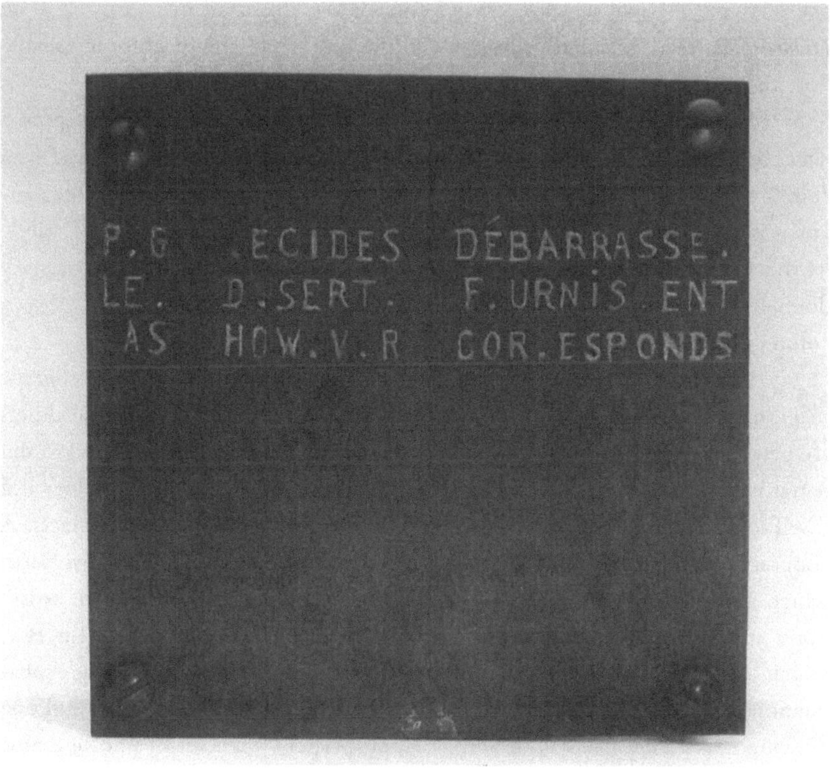

2.5 Marcel Duchamp. *With Hidden Noise* (detail of top plaque). Philadelphia Museum of Art: The Louise and Walter Arensberg Collection. Photo by Lynn Rosenthal, 1995. © 1997 Artists Rights Society (ARS), New York/ADAGP, Paris/Estate of Marcel Duchamp.

ball of twine, "I will never know whether it is a diamond or a coin."[18] *With Hidden Noise* is a "bilateral" allegory. On the one hand, the diachronic, pliable flow of language is disciplined into an imprisoning cage for an object—one is tempted to say a referent—while this hidden thing loses all identity except as a *noise.* It is transformed from a stable commodity or currency ("a diamond or a coin") to the primordial medium of language. On the surface of the work language is reified while at its center a thing regresses from the status of a commodity to a primitive form of exchange, the exchange of sound. In an extraordinary double move—or double *inscription*—language becomes a commodity,[19] as a commodity becomes language.

With Hidden Noise (as well as *"The"* and *Rendezvous*) performs a reflexive relationship between text and object, or commodity, in which material things are perpetually vulnerable to liquidation—a putting-into-motion related to the narrative function of text. But Duchamp's practice of the readymade does not dwell exclusively on the power of words to disrupt the integrity of objects. A countervailing logic of linguistic reification also characterizes *With Hidden Noise,* which is brought to the fore in Duchamp's re-presentations of his own artist's notes and jottings as readymades in *The 1914 Box.* The contents of this *Box,* which was published in an edition of three in 1914, include photographic reproductions of sixteen manuscript notes largely pertaining to project ideas and one drawing, *Avoir l'apprenti dans le soleil.*[20] Appropriately, each set of photographic reproductions was stored in the kind of commercial cardboard box, imprinted with the trademarks and slogans of photographic processing companies, used to store industrially produced photographs. In fact Duchamp purposely called attention to the commodity status of these pictures. On the cover of one Kodak container, he altered the label "so as to read that the box contained '15/16 industrial photographs.' The word 'photographs' was underlined three times."[21] Paradoxically Duchamp emphasized the role of the photograph as the residue or means of gaining access to his own original and highly personal notes: he sought to reveal his mental processes—as well as his handwriting—as industrial processes. Duchamp's second major collection of notes, most of which pertain to the conceptualization and generation of his *Large Glass* from 1913 to 1923, was published in 1934 as *The Green Box.* As in *The 1914 Box* he treated his own mental processes and musings as readymades:

> Twelve years after finishing or rather after putting aside my Glass, I fell upon my working notes, scribbled at random in some hundred scraps of paper. I wanted to reproduce them as exactly as possible. So I had all these thoughts lithographed in the same ink which had been used for the originals. To find paper that was exactly the same, I had to ransack the most unlikely nooks and crannies of Paris. Then we had to cut out three hundred copies of each lithograph with the help of zinc patterns that I had cut out on the outlines of the original papers.[22]

In *The Green Box,* as in the earlier collection, Duchamp took extraordinary pains to mass-produce what is generally assumed to be unique or original—the artist's cognitive processes. It was not enough to publish transcripts of his texts. Rather he sought to reproduce as precisely as possible each torn piece of paper, each different ink, so that every one of the proposed three hundred editions of *The Green Box* would appear to share the spontaneity, the immediacy of the original process—as though he had undertaken to mass-produce his own subjectivity discovered readymade.[23]

The mediation in both *The 1914 Box* and the later collection of notes between a handwritten text by the artist and its capture through various reproductive technologies may throw some light on a cryptic note contained within *The Green Box:* "*The bride stripped bare by her bachelors even.* to separate the *mass-produced readymade* from the *readyfound*—The separation is an operation."[24] The distinction between the *readymade,* here associated with the mass-produced, and the *readyfound* is highly suggestive. If we link the readymade to the world of objects—as Duchamp's emphasis on its mass-produced quality hints—and identify the ready*found* with mental forms of production like language or thought, which is recovered through mechanical reproduction in Duchamp's own notes, then both the meaning of this text and the motivations for producing the two

Boxes are clarified.[25] For Duchamp the object and the subject, the readymade and the readyfound, are profoundly imbricated in one another, so nearly inextricable that "the separation is an operation." Yet despite the close association of these terms—of mind and body—Duchamp's short texts and readymades suggest a self that is radically fragmented, perpetually falling into pieces. For instance in a note titled "Deferment" from *The 1914 Box* he imagined a body dramatically dispersed: "Against compulsory military service: a *'deferment'* of each limb, of the heart and the other anatomical parts; each soldier being already unable to put his uniform on again, his heart feeding *telephonically,* a deferred arm, etc."[26] In this extraordinary text a soldier's anatomy[27] floats out of alignment: each limb, each organ becomes a separable and separated object that may only relate to the others through a technical apparatus for speaking. Language drains away from the collapsed body, only to be retrofitted *telephonically.*

Duchamp's readymades are presumed to have terminated and displaced his cubist fascination with the nude by shifting the function of art from an artisanal practice of representation to a philosophical debate over what constitutes an art object. As these arguments go, the mass-produced readymade calls into question the transcendental process of creation by replacing it with a strategic logic of naming.[28] Making art is displaced by the struggles to define its terms. But Duchamp's readymades not only restage the drama of immensurability and mensuration that lay at the heart of his cubism, they also explicitly reintroduce his cubist poetics of a fragmented modern body. *Pulled at 4 Pins,* for instance, which is now lost, consisted of an unpainted tin chimney ventilator inscribed with the phrase "Pulled at 4 Pins" and presented to Louise Varèse in 1915. The inscription is a literal and consequently meaningless translation of the expression *tiré à quatre épingles,* which means "dressed to the nines." Not only does the English translation initiate a slippage between two languages that is also a slippage between nonsense and sense, but "pulled at 4 pins" implies a visceral disjunction—a kind of drawing and quartering reminiscent of outmoded techniques of torture. The superimposition of the English onto the French therefore takes on a sinister cast: the suggestion of violent dismemberment undermines dandyish self-possession, just as in the text "Deferment" a male body undergoes collapse and (re)constitution, is both "pulled apart" *and* dressed up. *Pulled at 4 Pins* thus manifests several levels of dissociation: between languages, within bodies, and between a commodity and its inscription. This latter alienation between words and objects occurs in virtually all of Duchamp's readymades,[29] but the lesson of this particular work is that each of the three disjunctions informs the others: the cutting apart of objects and words that Duchamp's readymades enact is haunted by the dissolution and dispersal of anatomies.

As *Pulled at 4 Pins* suggests, the logic of dissolving bodies that had been explicitly gendered in Duchamp's cubism persists in his practice of the readymade. In paintings like *Nude Descending a Staircase, The Passage from Virgin to Bride, Bride,* and *Network of Stoppages,* collapsed feminine anatomies are contained by diagrammatic armatures coded as masculine or framed, through the allusions of their titles, by an economy of marriage premised on the exchange of women. This often agonistic imposition of a poetics of mensuration onto immensurable flesh, which in *Network of Stoppages* suggests an erotic struggle, is mirrored by a countervailing semioticization of the feminine body, particularly in paintings like *Passage* and *Bride.* Such an immanence of language to femininity characterizes a series of ribald works in the mid-teens, some making use of the mechanized script of the typewriter that Duchamp had used to produce *Rendezvous of Sunday, February 6, 1916.* In these works the relatively neutral discipline of the body's architecture in the cubist paintings reemerges as a much more explicit and indeed misogynist coupling of feminine biology and language. In a 1916 "portrait" drawing of Fania Marinoff, Carl Van Vechten's wife, the dispersal of the body is explicitly attendant upon linguistic entropy. *Fania (Profile)* establishes a violent disjunction between the overlapping registers of a drawn profile and typewritten characters. A stepped diagonal moving from the upper right to the lower left of the drawing is composed of upside-down typewritten letters either singly or in nonsignifying chains corresponding to no word in either English or French. Weaving back and forth along this diagonal is the crude contour of a profile whose grotesque forms include a deeply shaded, beaklike nose and a virtually

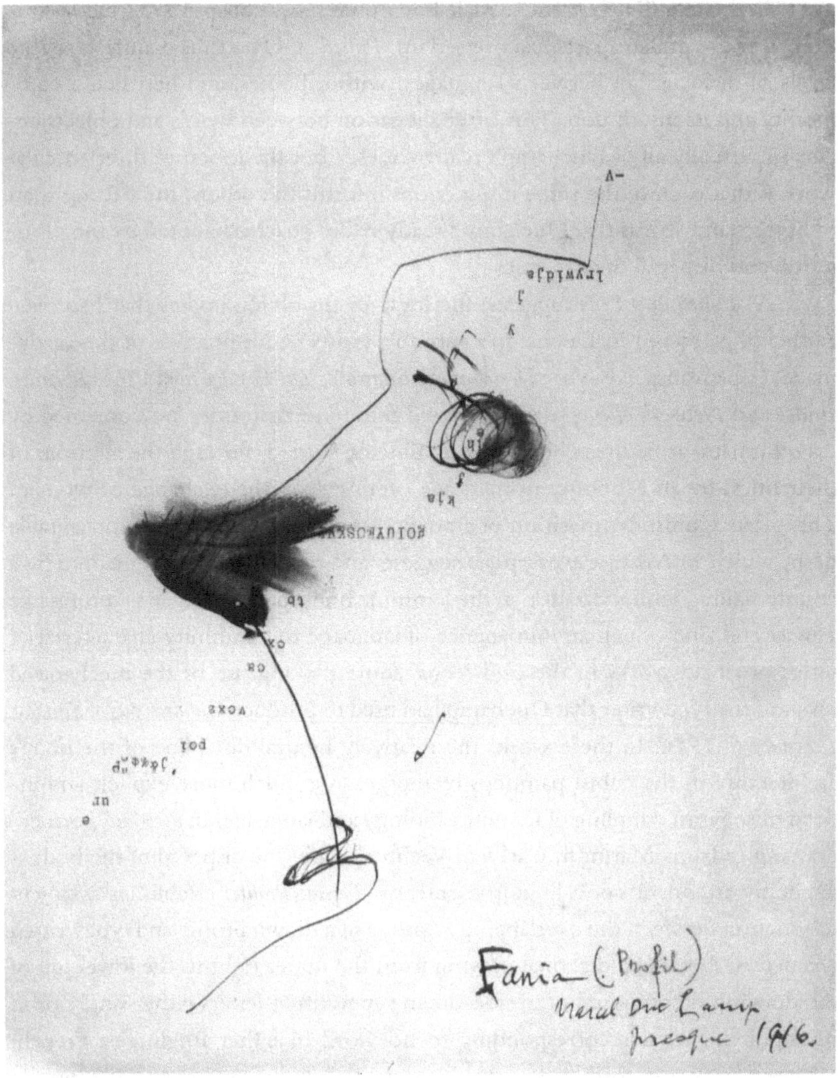

2.6 Marcel Duchamp. *Fania (Profile)*. 1916. Brown ink and wash with typed letters on ivory wove paper, 11 × 8 ½″. Philadelphia Museum of Art: The Louise and Walter Arensberg Collection. Photo by Lynn Rosenthal, 1992. © 1997 Artists Rights Society (ARS), New York/ADAGP, Paris/Estate of Marcel Duchamp.

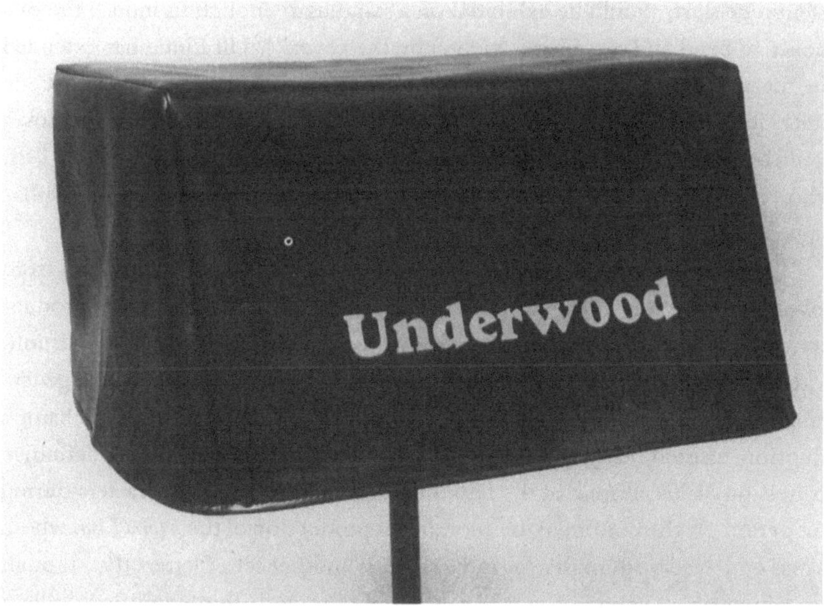

2.7 Marcel Duchamp. *Traveller's Folding Item* (original lost). New York, 1916. Underwood typewriter cover, 9″ in height. Photo Arturo Schwarz Collection, Milan. Photo: S.A.D.E. archives. © 1997 Artists Rights Society (ARS), New York/ADAGP, Paris/Estate of Marcel Duchamp.

obscene protruding tongue. The face is completed with an "eye" composed of several overlapping circles partly darkened by wash. Like *Rendezvous* this drawing was provoked by Duchamp's purchase of an Underwood typewriter, but unlike the other work of 1916, neatly organized into a linguistic and pictorial grid composed of actual words—even if combined to avoid coherent sense—this combination of woman and text exhibits a gestural crudeness not typical of Duchamp, particularly during this period. The typewriter seems to have suggested obscenity—even misogyny—when combined with femininity. In *Traveller's Folding Item* of 1916 Duchamp presented the cover of the Underwood typewriter as a readymade. According to Schwarz, "This item, which Duchamp identifies with a feminine skirt, should be exhibited on a stand high enough to induce the onlooker to bend and see what is hidden by the cover."[30] Ulf Linde has extended the metaphor: "If one considers that the Bride's task is to produce 'alphabetic units,' it might be possible to see her as a typewriter—and the Underwood cover could be her clothes."[31] Linde is referring to the bride in Duchamp's *Large Glass,* who, as part of her orgasmic blossoming, produces an inscription of "alphabetic units."[32]

In *Traveller's Folding Item,* machine-generated characters emanate not from a woman's hand but (metaphorically) from beneath her skirt: language production appears at the site of biological production. The portrait of Fania Marinoff, with its graphic language of clefts, depressions, and clitoral protuberance, generating a flow of meaningless letters, reinforces this interpretation.[33] Duchamp's notorious assisted readymade of 1919, *L.H.O.O.Q.,* may provide the definitive expression of his alliance of the feminine body and linguistic characters during this period. At the bottom of this modified reproduction of the *Mona Lisa,* whose face is endowed with mustache and goatee, is another set of letters that, though describing no meaningful word, is homophonic with the expression "Elle a chaud au cul" ("She has a hot ass [or cunt]"). As in *Fania* the letters are identified with the body, but in this case through connotation rather than graphic proximity. A similar inversion occurs with the mouth, which through the addition of facial hair has often been considered a vagina dentata.[34] The source of language is vaginalized, just as the letters themselves point to this region of the anatomy. If Mona Lisa has a hot ass, she also has a hot mouth—she's a good talker.

L.H.O.O.Q. and *Fania* demonstrate a means of materializing language different from the coolly cerebral exercises of *"The"* and *Rendezvous.* The former works imagine the liberated and materialized signifier in terms of an obscene and disruptive feminine body. But in fact this "feminine" characteristic of language comes to stand for linguistic regression in the speech of either gender. Duchamp retrospectively declared: "The curious thing about that moustache and goatee is that when you look at it the *Mona Lisa* becomes a man. It is not a woman disguised as a man; it is a real man, and that was my discovery, without really realizing it at the time."[35] As *Traveller's Folding Item* and *L.H.O.O.Q.*

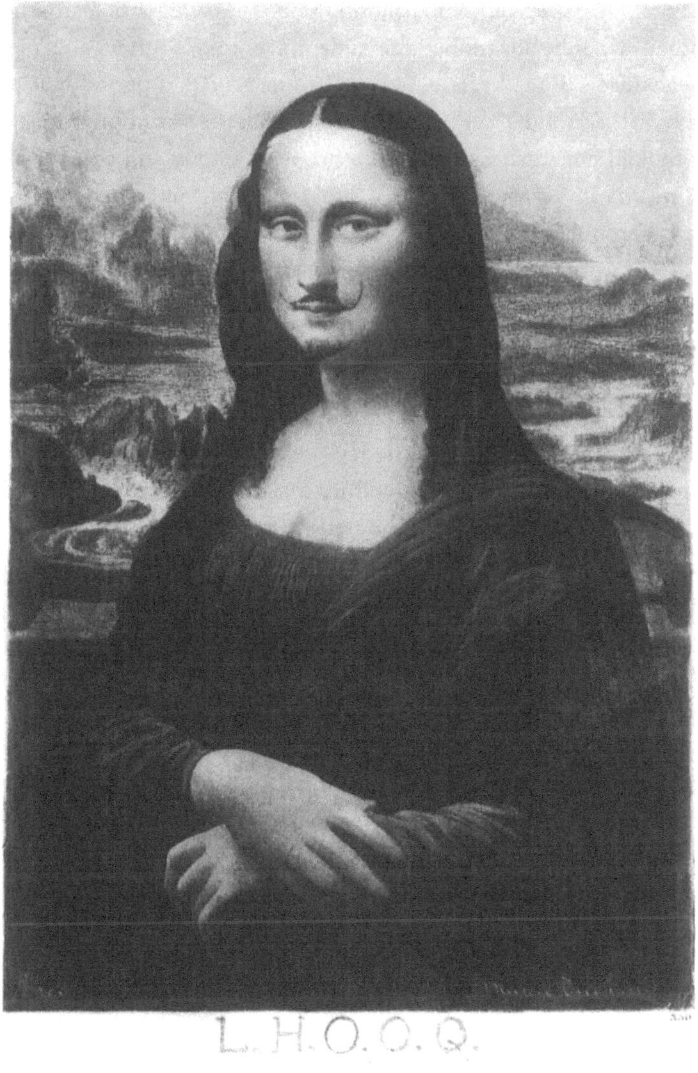

2.8 Marcel Duchamp. Replica of *L.H.O.O.Q.* 1919. Collotype hand-colored with watercolor, 7 5⁄8 × 4 13⁄16″. Philadelphia Museum of Art: The Louise and Walter Arensberg Collection. Photo by Lynn Rosenthal, 1992. © 1997 Artists Rights Society (ARS), New York/ADAGP, Paris/Estate of Marcel Duchamp.

demonstrate, Duchamp did not abandon the body—and particularly the feminine body—when he abandoned the nude in painting. Rather his explorations of the readymade in the years between 1914 and 1918, a period bracketed by *Network of Stoppages* and *Tu m'*, may help to explain the transition from a dichotomous, though chiasmatic, relationship between a body and that which measures it in *Network* to an open-ended proliferation of interchangeable objects and inscriptions in *Tu m'*, where each thing represented is both an object to be measured and a form of measurement. Just as Duchamp's cubism centered on a dynamic of mensuration in which an acephalous, aleatory libidinal field was submitted to various forms of immanent and external measurement, the readymade is premised upon an analogous dialectic of object and inscription. The fundamental insight of Duchamp's cubism between 1911 and 1914—that the nude may function as a "visceral currency"—led him to substitute commodities for bodies, bodies caught up in linguistic, social and scientific "mensuration." Indeed, Duchamp's readymades of this period, from *In Advance of the Broken Arm* and *Fountain* to *Pulled at 4 Pins* and *Traveller's Folding Item*, are haunted by a vestigial anthropomorphism, a metaphorical and often literal dispersal or dismemberment of the body. In them, the dissolving and visceral anatomies of Duchamp's cubism are transposed into commodities that are equally adrift: "pulled at 4 pins" as well as "dressed to the nines."

Such a reading of the readymades as informed by Duchamp's cubist thematization of the gendered body runs counter to the most powerful account of the passage from painting to the readymade in his art. For Thierry de Duve this metamorphosis occurs through the detachment of a name—*painting*—from the process of applying pigment onto canvas that it has traditionally signified. De Duve summarizes his argument at the outset of his book *Pictorial Nominalism:*

> The ruse of this book should make itself transparent. Its real object is tradition, that particular tradition that has been called modern art, modernity, or modernism, which has all the appearances of an antitradition and which is to be "photographed" in the privileged instant when it reveals what it transmits: a name, the name *painting*.

> This revelation can be recognized in two faces, or two phases. The "abandonment" of painting is the passage by which its name is detached from the specific craft that legitimated it. The "invention" of the readymade is the transition by which the name *painting*, having lost its specific legitimacy, nonetheless connects with the generic name *art*.[36]

De Duve's argument is compelling. Avant-garde painting repeatedly challenged that which could be legitimately called a painting. Around 1912, when artists like Kasimir Malevich or Robert Delaunay were inventing a rigorous abstraction composed of paints taken readymade from mass-produced, mass-marketed tubes, applied with the limited skill of factory workers onto expanses of canvas that were themselves readymade commodities, de Duve reasons that Duchamp's presentation of a mass-produced product as art belonged precisely to the newly "industrialized" discourse of painting.[37] But de Duve is at pains to demonstrate that Duchamp's gesture does not constitute a simple "murder" of painting by the readymade: at the heart of his "nominalist" gesture is a permanent instability, an undecidability. If the readymade begs to be considered a painting, it is also ultimately *not* a painting because of its status as a mass-produced commodity:

> Thus, the readymade ought to be called a painting/the readymade cannot be called a painting. One cannot get out of this contradiction by saying that it is both "painting" and "something else" or that it is neither "painting" nor "something else." The readymade does not put the concept of painting in contradiction with itself; it renders the act of naming the painting undecidable.[38]

De Duve's argument captures two fundamental aspects of Duchamp's oeuvre in the teens: first, the readymade constituted not a rejection but rather a "secession" from and continuation of the traditions of painting.[39] Second, Duchamp's works in this period—both his cubist paintings and the readymades that succeeded them—are characterized by paradox: they embody contradictions without resolving them. However, despite these insights, by locating the relationship between painting and the readymade within the act of naming, de Duve establishes an irreversible vector leading from one to the other that suppresses the "multilateral" or cyclical nature of Duchamp's metaphors.

In de Duve's formulation, the passage from painting to the readymade is oedipal. He establishes a parallelism between the transformations that Duchamp *represents* as an artist and his own biographical struggle to prove himself as an artist: "To the becoming-woman announced in *The Passage from the Virgin to the Bride* corresponds the desire of Duchamp to become a painter. A becoming-painter for a becoming-woman."[40] Within this logic, Duchamp's desire to become a painter is metaphorically and psychically collapsed onto his desire *for* a woman, figured as painting: "We will assume the word *painting* every time that Duchamp says *woman*." Importing the Lacanian schema, de Duve sketches the following progress: Duchamp's desire leads him to an imaginary identification with his painterly father figures (Cézanne, the cubists) but his pursuit of woman/painting results in what de Duve calls a crisis of revulsion/revelation. The image of woman that Duchamp finds/invents consists of a terrifying encounter with the real—a revulsion—resolved through Duchamp's passage into the realm of the symbolic, of language. De Duve describes this event by comparing Duchamp's *The Passage from Virgin to Bride* to Lacan's commentary on Freud's famous dream of "Irma's injection" in *The Interpretation of Dreams:*

> It has been said repeatedly that *The Passage* is the strangest and most disturbing of Duchamp's paintings from this period (and maybe of his whole career), the most *unheimlich* (uncanny) one. Like Irma's throat in the dream, it shows a misshapen flesh, a broken-up figuration, a scarred body, the limits of an unnameable Real in the face of which words abdicate their power. But these words take force again—and this is the second acme of the dream, as of *The Passage*—at the point where the Symbolic surges up as such: "At the point where the hydra loses its heads, a voice that is no longer anything but *the voice of no one* makes the formula for the trimethylamine surge

> up, as the final word for what this is all about, the word for everything. And this word says nothing but that it is a word."[41]

According to de Duve, the passage represented by this work is equally a passage from Duchamp's figuration of the real to an aesthetics of the symbolic: a passage from "misshapen flesh" to language. This disjunction is signified in the painting itself by the gap between its visceral figuration and its title, written out in Duchamp's hand in the lower left-hand corner of the canvas.[42]

De Duve therefore implies that the passage from an immensurable body to language is unidirectional and that the paradigmatic quality of the readymade lies in its definition of art as a *discursive* function.[43] Its scandal is therefore the complete circumvention of transcendental or universal qualities: the revelation that modern art is nothing more than a social and institutional struggle over the authority to name. But the seemingly irreversible passage from the Real to the Symbolic by which de Duve explains Duchamp's transition from painting to the readymade masks the extent to which a fragmentary or acephalous carnality irrupts within the readymades themselves. Even when he seems at his most nominalist, as in the entirely textual objects *"The"* and *Rendezvous of Sunday, February 6, 1916,* Duchamp is never far from what de Duve classifies as the Real. In these works the nominalist schema is reversed—instead of the Symbolic irrupting within the Real, the Real irrupts in the Symbolic: signifiers unhinged from their signifieds attain the mute materiality and incoherence of irrational bodies. For Duchamp the line between the Real and the Symbolic is completely porous and repeatedly transgressed. Moreover, this dialectical slippage *predates* the invention of the readymade; Duchamp's cubism already performs a paradoxical process of mensuration in which an abstract libidinal field is disciplined into form as the various modes of geometric measurement applied to it fall into carnality. This bilateral crossing and recrossing of the border between the body and the sign—or to import Lacan's terms, the Real and the Symbolic—is transposed, *not* transcended, in the readymades of 1914 to 1919. In the latter a spiraling interplay occurs between commodities and language that in the paintings took place between the body and its measure. As in Duchamp's cubism, in the readymades an ostensible "object" and its "inscription" both occupy simultaneously, and paradoxically, the position of Symbolic discourse and irrational dispersed carnality. De Duve's strongly teleological reading of the movement from painting to the readymade, with its persistent overtones of oedipal passage, fails to capture the permanent oscillation back and forth across the threshold of the Symbolic that characterizes both Duchamp's "nudes" and the readymade strategies that succeeded them.

If Duchamp's paintings of 1911 to 1914 and his readymades dating from 1914 to 1919 are structurally homologous, then the epistemological significance of the readymade lies not in its performance of the interplay between the Symbolic and the Real—which as we have seen occurs already in cubism—but rather in the displacement of the biological body by the commodity as the figure of carnality. This gesture makes explicit what was implicit in Duchamp's rhetoric of the virgin and bride—that the nude is already an object of exchange existing in the modernist discourse of prostitution initiated by Manet's *Olympia.* It was virtually inevitable that once Duchamp had attenuated the feminine body into an abstract flow, a decentered net of viscous pulsions subject to exchange, he would recognize the commodity—Marx's Maritornes—as its next logical representation. But in Duchamp's hands the commodity does not restabilize the collapsed anatomies of 1912. On the contrary, just as he had unwrapped the body into an unconscious libidinal band in *Bride* and *The Passage from Virgin to Bride,* the subsequent readymades disperse both language and commodities into atomized material fields, breaking apart all of the assumed links between things in order, as Duchamp declared to Schwarz with regard to *Rendezvous of Sunday, February 6, 1916,* to avoid any "echo of the physical world." Duchamp's desire to pulverize the world must not be mistaken as a metaphysical project. His strategy for escaping the "physical" lay precisely in putting a nearly intolerable emphasis on pure materiality, divorcing commodities and language from any function or signification, so that the world of things and the domain of words begin to resemble the claustrophobic, unknowable territories of Lyotard's "great ephemeral skin."[44]

If the goal of Duchamp's readymades was to enact a massive dismemberment of commodity and language networks, a "deferral of limbs" or an overwhelming aphasic vertigo in which one could "*lose the possibility of recognizing* [Identifying] *2 similar objects*," the significance of this operation had shifted over the course of the decade. While it may appear that gestures like extracting a snow shovel from its commercial and functional context or undermining the instrumental value of language constitute critical challenges to the capitalist order, this ultimately is not the achievement of the readymades. Instead, Duchamp projected upon the discrete commodity—and its linguistic analogue—the figure of its own regression: he performed its genealogy upon the very body of the final product. Duchamp looked behind the reified precipitates of capitalist production and found nothing but streams of matter—words that no longer meant anything and objects whose difference from one another was indiscernible.[45] He found what Gilles Deleuze and Félix Guattari call, in their *Anti-Oedipus,* the deterritorialized flows of capital. As Duchamp had, Deleuze and Guattari understand modern capitalism as an ever-expanding operation of decoding in which ritualized or collective inscriptions upon organs or objects dissolve, leaving a world of privatized matter subject to infinite exchange.[46] Behind the readymade, behind the effort "*To lose the possibility of recognizing* [Identifying] *2 similar objects*" through the transformation of commodities into "prime objects" and of language into "prime words," Duchamp returned the products of capitalism to their status as pure material flux.

If works like *With Hidden Noise* deterritorialize language and the commodity through an oscillating spiral of regression and reification in which language becomes object and an unknowable object becomes noise, Duchamp's last linguistic work of the teens, *Tzanck Check* of 1919, not only decodes the body but reterritorializes it as an explicitly financial flow. The *Tzanck Check* is an apparently authentic but hand-drawn check, somewhat larger than "life-size," with which Duchamp paid his dentist, the Parisian collector Daniel Tzanck, on December 3, 1919.[47] The check is drawn on an account at The Teeth's Loan & Trust Company Consolidated of New York for the amount of $115.00; the bottom half of the paper is stamped with the phrase "the teeth'sloanandtrustcompanyconsolitated" [sic] in successive lines and across the center of the check, perpendicular to its other writing is the word *ORIGINAL.* As in Duchamp's text "Deferment" from *The 1914 Box,* which suggests "a *'deferment'* of each

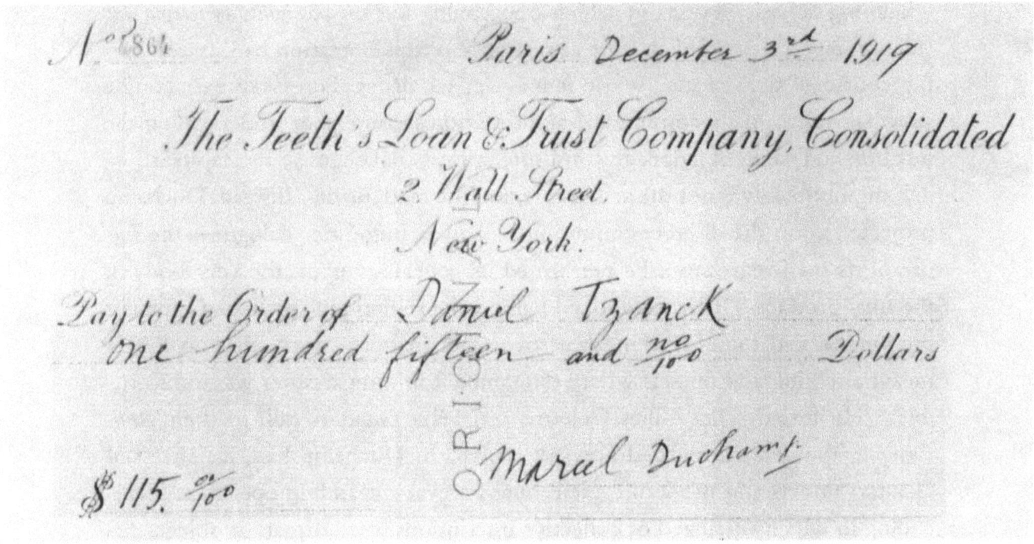
No 864 Paris December 3rd 1919

The Teeth's Loan & Trust Company, Consolidated

2 Wall Street,

New York.

Pay to the Order of Daniel Tzanck

one hundred fifteen and no/100 Dollars

ORIGINAL

Marcel Duchamp

$115. 00/100

2.9 Marcel Duchamp. Replica of *Tzanck Check* (from the *Boîte-en-Valise*). 1919. Color lithograph, 8 ⅞ × 15 $\frac{9}{16}$″. Philadelphia Museum of Art: The Louise and Walter Arensberg Collection. © 1997 Artists Rights Society (ARS), New York/ADAGP, Paris/Estate of Marcel Duchamp.

limb, of the heart and the other anatomical parts; each soldier being already unable to put his uniform on again, his heart feeding *telephonically*," the *Tzanck Check* suggests a body that has been blasted apart. The care and perhaps extraction of Duchamp's teeth is paid for through the funds of a bank—of teeth? At the heart of a financial transaction is an exchange of dismembered organic parts, of teeth,[48] and therein lies the particular irony of Duchamp's fictive bank declaring itself "consolidated." But the check itself does perform an act of consolidation: the field of disembodied parts is organized into an exchange of "liquid" funds; the deterritorialized body is stabilized as currency.

As Lyotard remarks in a passage reminiscent of Deleuze and Guattari:

> Capital is not the denaturation of relations between man and man, nor between man and woman, it is the wavering of the (imaginary?)

> primacy of genitality, of reproduction and sexual difference, it is the displacement of what was in place, it is the unbinding of the most insane pulsions, since money is the sole justification or bond, and money being able to justify anything, it deresponsibilizes and *raves* absolutely, it is the sophistics of the passions and at the same time, their energetic prosthetics; and if the "unity" which it wants to apply to the social body so frightens Marx, it is because it has certain *anti-unitary* and *anti-totalizing* traits, amongst which the great libidinal skin may be discerned.[49]

Precisely mirroring Lyotard's later description of money under capitalism, *Tzanck Check* projects the simulated unity of currency—"the sole justification or bond"—onto a shattered or dispersed anatomy. A financial grid is erected along which the body, displaced and unbound by *insane* pulsions, may be reconstituted. The cubist dynamic between a body and its measure—whose terms are transposed in the readymade into the embodied commodity and its inscription—is now imagined as the interplay between an atomized body and financial currency. This transformation is further allegorized in the check by its various graphic "scripts." For although the official form of the document appears industrially printed, the formalized typography of the check itself remains reminiscent of Duchamp's own handwriting, most notably his authorizing signature in the lower right corner of the work. Rotating around the vertical axis established by the word *ORIGINAL,* which bisects the check, is an oscillation between the subjective identity invested in a signature and the interchangeable anonymity of a printed document, each in different ways the product of the same man.

Duchamp's *Monte Carlo Bond* of 1924 pushes the relationship between multiple identities and financial flow even further. The *Monte Carlo Bond* was a "collaboration" between Duchamp and his feminine alter ego Rrose Sélavy.[50] As Robert Lebel recounts, the bond was conceived as a joint stock company designed to raise 15,000 francs "divided into thirty bonds of 500 francs each redeemable by 'artificial drawings' and bearing the somewhat exorbitant interest of twenty percent."[51] The purpose of this capital was to fund a system devised

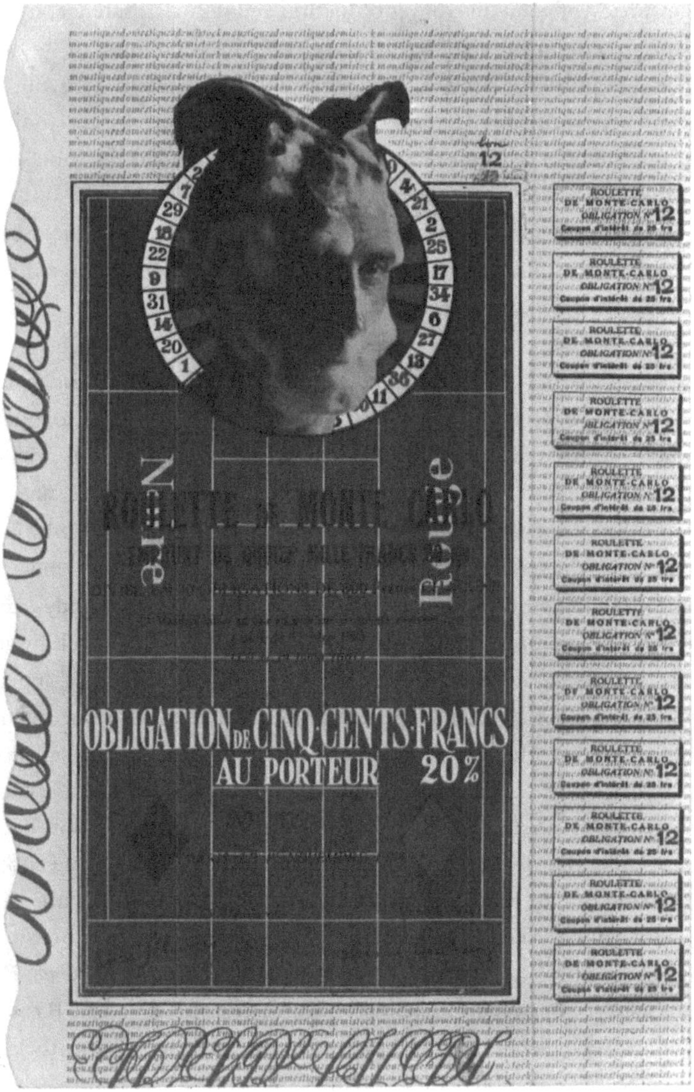

2.10 Marcel Duchamp. *Monte Carlo Bond.* Paris, 1924. Photocollage on colored lithograph, 12 ¼ × 7 ¾". The Museum of Modern Art, New York. Gift of the artist. Photograph © 1997 The Museum of Modern Art, New York. © 1997 Artists Rights Society (ARS), New York/ADAGP, Paris/Estate of Marcel Duchamp.

by Duchamp for winning at roulette. Such a conjunction of the activities of the "company" with the production of art is fundamental to the meaning of the *Monte Carlo Bond:* Duchamp's martingale was as much intended to produce works of art as to generate cash profits. The very bond note itself—a lithograph including a portrait by Man Ray of Duchamp transformed through shaving cream into a chimerical figure, perhaps resembling a faun or devil—was a "masterpiece" of sorts. As *The Little Review* somewhat guilelessly reported in 1924–25, "If anyone is in the business of buying art curiosities as an investment, here is a chance to invest in a perfect masterpiece. Marcel's signature alone is worth much more than the 500 francs asked for the share."[52] Duchamp himself made the connection with painting explicit in a letter to Picabia in 1924: "The Martingale is without importance. They are all either completely good or completely bad. But with the right number even a bad Martingale can work and I think I've found the right number. You see I haven't quit being a painter, now I'm sketching on chance."[53] The *Monte Carlo Bond* was a specific kind of machine: a painting machine whose elaborate, monotonous activity, the repetitive spinning of roulette discs, inevitably reminiscent of the optical pulse of Duchamp's rotary reliefs, was to generate a new kind of painting, "sketched on chance."

Duchamp's accounts of his "work" at the roulette table emphasize not the glamour of his occupation in a mythic Mediterranean capital but rather a killing monotony and sameness: to Picabia he wrote "It's delicious monotony without the least emotion;" and to Jacques Doucet: "I'm beginning to play and the slowness of progress is more or less a test of patience. I'm staying about even or else am marking time in a disturbing way for the aforementioned patience. But still, doing that or something else. . . . I'm neither ruined nor a millionaire and will never be either one or the other."[54] We are indebted to Lebel for amplifying this last line of Duchamp's letter to Doucet with an apparently trivial but fundamental piece of evidence: "He considers his martingale infallible in this respect but he also admits that if one perseveres long enough one can hope to win an amount equal to the wages of a clerk who works in his office as many hours as the gambler does in the casino.[55]

What kind of machine, then, is the *Monte Carlo Bond?* On one level it invents an entire discursive structure—bonds, thousands of spins of the roulette wheel—in order to double back to its starting point. It is premised on a death and rebirth of painting. When one—let's say Jacques Doucet—buys a share of the *Monte Carlo Bond,* he buys a work of art, for as *The Little Review* gushed, "Marcel's signature alone is worth much more than the 500 francs asked for the share." If he sells, he receives an "artificial drawing." Like other works of art his purchase of the *Monte Carlo Bond* is meant to appreciate (at an interest of 20 percent); but the only thing produced by Duchamp's martingale is precisely another work of art, a "painting sketched on chance." There are no profits, only a return to the same: "I'm neither ruined nor a millionaire and will never be either one or the other."

In creating a complex discursive line whose only purpose is to circle back to its point of departure, Duchamp's painting machine is strikingly reminiscent of Louise Montalescot's painting machine in Raymond Roussel's novel *Impressions d'Afrique.* Louise (perhaps like Rrose) is a clever young woman who has ingeniously invented a machine that can paint. Roussel described its mechanisms at length in several pages of description:

> Deprived of its shutter, which the young woman still held between her fingers, the plate now stood exposed, revealing a smooth, brown, shiny surface. All eyes were fixed eagerly on this mysterious substance, endowed by Louise with strange, photo-mechanical properties. Suddenly, opposite the easel, a slight shudder ran through the automatic arm, which consisted of an ordinary, bright, horizontal blade, bent in the middle; the adjustable angle of the elbow tended to open as wide as possible, owing to a powerful spring, whose effect was counteracted by a flexible metal wire, which, emerging from the sphere, was fastened round the furthest tip of the arm and thus regulated the gap; at present the wire was being stretched to allow the angle to become progressively greater.[56]

The result of this miraculous machine was nothing more or less than an exact transcription of the landscape: "The finished work, seen as a whole, gave an impression of uncommonly intense colouring and remained strictly true to the original."[57] As Foucault argues of Roussel, such machines present an allegory of the identity of language: "In their wealth of poverty words always refer away from and lead back to themselves."[58] And so, Marcel, Louise, and Rrose seem to imply, do paintings. The *Monte Carlo Bond* establishes a flow of desire—of infinite spins of a disc and settlings of a ball—that departs from and returns to the same position: the process of representation itself. As Pierre Klossowski has written with regard to Nietzsche's concept of the eternal return, "How can meaning be constituted within the intensity? Precisely in returning upon itself . . . by repeating and imitating itself, it would become a sign."[59]

If Duchamp's *Monte Carlo Bond* is a painting machine, it, like *Tzanck Check,* is premised on a metaphorical association of representation and currency. In the role of artworks, these simulated financial instruments assume the unique power of money: to decode and reinscribe matter and thus to effect an infinite chain of transformations between liquid funds and fossilized objects. But this Duchampian currency also maintains its primitive roots in carnality, as I have demonstrated in *Tzanck Check.* If the latter work projects a field of dismembered organic parts—of teeth—as the units of exchange, the *Monte Carlo Bond* associates its delirious flows of capital with a multiplication of identities, notably the dyad of Rrose Sélavy and Marcel Duchamp. More precisely, the bond issue is a *family* business: Rrose is mother and chairman of the board, while Marcel is father and worker. In Man Ray's portrait reproduced on the face of the bond, Marcel, like Rrose, is masquerading as a hyper-masculine devil or faun. But his mask is made of shaving cream, echoing Sélavy's "Complete Line of Whiskers and Kicks."[60] He may be about to lose his whiskers, and he might be in for some kicks from Mother. Marcel's face is obscured by the frothy stuff: as though his identity were being erased. Oedipus—the child—is there too. The entire background of the bond is covered with a text printed in green italics: "moustiques domestiques demistock." While the primary meaning of "moustique" is mosquito, it may also be an idiomatic term for a child or brat. "Stock" additionally contains the double meaning of family and goods. Distributed throughout the field of the *Bond* is a domestic brat, a "half-share;" the product of a bond issue.

In a fragment of 1922 Duchamp made an analogous conjunction, an equivalent play on words, between "insects" and "incest": "Rrose Sélavy trouve qu'un incesticide doit coucher avec sa mère avant de la tuer; les punaises sont de rigueur [Rrose Sélavy finds that an incesticide must sleep with his mother before killing her; bedbugs are de rigueur]."[61] Oedipus, the "incesticide" (and linguistic ghost of *insecticide*) is killing insects, (children, as well as parents?) yet also *producing* such progeny: "bedbugs are de rigueur." The flowing desires of capital are displaced onto the representation of the Oedipal family in the *Monte Carlo Bond,* joined most explicitly in the single word *demistock:* the child who is a share.

In *Anti-Oedipus* Deleuze and Guattari propose a similar relationship between finance and oedipalization. They assert that Freud's Oedipus complex is not immanent in the unconscious of individual subjects but rather arises only with the historical emergence of capitalism, as a figure of repression within the deterritorialized flux of its financial and material flows. Of the three economic epistemes or social machines that Deleuze and Guattari describe, capitalism comes closest to occupying what they theorize as the limit of the social: a complete decoding of desire in its transposition to an infinitely polymorphous cash economy. If capitalism is the relative limit of every socius, schizophrenia—the utter decoding of desire—is the absolute limit: "One can say that schizophrenia is the *exterior* limit of capitalism itself or the conclusion of its deepest tendency, but that capitalism only functions on condition that it inhibit this tendency, or that it push back or displace this limit by substituting for it its own *immanent* relative limits, which it continually reproduces on a widened scale."[62] Schizophrenia is both capitalism's ultimate expression and its limit: its dream and its nightmare. The structure of the Oedipus complex arises in the space between capitalism and schizophrenia: it enforces the boundary and "maintains the energy of the flows in a bound state." Oedipalization provides the mechanism for rewilling the self from its periodic dissolution into pure intensity (or schizophrenia). The family thus serves a new function: "Oedipal desires are the bait, the disfigured image by means of which repression catches desire in the trap,"[63] making the subject believe that all of his or her desires can be reduced to "Mommy and Daddy." Earlier forms of social repression associated with myth, or the law of the despot, are consequently resituated in the psychic economy of the individual.

In the spins of the roulette wheel and the production of dividends, Duchamp's *Monte Carlo Bond* projects a field of capitalist deterritorialization only to collapse or reterritorialize it within the repressive family formation of Oedipus. Thierry de Duve has identified a similar play of identities—produced like a family from the material of a single biological self—as a function of capitalist flows in *Fountain,* the urinal that Duchamp presented to the American Society of Independent Artists in 1917:

> At the beginning of the story Marcel Duchamp is R. Mutt, but this we won't know until the end. R. Mutt is like the little nobody who proclaims himself an artist in taking out his membership in the Society; he divides himself into a stockholder and an artisan, Richard and Mutt. Richard is like Arensberg, both of them "big" stockholders in the Society (both founding members) and both collectors (Richard is president of the hanging committee and future founder of the Société Anonyme). Mutt is like Mott, artisan-painter or small industrialist. As artisan Mutt suffers from his person's being divided into an exploited worker and a merchant who pockets surplus value. As industrialist Mott doesn't suffer, he exploits his workers. Mutt envies Mott and fears for his trade.[64]

As de Duve demonstrates, Duchamp's experience as a capitalist was radically divided and contradictory. He occupied several identities ranging from financier to laborer, therefore placing the "subject itself . . . not at the center . . . but on the periphery, with no fixed identity, forever decentered, *defined* by the states through which it passes."[65] But this delirious, dissolving family (which anyway collapses back onto just one man) is not the efficient laboratory of repression that Deleuze and Guattari identify. Duchamp reinvented the capitalist machine in the image of Roussel's painting machine: the *Monte Carlo Bond* leads to a long journey filled with spins of the wheel and the production of "demi-stock;" yet its destination is identical to its starting point. Or perhaps not quite. For in the *Monte Carlo Bond* Duchamp began with capitalism, the relative limit of social machines, and ended with schizophrenia—what Annette Michelson has called "autism considered as a language system"[66]—as the absolute limit of any socius. In his bond, Duchamp represents two kinds of pure intensity: that defined by Nietzsche as the "vicious circle," the cycle of alternate identities through which one must pass to will the self out of its lavalike formlessness; and second, the equally deterritorialized flows of money, which likewise eternally return to the same—to the point of breaking even. With his wry choice of the roulette wheel as the vicious circle par excellence, Duchamp inscribed one spinning disc within another: the cycle of identity meshes with the cycle of capital. Through the figure of Oedipus, the *moustique domestique demistock,* these two wheels of chance communicate, and in this conjunction a painting machine emerges in which the process of representation is projected as a transactual field of exchange.

If the *Tzanck Check* introduced currency as a means of stabilizing a dispersed field of body parts, the *Monte Carlo Bond* literally raises the stakes by instituting a double process in which the identity of the artist is fragmented through multiplication—he is a man, a woman, a child, a worker, a financier, etc.—and then reterritorialized around the dual axes of filiative and alliance capital.[67] As Deleuze and Guattari declare: "Father, mother, and child thus become the simulacrum of the images of capital ('Mister Capital, Madame Earth,' and their child the Worker), with the result that these images are no longer recognized at all in the desire that is determined to invest only their simulacrum. The familial determinations become the application of the social axiomatic."[68] Duchamp's adoption of a feminine identity in Rrose Sélavy may therefore have a significance beyond—but also incorporating—its challenges to conventional heterosexual masculinity.[69] By projecting a feminine self onto his masculine identity Duchamp made possible, as in the *Monte Carlo Bond,* an exploration of the compulsive replication and slippage of selves that calls for stabilization through oedipalization. Indeed, following Deleuze and Guattari's assertion that "familial determinations become the application of the social axiomatic," we might read Duchamp's *Wanted: $2,000 Reward* of 1923 as a particularly apt companion piece

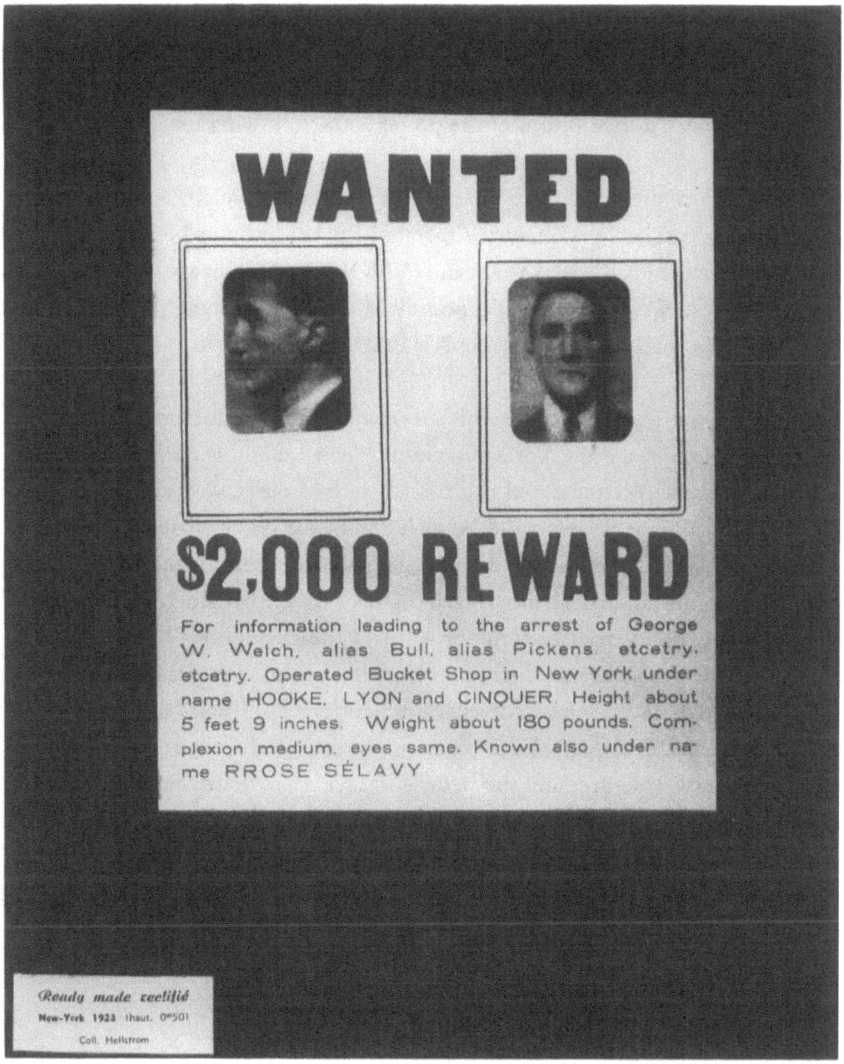

2.11 Marcel Duchamp. Replica of *Wanted: $2000 Reward* (from the *Boîte-en-Valise*). New York, 1923. Color lithograph, 8 ⅛ × 6 ⅜". Philadelphia Museum of Art: Louise and Walter Arensberg Collection. © 1997 Artists Rights Society (ARS), New York/ADAGP, Paris/Estate of Marcel Duchamp.

to the *Monte Carlo Bond* of the following year. The top two-thirds of *Wanted* consists of two grainy photographs of Duchamp, one face-on and the other in profile, sandwiched between two bold headlines: "Wanted" above and "$2,000 Reward" below. At the bottom of the poster is the following text:

> For information leading to the arrest of George W. Welch, alias Bull, alias Pickens, etcetry, etcetry. Operated Bucket Shop in New York under name HOOKE, LYON and CINQUER. Height about 5 feet 9 inches. Weight about 180 pounds. Complexion medium, eyes same. Known also under name RROSE SÉLAVY.

According to Schwarz this work, which is now lost, was made from a joke poster Duchamp found in a New York restaurant. He attached his own photographs within two blank rectangles and had the last line of the lower text altered by a printer so that Rrose Sélavy could be included in the list of aliases. While both *Wanted* and *Monte Carlo Bond* invoke a virtually schizophrenic profusion of selves as the limit condition of deterritorialized capital,[70] the earlier work adopts a disciplinary mode of interpellation in order to stabilize identity[71] (the criminal poster), whereas the later one does so through the oedipal introjection of capital's exigencies. Each nevertheless centers around currency—*Wanted* offers a reward, and *Monte Carlo Bond,* a dividend—and, as Deleuze and Guattari demonstrate, repressive social structures and the oedipal drama are structurally indistinguishable in capitalism: each simulates and masks the other.

With regard to the *Monte Carlo Bond* Duchamp wrote to Picabia, "You see I haven't quit being a painter, now I'm sketching on chance."[72] Despite its apparently offhand or ironic nature, this statement has much to teach us. For if, as I have argued, Duchamp's cubism consisted of dissolving the nude into a libidinal form of currency where the language of marriage—the bride and the virgin—organize exchange, then works like *Wanted* and *Monte Carlo Bond* are the legitimate heirs to Duchamp's painterly themes. In place of a body collapsed into indefinable carnal anatomies in *Bride* and *The Passage from Virgin to Bride,* the poster and the bond mobilize a different mode of fragmentation—one that multiplies the self rather than dispersing its constituent limbs. The earlier metaphors of bulbs and stems, nerves and telegraph wires are succeeded by a crowd of superimposed simulated selves riding the raucous rapids of financial flows.[73] If in 1912 the collapsed anatomies of the nude were the locus of "the most insane pulsions," by 1924 Duchamp knew that it was money which in Lyotard's words "deresponsibilizes and *raves* absolutely," and it is money which "has certain *anti-unitary* and *anti-totalizing* traits amongst which the great libidinal skin may be discerned."[74] The self returns only as a function of capital, not, as in the paintings of 1912, as its raw material. Duchamp could not have arrived at this fantastic inversion of his cubist preoccupations "sketched on chance" without his extended exploration of the readymade. What his gesture of radical displacement teaches us about objects and words has less to do with their status as reified commodities than with the massive capitalist project of deterritorialization that makes this reification possible. Duchamp's readymade gesture is both an act of inscription and a ruthless act of decoding: the thing loses its identity only to gain another . . . and another. This revelation of what Deleuze and Guattari identify as a perpetual cycle of deterritorialization and reterritorialization allowed Duchamp to transform the decoded *anatomies* of his cubist paintings into the decoded *selves* of his conceptual projects of the 1920s and inspired him to assure Picabia, "You see, I haven't quit being a painter."

3

Modern Machines: From the Virgin to the Widow

Painting's washed up. Who'll do anything better than that propellor? Tell me, can you do that?[1]

—*Marcel Duchamp to Constantin Brancusi and Fernand Léger, 1912*

In cubist painting Duchamp produced a diagrammatic idiom that simultaneously emerged from the body and was imposed from outside it. The readymades of the teens restaged this drama of mensuration in the field of commodities, but in *The Bride Stripped Bare by Her Bachelors, Even* or *Large Glass,* executed between 1915 and 1923, the diagram and the commodity come together. The bachelor machine in the lower half of the *Glass* combines a series of objects, reminiscent of readymades, in a mechanistic apparatus that revivifies Duchamp's cubist metaphors of virginity and marriage. In place of the different iterations of the graph that organize paintings like *Bride, Nude Descending a Staircase,* and *Network of Stoppages,* alluding respectively to skeletal structure or spatialized motion studies, in the *Large Glass* the diagram—along with the readymade—is associated with machines.

But what kind of machine is the bachelor apparatus of the *Glass?* Is it possible to perceive in the hybrid assemblage of antiquated mechanisms like a chocolate grinder and a watermill that compose the bachelors' realm an image of twentieth-century industrial progress? How can one reconcile such quaint anachronisms as Duchamp's "chariot" with the futurist's violent romance with the car or, closer to home, Picabia's attraction to engine parts? *The Bride Stripped Bare by Her Bachelors, Even* is often considered a manifestation of the early twentieth-century machine aesthetic, but its lower half represents an almost comical retreat from the most advanced manifestations of modern technology. Nor may we explain the discrepancy between the pessimistic, jerry-rigged Duchampian machine and the heroic technological phantasms of other avant-gardists in the years between 1915 and 1923—the period during which the *Large Glass* was produced—solely in terms of parody or subversion. In fact, the more rigorously we apply technological metaphors to the *Glass,* the less it seems to represent a machine at all, to have anything to do with the myth of progress and rationalization that crystallized around the airplane, the automobile, and the assembly line during this period. For this reason Duchamp's exclamation to Brancusi and Léger at the Salon de la Locomotion Aérienne in 1912—if indeed he ever made it[2]—must have been largely ironic. For his own machines have little in common with an airplane propellor: they are characterized not by sleek efficiency but by a conspicuous *failure* to function. The *Large Glass* is an elaborate trip to nowhere: not only is the erotic encounter between motorized bride and mechanical bachelors never consummated, the apparatuses themselves have no rational program. What then, could the machine possibly mean to Marcel Duchamp? The answer to this question lies in the relationship between Duchamp's mechanistic idiom and a dense network of economic, psychoanalytic, and literary discourses surrounding it in the period between 1880 and 1925—discourses in which the ostensible failure of the machine is identical to its success.

The Duchampian mechanism embodies a function even more fundamental to modernity than the advances of technological rationalization on the factory floor or in the airplane hangar: it allegorizes the introjection of a mechanical mind within an already mechanized body. This representation of an *irrational* psychic machine, fueled on desire, lies at the heart of the motorized romance of *The Bride Stripped Bare by Her Bachelors, Even.* Duchamp's *Glass* is a mechanism

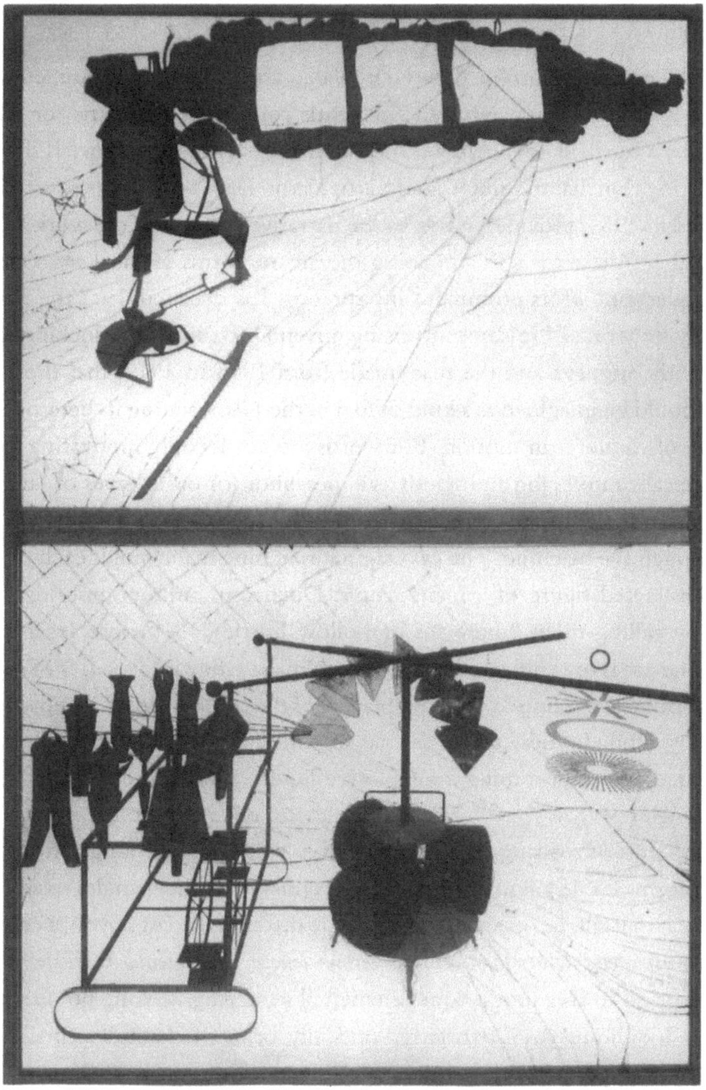

3.1 Marcel Duchamp. *The Bride Stripped Bare by Her Bachelors, Even (The Large Glass).* 1915–23. Oil, varnish, lead foil, lead wire, and dust on two glass panels (cracked), each mounted between two glass panels, with five glass strips, aluminum foil, and a wood and steel frame, 109 ¼ × 69 ¼". Philadelphia Museum of Art: Bequest of Katherine S. Dreier. Photo by Graydon Wood, 1992. © 1997 Artists Rights Society (ARS), New York/ADAGP, Paris/ Estate of Marcel Duchamp.

in which anthropomorphic flows circulate, are broken, and are conjoined through a variety of apparatuses. The work consists of two parts, or regions, divided by a horizon line: below is the bachelor machine and above is the realm of the bride. Duchamp's notes, and particularly *The Green Box,* retrospectively published in 1934, provide a guide to the narrative patterns of the work.[3] In fact, so crucial are these texts in animating the arcane forms of the *Large Glass* that Jean Suquet, one of its prominent interpreters, has declared that "the machine runs only on words."[4] It is not surprising, given Duchamp's interlocking experiments with language and the readymade from 1915 to 1919, that the flow of words should be imagined as a kind of fuel in the *Glass,* setting its heterogeneous mélange of elements in motion. But words are not its only motivating force—language calls into being and stands as a metaphor for other types of "fuel."[5] In the bachelor sector of the work, a picaresque voyage of "illuminating gas" circulates through the machine. The gas originates in nine malic molds each of which is the abstracted figure of a man's trunk. Duchamp anthropomorphizes these molds by calling them "uniforms or hollow liveries"[6]—themselves a kind of mold. The gas is drawn from the top of each malic effigy into a series of capillary tubes, formed according to the "templates" of the three standard stoppages. Paradoxically, while in these tubes, the gas solidifies, is cut "in long needles *already* solid, since before becoming an explosive liquid, *it* takes the form of a fog of solid spangles of frosty gas."[7] These spangles are released into the mouth of the first of a series of rotating semicircular sieves whose disorienting action on the gas transforms it into a liquid: "The spangles [dissolve]; the spangles splash themselves each to itself, i.e. change (little by little through the last sieves) their condition *from: spangles lighter than air, of a certain length, of elemental* thickness with a determination to rise, *into:* a liquid elemental scattering, seeking no direction."[8] This splash of liquid gas is transferred optically, or in Duchamp's terms, mirrorically, to the upper or bride portion of the *Glass* via a series of three mirrored oculist's charts. The bachelor's flow of illuminating gas is therefore continuously transformed—from gas to solid to liquid and finally to an optical quality with no physical dimension whatsoever—by various types of equipment including molds, tubes, sieves, and charts. In the midst of this journey, two other apparatuses regulate two other types of flow. A chariot rides back and forth without friction, its parallelepiped chassis enclosing a watermill, and a chocolate grinder supports a pair of horizontal scissors.

The onanistic nature of Duchamp's bachelor apparatus has often been commented upon, especially with regard to the chocolate grinder, which Duchamp glossed with the masturbatory adage "*The bachelor grinds his chocolate himself—*,"[9] and the chariot, whose back-and-forth motion is accompanied by the following litanies:

—Slow life—
—Vicious circle—
—Onanism—
—Horizontal—
—Buffer of life
—Bach. life regarded as an alternating rebounding on this buffer.
—Rebounding = junk of life
—Cheap construction
—Tin
—Cords
—Iron wire
—Crude wooden pulleys
—Eccentrics
—Monotonous fly wheel[10]

But the extent to which Duchamp's machines and even his geometric schemas partake of a phallic logic has not been sufficiently recognized. The litanies of the chariots and several other of Duchamp's explanatory texts provide invaluable clues to this. In a note from *The Green Box* describing the malic molds Duchamp stated: "Each of the 8 malic forms is cut by an imaginary horizontal plane at a pnt. called the pnt. of sex."[11] The association of horizontality with the phallus, the point of sex, might seem merely an idiosyncratic way of stating the obvious fact that a male body may be bisected roughly at the level of its penis, if it were not for a series of other statements that amplify this metaphoric association. In the litanies of the chariot, for instance, "Horizontal" follows immediately upon "Onanism" in a juxtaposition that would otherwise seem incomprehensible. The scissors mounted on a bayonet rising from the churning drums of the chocolate grinder is referred to as a "horizontal column" whose monotonous opening and closing—reminiscent of the chariot's endless back-and-forth movement—is described in erotic terms:

> Horizontal column
> Sort of horizontal scissors, Working / like balance pans, by means / of the little upper wheels of the carriage. / In their alternating movement / these little wheels raise or / lower the horizontal column / according to / their contact with the **precision friction plate.** / Study the form of this friction plate. Its influence on the arrangement of the desire centers / in the dynamo. / P.T.O.[12]

The association of horizontality or the horizontal column and "desire centers" is stipulated in another note: "This explosion produced by the alternating presentation of the 'desire / centers' (these 'desire centers' belong to the **horizontal column** of the / bach. machine."[13] Both the husklike bodies of the malic molds and the scissors associate horizontality with male desire, the point of sex. This relationship is equally and perhaps even more explicit in the chariot, which Duchamp described in the following manner:

> The metal or (material)—of the chariot is *emancipated.* i.e: that it has a weight but a force acting horizontally on the chariot does not have to support this weight (the *weight* of the metal does not *impede* a horizontal traction (to be developed)). The chariot is *emancipated horizontally.* it is free of all gravity in the horizontal plane (property of the metal rods which compose the chariot)[14]

Its litanies explicitly link the chariot to a mechanics of onanism, but this association is further intimated by its miraculous horizontality. Like the erect penis that defies gravity in its tumescence, the chariot is "*emancipated horizontally,*" and "the *weight* of the metal does not *impede* a horizontal traction." It would be counter to Duchamp's delicate irony to suggest that the horizontal serves solely as a symbol of the phallus in the *Large Glass.* The particular genius of Duchamp's art is the way in which images attract a variety of metaphorical valences to themselves, the way objects adopt a range of contradictory colorations. But while the meaning of the mechanical assemblages of his bachelors is not exhausted by their links to a phallic logic, these associations provide one of many points of convergence between the body and the machine. It is striking then, that each of the units composing the bachelor machine—with the exception of the oculist witnesses—shares a similar structure. The malic mold-capillary tube-sieve complex, the chariot-watermill complex, and the chocolate grinder-bayonet-scissors complex join together two elements: a reservoir of fluid medium—gas, water, or chocolate—and a horizontal, or horizontally oriented unit that partakes of a back-and-forth movement—the tubes and sieves, the chariot armature, and the scissors. In Duchamp's vision male sexuality is geometric, disciplined into machinic matrices. Perhaps this is what he meant when he declared in one of his notes: "—don't forget the imaginary polygon of sex."[15]

If male sexuality is alternately a sequence of mechanical apparatuses and specific geometric figures, it also closely relates to the graphic language of perspective: correct perspective projections of three-dimensional bodies are conspicuously present in the realm of the bachelors and absent in that of the bride. As *Tu m'* demonstrated in 1918, perspective is no stable descriptive tool for Duchamp but rather a single term in an infinite regression of representation and measurement. His delirious fascination with the relativity of dimension led to a playful conviction that if three-dimensional reality may be projected in two dimensions, then it must be possible to project a four-dimensional reality in three, a five-dimensional in four, and so on.[16] Perspective belongs to the logic of anamorphosis *en abyme* as described by Jean Clair: "Each form is the projection of another form, . . . every apparition in the material world represents or repeats an appearance which is itself only the apparition of another form according to the circular chain of anamorphosis, without its ever being possible to say which form is first and which is second."[17]

But Duchamp's association of masculine desire with conventional perspective could not be arbitrary. Moreover, there must be some relationship between the three phallic machines of the bachelors' realm and the oculist witnesses that form their principal passage to the bride. The theory of anamorphosis developed by Jacques Lacan in his *Four Fundamental Concepts of Psycho-Analysis* may clarify these riddles. Lacan distinguishes two components within vision: one that he associates with perspective and a second that escapes the projections of geometry into a thoroughly optical realm. Perspective—including the illusions of anamorphosis—is, as Lacan argues, accessible to the blind, and therefore not inherently visual:

> What is at issue in geometral perspective is simply the mapping of space, not sight. The blind man may perfectly well conceive that the field of space that he knows, and which he knows as real, may be perceived at a distance, and as a simultaneous act. . . . The geometral dimension of vision does not exhaust, therefore, far from it, what the field of vision as such offers us as the original subjectifying relation.[18]

The other component of vision—that which escapes the spatial mapping of perspective—is what Lacan localizes around his concept of the gaze, in its "pulsatile, dazzling and spread out function."[19] One of the metaphors for the gaze that Lacan opposes to geometral perspective is the illusion, drawn from Sartre's *Being and Nothingness,* of *seeing myself seeing myself.*[20] For Sartre, the seeing subject, peering through a keyhole, attains a material body only through the sensation of being watched by an other. This surveillance—this gaze—transforms the looker from a disembodied eye to a desiring subject. Lacan takes the gaze to signify all that is outside and inaccessible to the seeing subject in vision: the impossibility of possessing one's own look. In fact, the gaze operates on the subject almost like a horizon in a picture: "From the moment that this gaze appears, the subject tries to adapt himself to it, he becomes that punctiform object, that point of vanishing being with which the subject confuses his own failure."[21] If the gaze is a kind of reverse vanishing point, ending in a "punctiform" subject occupying a *horizon,* what is the place of perspective in vision? Lacan's response is startling:

> How is it that nobody has ever thought of connecting . . . [anamorphic distortion] with . . . the effect of an erection? Imagine a tattoo traced on the sexual organ *ad hoc* in the state of repose and assuming its, if I may say so, developed form in another state.
>
> How can we not see here, immanent in the geometral dimension—a partial dimension in the field of the gaze, a dimension that has nothing to do with vision as such—something symbolic of the function of the lack, of the appearance of the phallic ghost?[22]

Years later Lacan proposes a schema strikingly homologous to Duchamp's bachelor machine in which the anamorphic system of perspective is elided with the phallic, and this elision occurs as a poetry of loss, of the endless onanistic deferral of erotic consummation. Such a reading is confirmed by the way in which Duchamp imagined the ejaculatory splashing of the bachelor's gas onto the register of the bride above. After exiting the rotating semicircle of sieves as a liquid, the gas is "dazzled across the oculist's charts, each drop acting as a point and sent back mirrorically to the high part of the glass to meet the 9 shots."[23] These nine shots—a splatter of spermatic gas—are precisely an anamorphic projection produced by shooting a series of paint-impregnated matches from a tiny canon onto the surface of the right side of the bride's territory. Duchamp described the process in the following terms:

Shots

> From more or less far; on a *target.* This target in short *corresponds* to the vanishing point (in perspective.)
>
> The figure thus obtained will be the projection (*through skill*) of the principal points of a 3 dim'l body.—With maximum skill, this projection would be reduced to a point (the target). . . .

> Repeat this operation 9 times—3 times by 3 times from the same point[24]

The bachelors' closest "shot" at breaking out of their onanistic trap—the closest they come to coming—is experienced through a performance of anamorphic perspective.

But in this transfer of the gas from the realm of the bachelors to that of the bride, the anamorphic mixes with the optical, the phallic elides with the gaze. The oculist *witnesses* suggest an invisible power of surveillance on the part of an other—a role reinforced by the original function of the images as *tests*. But these apparently optical figures are suffused by an anamorphic logic. Here is how Duchamp described the mirrorical transfer, after the splashes have been "dazzled across the oculist's charts":

> Mirrorical return—Each drop will pass the 3 planes at the horizon between the perspective and the geometrical drawing of 2 figures which will be indicated on these 3 planes by the Wilson-Lincoln system (i.e. like the portraits which seen from the left show Wilson seen from the right show Lincoln—)[drawing inserted] seen from the right the figure may give a square for example from the front and seen from the right it could give the same square seen in perspective—
>
> The mirrorical drops not the drops themselves but their image pass between these 2 states of the same figure (square in this example)[25]

Nothing like the Wilson-Lincoln illusion occurs in the *Glass,* but Duchamp's reference introduces an optical aporia, bringing the anamorphic into the heart of vision, suffusing the gaze with the phallus.[26] Nonetheless, the male essence, the splash of gas, can only enter into the realm of the bride as an *image,* and this too seems to converge with Lacan's theory of the gaze: "I apprehend the world in a perception that seems to concern the immanence of the *I see myself seeing myself.* The privilege of the subject seems to be established here from that bipolar reflexive relation by which, as soon as I perceive, my representations belong to me. . . . How can one deny that nothing of the world appears to me except in my representations?"[27] Yet Lacan argues that this pretense of the image *belonging* to the subject is impossible, that it masks his or her anxious inability to locate the self anywhere but in an infinite regress of images. Duchamp invested such a performance of loss through representation, through the superimposition of geometry onto seeing, in the scissors mounted above the chocolate grinder of the bachelor machine. The enigmatic function of this image is clarified by *To Be Looked At (from the Other Side of the Glass) with One Eye, Close To, for Almost an Hour,* a study of 1918.

In this small work on glass only the ends of the two squared-off scissor blades are visible, each of which balances a ball on its tip. These "horizontal columns" pivot around a lens embedded in the glass surface and supported illusionistically by an obelisk or *portillon*[28] rising from a radiating pattern similar to the oculist witnesses. While there is no such lens in the *Large Glass,* the outline of a circle marks the place it would have occupied between the blades. Among Duchamp's explanatory notes for the *Glass* there is one written under a sketch representing this section of *To Be Looked At,* identical to the final work, only reversed. In this drawing the ball balanced on the tip of the near blade is labeled "A," and the one on the far blade "B." The blades themselves are labeled "C" and "D." The text reads: "Magnifying glass / C and D scissors which / open. / In opening, A / and B no longer see / themselves through the / magnifying glass—Therefore . . . / consequences ad libitum"[29] The scissors' perpetual opening and closing successively accommodates and annihilates vision through a lens. Its seesaw focus offers a precise allegory of how the gaze may be spatialized—how it is locked in an embrace with the phallic logic of geometral projection. If phallus and gaze are theoretically separable, each carrying its own particular poetics of loss and alienation into vision, it is virtually impossible to divide them in practice. If the dynamic of tumescence and detumescence conditions vision, as in the seesaw of the scissors' "horizontal columns" around a lens, the converse is equally true: the bachelor apparatuses themselves are submitted to disciplinary

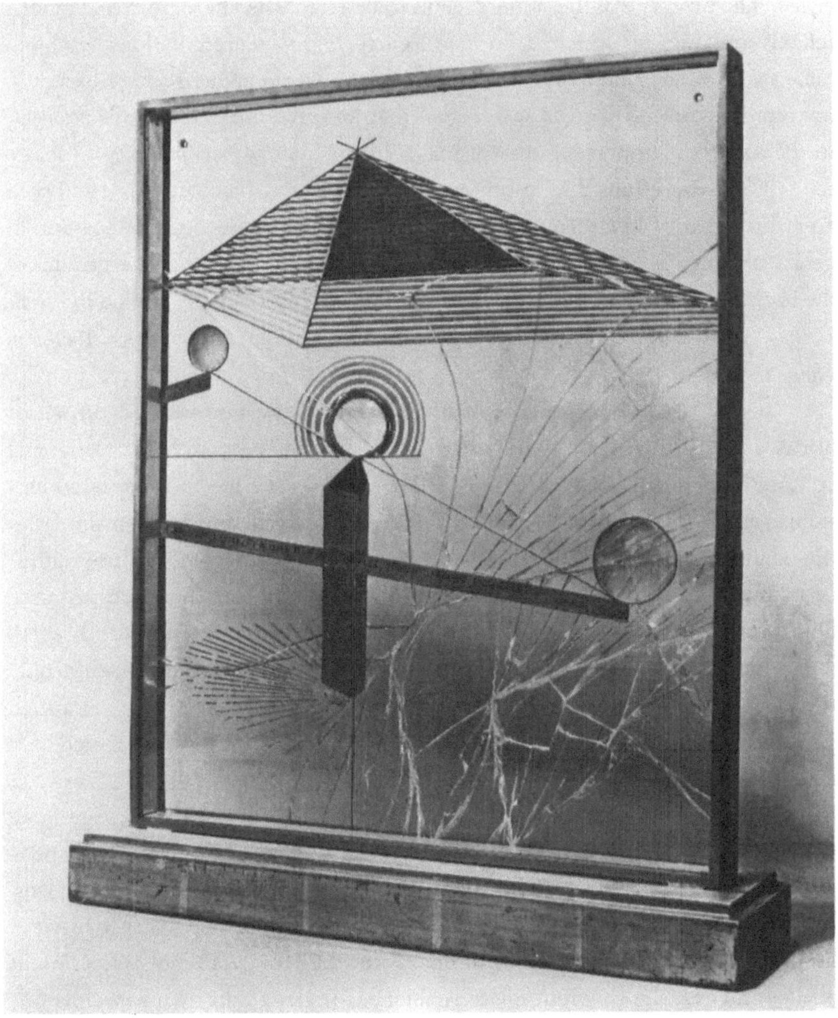

3.2 Marcel Duchamp. *To Be Looked At (from the Other Side of the Glass) with One Eye, Close To, for Almost an Hour.* Buenos Aires, 1918. Oil paint, silver leaf, lead wire, and magnifying lens on glass (cracked), mounted between two panes of glass in standing metal frame. Overall height 22"; glass (cracked) 19 ½ × 15 ⅝"; metal frame 20 ⅛ × 16 ¼ × 1 ½", on painted wooden base, 1 ⅞ × 17 ⅞ × 4 ½". The Museum of Modern Art, New York. Katherine S. Dreier Bequest. Photograph © 1997 The Museum of Modern Art, New York. © 1997 Artists Rights Society (ARS), New York/ADAGP, Paris/Estate of Marcel Duchamp.

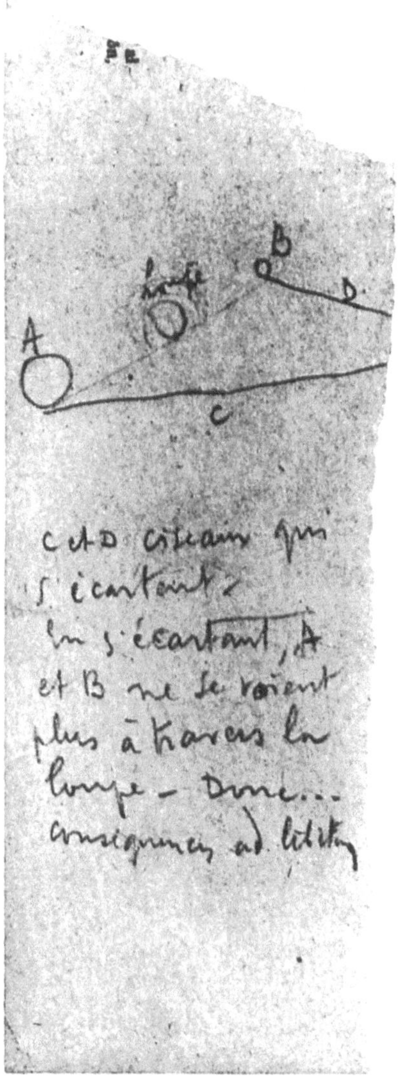

3.3 Note 129 from *Marcel Duchamp, Notes*. Boston: G. K. Hall & Company, 1983. © 1997 Artists Rights Society (ARS), New York/ADAGP, Paris/Estate of Marcel Duchamp.

surveillance by oculist *witnesses*—the stern presence of the other within vision—whose potential for causing humiliation within the paradigm of *seeing oneself seeing oneself* is literalized in *To Be Looked At (from the Other Side of the Glass) with One Eye, Close To, for Almost an Hour.* In this work the viewer obedient to the imperative of the title finds himself[30] ridiculously crouched behind the object, looking through it, only to become a spectacle himself, behind the glass.

It is not surprising then, given how the gaze and the phallus are imbricated in one another in Duchamp's formulation, that the relationship between the bachelors and their bride in the *Large Glass* has nothing to do with literal genitals and much to do with penetration by the eye: with her being *mise à nu.* This dynamic of visibility might seem contradictory in an artist whose disdain for the retinal in painting is legendary, but herein lies the great paradox and perversity of *The Bride Stripped Bare by Her Bachelors, Even.* The bride cannot be stripped because she is inaccessible to conventional vision: to see her requires inventing a new way of seeing that transcends the purview of her bachelors' gaze. Her *immensurability*—the impossibility of capturing her in representation—endows the bride with her special allure and drives the bachelors wild with desire. In contrast to the bachelors' intelligible geometric contours, the bride's form is flaccid, undisciplined, a *pendu femelle,* whose hanging is quite literal: "A shiny metal gallows could simulate the maiden's attachment to her girl friends and relatives. (the former and the latter corresponding graphically to a solid base."[31] This imagined death by hanging stands in for another kind of death: the death of her intelligibility. Unclothed, stripped of the moldlike uniforms and liveries that identify the bachelors, the bride escapes her status as an image just as the bachelors' compound gaze fails to capture her. She is outside of conventional representation and therefore cannot be *mise à nu.*

The upper component of the *Large Glass* consists primarily of two elements: an image of the bride or *pendu femelle* extracted from Duchamp's 1912 painting *Bride* and a "milky way" of flesh extending from it representing her orgasmic "blossoming." While the bride is described as a machine—fitted with gears, pistons, and motor—her mechanism has little in common with the antic sequence of apparatuses that composes the bachelor machine. A crossed-out but legible note in *The Green Box* summarizes how Duchamp may have conceptualized the difference: "(The bride has a life center—the bachelors have not. They live on coal or other raw material drawn not from them but from their not them."[32] This note, enigmatically canceled but retained makes a crucial distinction: if the bachelors are nothing but a series of empty molds linked together in order to channel a fluid medium through themselves, the bride mechanism spontaneously feeds upon itself—she is the machine "stripped" of its molds, imagined as nothing but the medium itself in undisciplined, "hung" form. The bachelors transform raw materials like gas or chocolate to produce sparks and splashes—explosions—but the bride *blossoms*. She is not alienated in the manner of the bachelors, who are fueled upon the "not them," but the price she pays for her tautological blossoming is *immensurability,* her ultimate inaccessibility. She is caged within herself: "Put the whole bride under a glass case, or into a transparent cage."[33] Nevertheless, the bride, as Duchamp declared, is explicitly a motor, if an organic one:

> The Bride basically is a motor. But before being a motor which transmits her timid-power.—she is this very timid-power—This timid-power is a sort of automobiline, love gasoline, that, distributed to the quite feeble cylinders, within reach of the *sparks of her constant life,* is used for the blossoming of this virgin who has reached the goal of her desire—(Here the desire-gears will occupy less space than in the bachelor machine.—They are only the string that binds the bouquet.)[34]

The contradiction embodied here suffuses Duchamp's concept of the bride: she is both a motor *and* a bouquet. Her "desire gears" may run on automobiline but they have no more mechanical sophistication than the devices of a florist shop, the string around a bunch of flowers. This duality is reflected in the Bride's *double* stripping: "The bride reveals herself nude in 2 appearances: the first, that of the stripping by the bachelors. the second appearance that voluntary-imaginative one of the bride. On the coupling of these 2 appearances of pure virginity—On their collision, depends the whole blossoming, the upper part and crown of the picture."[35] The stripping by the bachelors and the onanistic auto-stripping of the bride are accomplished through different technologies. The bachelor's stripping is electric and cinematic, whereas the bride's voluntary stripping is referred to in organic terms as the "arbor-type": "*the cinematic effects of the electrical stripping, transmitted* to the motor with quite feeble cylinders, leave . . . the arbor-type at rest . . . and do not touch. the desire gears. which by giving birth to the arbor type, find within this arbor type the transmission of the desire to the blossoming into stripping voluntarily imagined by the bride desiring."[36] The arbor-type, which "has its roots in the desire-gear, a constituent, skeletal part of the bride,"[37] is therefore not only the locus of the bride's onanistic stimulation but also a fundamental part of her anatomy, her skeleton. On the other hand, the electrical stripping of the bachelors does not penetrate to the core beneath the bride's flesh but rather to a "superficial organ."[38] Duchamp leaves no doubt as to the technological divergence between the bride's own desire and that inspired by the bachelors:

> Hence, this motor with quite feeble cylinders has 2 strokes. The 1st stroke (sparks of the desire-magneto) controls the immobile arbor type. This arbor-type is a kind of spinal column and should be the support for the blossoming into the bride's voluntary stripping. The 2nd stroke (artificial sparks of the electrical stripping) controls the clockwork machinery, graphic translation of the blossoming into stripping by the bachelors. (expressing the throbbing jerk of the minute hand on electric clocks.)[39]

Like the cartoonish conjunctions in the lower section of the *Glass,* the bachelors' stripping is clumsy and mechanical; it projects a foreign, masculine dynamic onto the bride. Her relationship to her own desire follows a different path: like sap rising through a tree. The arbor-type—a kind of spinal column—is the support for a blossoming of the bouquet which is the bride; in Duchamp's words, *The Bride Stripped Bare by Her Bachelors, Even* is a kind of "Agricultural machine" or "instrument for farming."[40]

These ostensibly contradictory blossomings share a quality fundamental to the bride: they are inaccessible to vision. That which makes cinema possible is the inability of the eye to distinguish between successive still frames, causing the illusion of continuous movement.[41] On the other hand, biological growth—organic blossoming—occurs on the opposite frontier of the visual: that which takes place too slowly to be discerned. Ironically only through the acceleration of time made possible through film—through the collapse of these two poles—has the growth of plants been visualized. As opposed to the plodding, back-and-forth motion of the bachelors—their chariot, their chocolate grinder, and their scissors—the bride brackets time from either end of consciousness: she is both too fast and too slow. Her existence beyond conventional forms of temporal measurement is mirrored by her spatial indeterminacy—by Duchamp's frequent suggestion that the bride belongs to a fourth dimension: "The Pendu femelle is the form in *ordinary perspective* of a Pendu femelle for which one could perhaps try to discover the true form—This comes from the fact that any form is the perspective of another form according to a certain *vanishing point* and a certain *distance*."[42] The bride's anamorphic projection has nothing to do with the geometric perspective of the bachelors: her "true form" cannot be grasped: she is necessarily invisible to the bachelors who are creatures of ordinary three-dimensional space and time. But her elusiveness does not prohibit contact between the bride and bachelors. In fact, through the bride's moving inscription, filtered through the three draft pistons of the milky way, she meets the anamorphic projection of the nine shots, the destination of the bachelors' spermatic splash of illuminating gas: "the *form* [of the draft pistons] permitting all combinations of letters sent across this said triple form, commands, orders, authorizations, etc. which must join the shots and the splash."[43] What is more, this inscription was to have had a cinematic logic: "Perhaps look for a way to obtain superimposed prints.—i.e. a first print—of the first alphabetic unit (for instance). hyposulphite.—make a second print of the second alphabetic unit. superimposing itself on the first. but printing only the essential without a background."[44]

If the logic of the bachelor machine is that of the mold or perspectival projection, the bride follows a dynamics of inscription. The two genders are imagined through inverse systems: the masculine is characterized by the imposition of structure, measurement, or containment from without, whereas the bride's structure emerges from within, through an "alphabetic" inscription. This immanence is signaled by the bride's own blossoming as distinct from the bachelors' stimulation of her and conveyed visually through the appearance of an *absence* in the draft pistons, as opposed to the fully developed perspectival *presence* of geometric volumes in the realm of the bachelors. The mold and the inscription are fundamental because through them undisciplined flows and mute flesh may be elevated to the status of an image. Only through the mediation of representation can the separate desires of bride and bachelors meet. The splash of the bachelors transfers mirrorically as an image to the bride, and her contact with her suitors is via the inscription, which (as I have discussed with regard to Duchamp's cubism and his readymades) is the transposition of a familiar linguistic alphabet into a new formal vocabulary: "(utilize colors—in order to differentiate what would correspond in this [literature] to the substantive, verb, adverb declensions, conjugations etc.)."[45] One fundamental lesson of the *Large Glass* is that the currency of erotic commerce is the image. Its poetics explores the arduous and even tragic project of bringing the self into representation. There is something unutterably poignant, for instance, about the tortured narcissism of the malic molds:

> The gas *castings* so obtained, would hear the litanies sung by the chariot, refrain of the whole celibate machine, But *they* will never be able *to pass beyond the Mask* = They would have been as if enveloped, alongside their regrets, by a mirror reflecting back to them their own complexity to the point of their being hallucinated rather onanistically. (Cemetery of [8] uniforms or liveries)[46]

Although the masks they build are differently constructed, neither the bride nor the bachelors are able to "pass beyond" them, and this is the searingly pessimistic message of *The Bride Stripped Bare by Her Bachelors, Even:* erotic contact is no more than mutual narcissism, "hallucinated rather onanistically." The body disappears into a mental universe of misrecognized masks and eroticism functions as a point of transfer between carnal reality and mental aporia.

A metaphorics of mechanization thus establishes two species or impasse in the *Large Glass:* a physical incapacity to copulate and a psychic encounter of mutual misrecognition. As I have argued, representing such duality was precisely Duchamp's accomplishment in his cubist paintings, *Bride* or *The Passage from Virgin to Bride,* where a conceptual system of mensuration falls into immensurability as the organic motifs that it seems to structure attain the status of signs. Similarly, in the readymades of the teens, an infinite regress is established between a material commodity and its textual inscription. With the machine, Duchamp's art finds a model in which the reversibility of mind and body—mensuration and immensurability—achieves great social resonance. For during the period between 1880 and 1925 economies of mechanization were central to *both* discourses of the mind and of the body. The self, whether conceived as a function of its physical labor or its unconscious desire, was comprehended through metaphors of the machine. Duchamp's work produces this mechanical self as a conjunction of energy flows, both emanating from and channeled through a mechanical apparatus. Illuminating gas—an ordinary form of fuel—circulates in the bachelor machine; the bride is fed with automobiline from her own reservoirs while her motor is ignited externally through sparks generated by the bachelors. In imagining human subjects—men and women—as machines, Duchamp attributed to them a fundamental bifurcation, the division between a fluid, energetic matter or fuel and a controlling mechanism or motor.

Such a structural division at the heart of the modern subject lies behind an impressive variety of theories of the self during this period, ranging from Henry Ford's concept of the division of *physical* labor to Sigmund Freud's "Project for a Scientific Psychology." While the opposition between flow and mechanism is constant in these theories, the specific significance of its terms is extraordinarily mobile. On the one hand, it may describe physical force, and on the other mental capacity. For instance, in 1923 Ford made a telling elision between physical and mental power when he declared in a typical demonstration of his homespun wisdom, "[A] ten-horsepower engine will not pull as much as a twenty. The man who keeps brain office hours limits his horsepower." And in more detail: "It is just like power: formerly every machine was run by foot power; the power was right at the machine. But nowadays we have moved the power back—concentrated it in the power-house. Thus also we have made it unnecessary for the highest types of mental ability to be engaged in the factory. The better brains are in the mental power-plant."[47] Ford here dramatized how the modern metaphor of the machine may encompass what appears to be an extraordinary contradiction: *power* may signify either a form of mental activity separated from physical exertion—"the mental power-plant"—or, alternatively, precisely that bodily force that mental activity leaves behind—"foot power." For although the ideal horizon of factory rationalization would be the complete disappearance of the human worker, this goal has never been achieved, and in Ford's time as in our own the worker's body must still be integrated, albeit ever more efficiently, with the machine.

Ford was unapologetic in his efforts to make sentient bodies into pure flows of force: "The net result of these principles [of the assembly line] is the reduction of the necessity for thought on the part of the worker and the reduction of his movements to a minimum. He does as nearly as possible only one thing with only one movement."[48] The industrial machine therefore regulates the intersection of two streams of human energy: mental "capital," expended in the conceptualization and management of entire enterprises, and physical force, which fuels each individual machine. But as different as the mental and physical power-streams are—exemplified by the discontinuous material and intellectual positions of the capitalist and the worker—each is closely tied to the metaphor of the machine and the economies of social, intellectual, and physical power it encompasses. Indeed, Freud, in his own attempts to theorize the relationship between the material and the mental, imagined psychic space as a kind of assembly line in which energies must be harnessed—cathected—and discharged. Behind his turgid scientistic prose is an uncanny echo of Ford's analysis of the "mental power-plant" and "foot power": "*Thus the process of thought would be characterized mechanically by this bound condition, which combines a high cathexis with a small flow of current.* We can think of other processes in which the current would run *parallel* to the cathexis—processes with an uninhibited discharge."[49] Uninhibited discharge of stimuli is the most primitive form of mental activity, which in its more sophisticated manifestations consists of a complex sequence of mechanical bindings, or cathexes, of "currents" of energy. In the domain of the mind, as on the factory floor, apparatuses are constructed that break, conjoin, and channel flows of pure energy.

If the metaphor of the machine was applied to both body and mind, this does not mean that the enormous class alienation resulting from capitalism's division of mental from physical faculties could be conjured away. On the contrary, one of the social functions of the exaltation of technology and the machine during this period was to mask class ruptures.[50] As Didier Deleule and Françǫis Guéry have shown, industrial rationalization proceeded along a double track. First, as Ford declared, mental force was drained away from the body of the worker and accumulated in the entrepreneurial class:

> If a body is defined as much by its divisions as by its unity, it is not the social division of labor, affecting the social body, that accomplishes the formative and repressive tasks [*tâches*], objectively identified, with regard to the biological body: it is the division of labor within manufacturing, affecting the productive body; it does not parcel out the biological body, it draws and quarters it [*l'écartèle*] by setting it apart from its powers, in turning the powers of the mind against it, concentrating and consolidating them. Capital hence accomplishes the migration of productive energy into the capital of the body which is the head, and thus begins to warrant fully its name.[51]

In conceiving the body not in monolithic or essentialist terms but rather as a triadic formation of social, productive, and biological dimensions, Guéry and Deleule clarify considerably the multiple rechannelings of human energy and will that compose industrial capitalism. Their somewhat startling conclusion is that it is not the division of labor per se that transforms or disciplines the biological body of the worker but rather the violent act of beheading that modern production performs on its subjects. As we have seen, this divorce of head from body is not merely a theoretical prognostication after the fact. Frederick Winslow Taylor and Henry Ford explicitly acknowledged the fundamental importance of consolidating mental capital. In *The Principles of Scientific Management* Taylor wrote:

> Thus all the planning which under the old system was done by the workman, as a result of his personal experience, must of necessity under the new system be done by the management in accordance with the laws of science; because even if the workman were well suited to the development and use of scientific data, it would be physically impossible for him to work at his machine and at a desk at the same time. It is also clear that in most cases one type of man is needed to plan ahead and an entirely different type to execute the work.[52]

According to Taylor, the ideological division between mind and body is inevitable—*of necessity*—and *in accordance with the laws of science;* it is *physically impossible* to imagine otherwise, because the capitalist and workman are *entirely different types*. In a manner seldom acknowledged as perspicaciously as Guéry and Deleule have, the most radical legacy of rationalization is not simply the reorganization of physical tasks but rather the *capitalization of the rational:* the harnessing of brain power in its own power plant, to use Ford's metaphor.

As in an actual beheading, the decapitated worker falls into two parts and consequently presents two problems. The first is easier to solve, requiring no more than an efficient application of physical force: "In order for the productive body to reveal itself, the biological body must be dissected, viewed in parts. . . . Productive activity has to be extracted from the body itself, from living labor, and relocated within the parcelization of physical motion."[53] This is the classic domain of factory rationalization: the body is analyzed—dissected—and reconfigured in the hybrid mechano-human complex of the assembly line. But a much more refractory problem remained: that of the worker's "vestigial" consciousness. For as much as industrial theorists like Taylor and Ford fantasized about a productive body parted from its mind, such a human monster was impossible to obtain in practice, and this meant that the worker's willful or involuntary resistance to his own mental evisceration emerged as a serious impediment to the smooth functioning of production. Reconciling the worker to his mutilated status required a new science of the mind:

> If the social body must delegate its powers more and more to the productive body, similarly the autonomy of the biological body is required at the heart of the individualized productive body; better, the mechanized status imposed on the former by the latter demands in may regards a certain type of separation that we must analyze. This separation—which signals the return of life in dominated form—requires in its turn the development of a specific discipline, itself in search of its problematic autonomy; in this way the scientific psychology of work comes to occupy a place that one could say was already *reserved* in the space of ideology, but which could only be filled with the actual evolution of modes of production.[54]

What Guéry and Deleule call "la psychologie à vocation scientifique" is very different in terms of its therapeutic subjects and objectives from psychoanalysis. If the former was a psychology of the productive body, often called the science of work,[55] the latter emerged as a science addressing pathologies of the will, directed not to workers but to their capitalist employers. The physiologically based and thermodynamically inspired science of work understood the mental life of its subjects—their consciousness—as an impediment to the efficient exploitation of productive bodies[56] while in psychoanalysis the *un*conscious of its bourgeois subjects was to be brought to light rationally in order to facilitate their uninhibited expenditure of mental capital.[57] These two different discourses of the mind perform a fundamental inversion at the fulcrum of class. To the extent that consciousness is foreclosed within the worker, it is imperialistically expanded in the bourgeois subject, as part of his or her accumulation of mental capital.

With the entry of neurasthenia, a multiform illness of nervous exhaustion, into the popular imagination of America and Europe at the turn of the century, the expenditure and consolidation of mental capital was invested with its own pathologized logic. While thermodynamically oriented physiological and psychological studies of workers were intended to "[adjust] the living machine to the lifeless machine, making the living machine function like a lifeless machine,"[58] the neurasthenic's affliction derived not from his or her difficulty adjusting to the relentless physical repetitions of factory work but rather from a failure to accommodate the analogously persistent shocks of fast-paced urban life. Neurasthenia encompassed a wide variety of complaints ranging from headaches and dyspepsia to a general and persistent feeling of fatigue, but while its manifestations were wide-ranging, the majority of its sufferers belonged to a single group—namely, the bourgeois capitalist classes, and particularly "brainworkers." As Tom Lutz has stated, neurasthenia was so much associated with the socially dominant that "nervousness . . . was therefore a mark of distinction, of class, of status, of refinement."[59] Indeed, in the writings of George M. Beard, an American physician whose pioneering theories of neurasthenia were influential both in the United States and Europe, the economy of the mind was often understood in terms of finance and industry:

> In finance, a man is rich who always lives within his income. A millionaire may draw very heavily on his funds and yet keep a large surplus; but a man with very small resources—a hundred dollars in the bank—can easily overdraw his account; it may be months or years before he will be able to make himself square. There are millionaires of nerve-force—those who never know what it is to be tired out, or feel that their energies are expended . . . and there are those—and their numbers are increasing daily—who, without being really sick, without being, perhaps for a lifetime, ever confined to the bed a day with acute disorder, are yet very poor in nerve-force; their inheritance is small.[60]

The striking analogy that Beard drew between nerve force and capital dramatizes the serious stakes underlying his ostensibly casual metaphor. For if, as Deleule and Guéry indicate, the real innovation of the modern factory was its isolation and capitalization of the rational—of mental energy—then the capacity of the bourgeois classes to become "millionaires of nerve-force" is of critical importance. Indeed, while Beard did not explicitly assert a direct connection between psychic wealth and success in business, he left little doubt as to their close relationship. In a subsequent passage he expanded his metaphor by imagining the mechanics of bourgeois bodies as urban infrastructure:

> An electric machine of definite horse-power, situated at some central point, is to supply the electricity needed to run a certain number of lamps. . . . If an extra number of lamps should be interposed in the circuit, then the power of the engine must be increased. . . . The nervous system of man is the center of the nerve-force supplying all the organs of the body. Like the steam engine, its force is limited. . . . and when new functions are interposed in the circuit, as modern civilization is constantly requiring us to do, there comes a period, sooner or later . . . when the amount of force is insufficient to keep all the lamps actively burning; those that are weakest go out entirely, or, as more frequently happens, burn faint and feebly . . . this is the philosophy of modern nervousness.[61]

Beard's choice of metaphor links a neurological territory to a technological one: the modernization of cities is made to represent a retooling of the bourgeois body. Nor is this elision of neural topography and urban landscape arbitrary. For Beard, as for virtually all experts on neurasthenia, the distinctively modern stimuli of the great city, with its crowds and its distractions, were a major cause of nervous exhaustion. His metaphor thus contains a literal dimension: improvements like the installation of electric street lamps and the attendant blurring between day and night were thought to be causes of increased nervous stimulation that required appropriate mental adjustment and accommodation. It is impossible therefore to determine the priority of cause and effect in this half-figurative and half-literal metaphor: the neural network may be the introjection of urban modernization, but it is equally true that the city is nothing more than the body turned inside out. The modernization of the body and the modernization of the city are presented as continuous processes of adaptation to an homologous technology.

Although few wrote as colorfully as Beard, most American and European experts agreed that the causes of neurasthenia were rooted in the exigencies of urban capitalist life. For instance, Achille-Adrien Proust, father of Marcel and the most important authority on neurasthenia in France, concluded with his collaborator, Gilbert Ballet: "Thus may be explained the increasing frequence of neurasthenia in our time and its predominance in towns, among the middle and upper classes, in a word, in all circumstances where intellectual culture or commercial and industrial traffic are carried to the highest degree of intensity."[62] But, as Anson Rabinbach and Tom Lutz have demonstrated, the thermodynamically derived energetic economy of neurasthenia was more complex than Beard's simple vision of accumulation and expenditure. Rabinbach argues that nervous exhaustion, far from having an unambiguously negative impact on the progress of industrial capitalism, was rather a means of preserving and replenishing the nervous energy requisite for its development. Just as the science of fatigue, developed in the late nineteenth and early twentieth centuries, maximized the physical labor of workers by ascertaining precisely how much they could produce before their bodies began to tire, research into mental fatigue—neurasthenia—enforced a salubrious form of nervous *regulation* making possible an optimal expenditure of "nerve-capital."[63] The apparent contradiction, then, of a powerful and dynamic industrialist's suffering from neurasthenia dissolves: nervous complaints were one means of managing psychic resources. As Lutz concludes,

> The disease was related to changing notions of work. Neurasthenia helped some newly upper-class Americans, swelling from the wealth created by industrialism and expansion, accept a leisure-class ethic at odds with the still-dominant work ethic. It suggested to others a redefinition of the social roles of upper-class men in ways that curtailed their leisure and created, among other things, a new sanction to work in the formerly "vulgar" world of business, finance, and industry and thereby profit from ongoing modernization.[64]

The bourgeois mind, like the worker's body, was envisioned as an economy of force. The metaphor of the machine, with its bifurcation into a mechanistic apparatus and a motivating energetic stream, unified ideologically the explosively divergent paths of bourgeois and worker. But if businessman and factory hand were each imagined as machines, their subjective mechanisms ran on completely different fuels: "brain-power" for the capitalist, and "foot-power" for the worker. Duchamp, too, in a characteristically elliptical statement, acknowledged the structural parallel between the energetic economy of the mind and that of the body. As we have seen, onanistic repetition was fundamental to the operation of the bachelor machine in the *Large Glass*. So when Duchamp tied neurasthenia to repetition, he also implicitly associated it with the machine: "See Nietzsche's eternal Return, neurasthenic / form of a / repetition in succession to infinity."[65] By folding neurasthenia's mental economy into the physical economy of repetition that characterizes technology, Duchamp explicitly acknowledged the link between mental and physical capital underlying the metaphorical universe of *The Bride Stripped Bare by Her Bachelors, Even.*[66]

It would appear that by staging the private erotic drama of the *Large Glass* as an encounter among machines, Duchamp was able to mesh the paradoxical imbrication of physical attraction and psychic misrecognition of bride and bachelors with modern class-bound capitalizations of mental and physical capital—brain power and foot power. But such an assessment, rooted in the logic of industrialization, captures only half of the story of the *Glass*. Suffusing the iconography of the machine—and literally projected upon it—is a second metaphorical universe that seems to cancel it out. If Duchamp envisioned his great work as a thermodynamic factory of desire, it was also, in his eyes, a shop window, as is suggested in an extraordinary note of 1913:

> The question of shop windows∴
> To undergo the interrogation of shop windows∴
> The exigency of the shop window∴
> The shop window proof of the existence of the outside world∴

> When one undergoes the examination of the shop window, one also pronounces one's own sentence. In fact, one's choice is "round trip." From the demands of the shop windows, from the inevitable response to shop windows, my choice is determined. No obstinacy, ad absurdum, of hiding the coition through a glass pane with one or many objects of the shop window. The penalty consists in cutting the pane and in feeling regret as soon as possession is consummated. Q.E.D.[67]

In this text the shop window embodies a monumental image of erotic frustration: the alienation and cyclical nature of desire central to the dual onanisms of bachelors and bride in the *Large Glass*. Here, in one of his few explicit discussions of glass as a medium and a membrane, Duchamp described "coition through a glass pane with one or many objects of the shop window," suggesting that the grand amorous narrative of his own "glass" might be read more accurately as a perversion of the department store rather than of the factory floor. Nor is this the only clue that the *Glass* itself might be a site where promiscuous commodities may be apprehended, a place where subject and object gyrate around the hymenal glass—"From the *demands of* the shop windows, from the inevitable *response to* shop windows" [my emphasis].

Robert Lebel, one of Duchamp's best informed and most perspicacious critics, explicitly described the *Large Glass* as a shop window: "What strikes us when we first examine the *Glass* is the fact that Duchamp did everything to make it inconspicuous, for it is no more visible in broad daylight than a restaurant window encrusted with advertisements, through which we see figures moving within."[68] If Lebel saw Duchamp's work as a collage of images reminiscent of advertisements, the use of perspective in the bottom sector of the *Glass* has suggested a different type of commercial metaphor, in which a jumble of objects is visible *behind* the glass. As paraphrased by Richard Hamilton: "Each part is dimensioned and so completely developed that the perspective projection onto the glass is an ideal demonstration of classical perspective, that is to say, the elements of the Bachelor Apparatus were first imagined as distributed on the floor behind the glass rather than a composition of a two-dimensional surface."[69] This illusion of lying *behind* the glass causes the image's support to transform itself into an imprisoning vitrine—an effect accentuated through comparison to the bride whose "four-dimensional" anatomy does not conform to perspective but rather appears like a viscous transposition of the glass itself. It is well known that the model for Duchamp's chocolate grinder had been glimpsed through the window of a candy shop in Rouen: "The chocolate grinder is only a reproduction in two dimensions of an authentic chocolate grinder that I saw everyday in Rouen through the window [*derrière la vitrine*] of a confectioner."[70] In his description of the label to be appended to the drawing of *Chocolate Grinder, No. 1* Duchamp accentuated its nature as a commodity rather than an industrial machine: "*commercial formula, trade-mark, commercial slogan inscribed like an advertisement on a bit of glossy and colored paper (have it made by a printer).*"[71] Moreover, the "uniforms" of the malic molds ("Je pouvais fignoler un agent de police mais la paresse m'inclinait à considérer comme suffisant et tout aussi significatif le dessin de son enveloppe [I could have managed a policeman but laziness inclined me to consider as sufficient, and significant too, the pattern of his encasement]"[72]) could themselves suggest the display dummies of a shop window. Lebel recounts such an argument:

> Jean Reboul's very persuasive hypothesis, according to which [the malic moulds] could have been suggested by the show window of an American dry-cleaner's, can scarcely be proven chronologically, for the *Malic Moulds* antedate Duchamp's trip to New York, but an ordinary Parisian cleaner's would perhaps have been sufficient. The malic clothing, in short, was first 'pressed,' like those of 'bridegrooms' whom you see stuffed into their wedding garments.[73]

Duchamp also proposed developing colors for the *Glass* from a range of everyday commodities. A note published in *A l'infinitif* reads: "Use tooth paste / make a test on the glass / also Brilliantine, Cold cream, etc.?"[74] Aside from Duchamp's text on the "question of shop windows," the most evocative fragment tying the

Glass to commodity culture is a remark he made to Katharine Kuh about *The Green Box,* his collection of "explanatory" notes: "The Green Box is a very incomplete realization of what I intended. It only presents preliminary notes for the Large Glass and not in the final form which I had conceived as somewhat like a Sears, Roebuck catalogue to accompany the glass and to be quite as important as the visual material."[75] The metaphor of the Sears catalogue is more than a self-deprecating joke: by extracting the *Glass* from the realm of production—where critics and historians traditionally place it—and inserting it into the fantasmatic world of consumption, Duchamp hinted at the differences between his kind of machine and that of the factory. The Sears catalogue orders the world of things (for sale) in at least two ways: first, through the abstract and universal yardstick of price; and second according to categories of use, divided into "families" of commodities, like housewares and clothing. Objects unroll cinematically from page to page but without any necessary narrative link between one "spread" and the next. This logic—the logic of commodities or the shop window—differs from the synthetic or even organic organization of the assembly line or industrial machine, in which each part—each gear or piston—belongs to a coordinated economy of force. The circulation of commodities, like the bizarre interrelationships of the apparatuses in Duchamp's bachelor machine, is unpredictable, ordered not according to industrial production but to the deterritorialized desires of consumption.[76]

Duchamp therefore established a metaphor of the shop window alongside that of the industrial machine in his *Large Glass.* But this conjunction of commodity and machine is not necessarily contradictory. Only twenty years before the initial conception of the *Bride Stripped Bare by Her Bachelors, Even,* Emile Zola, in his epic novel of the department store, *The Ladies' Paradise,* used the metaphor of industrial machinery to convey revolutionary new networks of consumption. In an uncanny metaphorical elision, he consistently described the department store as a kind of factory, a great glowing dynamo of consumption:

> But opposite, the gas-lamps were being lighted all along the frontage of The Ladies' Paradise. She moved nearer, again attracted and, as it were, warmed by this wealth of illumination. The machine was still

> roaring, active as ever, hissing forth its last clouds of steam; whilst the salesmen were folding up the stuffs, and the cashiers counting up the receipts. It was, as seen through the hazy windows, a vague swarming of lights, a confused factory-like interior. Behind the curtain of falling rain, this apparition, distant and confused, assumed the appearance of a giant furnace-house, where the black shadows of the firemen could be seen passing by the red glare of the furnaces.[77]

It is easy for us to forget how innovative and aggressive the developing consumer culture of the 1880s and '90s must have looked to contemporaries: the machine and the factory were perhaps the most appropriate images to represent the brash and intimidating bazaar of Zola's fictional emporium, The Ladies' Paradise. Indeed, as Rosalind Williams points out, between 1894 and 1905 the journalist Georges d'Avenel wrote a series of articles titled "Le Mécanisme de la vie moderne" in which the "word *mechanism,* traditionally associated with means of production, was applied . . . to means of consumption."[78] Zola, however, did not simply superimpose factory onto department store; he also established a gendered opposition between them.[79] For if the "raw material" of a factory is inanimate, the department store is a "machine for devouring . . . women."[80] Zola was explicit in this: "The moment of the formidable afternoon rush had arrived, when the over-heated machine led the dance of customers, drawing the money from their very flesh."[81] In *Germinal,* his novel based on the coal-mining industry, Zola described the mineshaft as a kind of man-eating monster,[82] but in *The Ladies' Paradise* it is no longer the worker—often but not always a man—who is devoured but the feminine shoppers: "Bleed the women, work them as you would a coal mine."[83] Zola transformed women, in their overpowering desire, into a kind of force of nature that makes the great machine run:

> The ladies, seized by the current, could not now go back. As streams attract to themselves the fugitive waters of a valley, so it seemed that the wave of customers, flowing into the vestibule, was absorbing the passers-by, drinking in the population from the four corners of Paris. They advanced but slowly, squeezed almost to death, kept upright

> by the shoulders and bellies around them, of which they felt the close heat; and their satisfied desire enjoyed the painful entrance which incited still further their curiosity.[84]

For Zola, then, the difference between industrial machinery and consumer culture was not the suppression of the machine in favor of the commodity but rather a shift in the nature of the machine itself. While the mineshaft feeds on its workers to extract wealth from the land, the department store feeds on its consumers to extract wealth from their bodies. They become the "fugitive waters of a valley" but also the steam that propels an engine. Through the capture of commodities—a kind of perpetual "coition through the glass"—this fluid fuel circulates and makes the great machine run.

In the *Large Glass,* as in Zola's novel, metaphors of production and consumption interpenetrate. As I have argued, the significance of virtually every element in the composition, including the glass support itself, alternates between an industrial apparatus and a commercial shop window. But both sets of associations are subsumed within a single event: the failed erotic encounter of bachelors and bride. Indeed, Duchamp's choice of a sexual drama as the "ground" for his complex imbrication of production and consumption is prescient. For as psychoanalysis has established, erotic desire is precisely the domain in which the force of the body is most intimately united with the psychic formations of the mind: the perfect union of "foot-power" and "brain-power." Indeed, sexual intercourse has long functioned ideologically as the exemplary form of production—*the production of children*—which is presumed to exist prior to and outside of the alienating procedures of industrial rationalization. Yet this belief in a primordially pure biological mode of production is precisely what Duchamp attempted to foreclose in his *Large Glass*. In *The Bride Stripped Bare by Her Bachelors, Even* the mechanized body or anthropomorphized machine (it is impossible to decide which describes the protagonists most accurately) *no longer functions:* the productive act of sexual intercourse collapses into barren onanistic repetition. This failure of production, however, is identical to the successful dynamic of consumption. For as Zola understood at the time of the department store's infancy, the purchase of an object never satisfies desire and was never meant to; rather it incites an unfulfillable desire. It creates, as it were, a regular customer. Indeed, as he declared indirectly in *The Ladies Paradise,* biological production is displaced by consumption: "the over-heated machine led the dance of customers, drawing the money from their very flesh." As in Duchamp's *Monte Carlo Bond,* currency, drawn like a child from women's flesh, becomes offspring.

Like the Wilson-Lincoln optical illusion that had captured Duchamp's imagination, the *Glass* therefore looks different from different points of view: it is both a factory and a shop window. But as I have demonstrated, these alternative meanings do not simply coexist: Duchamp introduced alienated desire into production through his allusions to consumption. He accomplished this structurally through a logic of delay. In a well-known note he suggested that the *Glass* be subtitled a *Delay in Glass:*

> Kind of Subtitle
> **DELAY IN GLASS**
>
> Use "delay" instead of picture or painting; picture on glass becomes delay in glass—but delay in glass does not mean picture on glass—
>
> It's merely a way of succeeding in no longer thinking that the thing in question is a picture—to make a delay of it in the most general way possible, not so much in the different meanings in which delay can be taken, but rather in their indecisive reunion "delay"— / a delay in glass as you would say a poem in prose or a spittoon in silver[85]

Delay, or perhaps more accurately, *deferral,* is for Duchamp, a fundamental characteristic of both desire and the shop window. Indeed, as he declared in his text on shop windows, "The penalty consists in cutting the pane and feeling regret as soon as possession is consummated." If possession entails the penalty of regret rather than the "reward" of satisfaction, then desire must be the converse of consummation—a state of perpetual postponement or "coition through the glass." The membrane of the glass brings the commodity into being by establishing a paradoxical relationship of proximity and distance that produces desire in the viewer/consumer. It is the nature of a commodity to frustrate a desire as well as, and often instead of, satisfying a need. The poetics of deferral is not however limited to the commodity but characterizes modern industrial production as well. In the *Glass,* for instance, the conjunction of machines initiates a circulation of force that is never discharged. The illuminating gas follows its circuit, the bride is in the throes of her blossoming, but these onanistic bachelor machines never consummate—they embody industrial production as a delay.

Duchamp's understanding of production as a function of deferral is consistent with an epistemological shift in economic theory around the turn of the century. Between 1880 and 1925 an economy of desire, conceived in both financial and sexual terms, emerged that defined industrial production not in terms of the ever-increasing capacity to manufacture goods but rather as a function of the fluctuating demand for commodities within the marketplace. Selling took over from making, and just as mental capital had gained precedence over physical capital in the course of industrial expansion, the new apparatuses of consumption prospered through appeals to the mind—and particularly to desire. Lawrence Birken has argued that the development of sexology and psychoanalysis in the late nineteenth century, in which desire is erected as a scientific object, is inseparable from the contemporaneous redefinition of economics in terms of consumption.[86] Understanding commodities in terms of their "desire value"—in contradistinction to their "exchange value" or "use value"—paradoxically introduces the notion of delay or deferral within the closely communicating spheres of economic and erotic desire. This delay arises with the marketplace, which temporally divides the formerly inseparable operations of production and consumption. With the development of capitalism, the apparatuses for producing goods were extracted more and more completely from the networks for selling them, which meant that between the moment of production and that of consumption, the marketplace was opened up as a space of desire and delay. In fact, according to Guéry and Deleule the terms *production* and *consumption* are meaningless until the processes they signify are divided from one another. In their words,

> Production and productivity are names given by consumers; they are signs in the discourse of the consumer. . . . The productive body exists only in an economy of the market or in a commercial mode of production. The secret of the initiation or suspension of production, in the form of productivity, is that production occurs not for direct consumption, second moment of the cycle, but for the market, for the temporary appropriation of products, for exchange.[87]

Far from being the condition of possibility, as classical economics believed, production is actually a function of consumption. By the late nineteenth century manufacturing had achieved a level of efficiency that paradoxically submitted the factory to the stops and starts of consumer demand. Industry, like psychoanalysis, became a science of desire, whose objective was to anticipate, and often to produce, consumer demands. Consequently, within the dynamic of exchange, the material infrastructure of manufacturing was attenuated into a temporal interplay of deferral and acceleration:

> The emergence of this ecological conception should thus be associated with the shift in emphasis toward consumption in the late nineteenth century. From the perspective of the consumer, there can be no objective production but only the satisfaction or frustration of desire. The consumer recognizes production not as something real in itself but only as the deferral of consumption. In any case, from the point of view of the consumer, objects simply appear or do not appear; they are available or not available, however they are produced.[88]

Duchamp's intuitive superimposition of the conventionally distinct realms of production and consumption belongs to this elision of the productive process under the regnant desire for commodities; his *Glass* submits an industrial metaphorics of the machine to the logic of delay that characterizes the commodity. If the *Glass* can masquerade as *both* factory and shop window, it is because the one relates to the other "with all kinds of delays."[89] Duchamp did not so much oppose production to consumption as demonstrate their functional interdependence: just as the bachelor machine is composed not of conventional gears and pistons but of ambiguous elements that often appear as commodities, production is represented "not [as] something real in itself but only . . . the deferral of consumption." If production is the deferral of consumption, Duchamp also insisted that consumption is itself an endless deferral of satisfaction. For him economics—both production and consumption, like "coition"—is an infinite regress of delay, and delay is the source of desire.

The introduction of "desire value" and its accompanying dynamics of delay or deferral links the picaresque transformations of the commodity to the dual onanisms of the *Large Glass;* as Duchamp implied in his text on shop windows, the failure to possess *objects* is completely imbricated in the blockage of coition between *subjects*. And like the circulation of commodities, the science of desire, developed by Freud and others, shares the thermodynamic metaphors that motivated both the science of work and the discourse of neurasthenia. Sexuality, like "foot-power" and "nerve-power," was typically conceived as an energetic economy:

> Sexologists, including [Havelock] Ellis, tended to attribute to women, as well as to children and primitives, a more extensive though less intense sexuality than that possessed by men. Actually, it is probably more accurate to say more extensive and *thus* less intensive because sexual energy was supposed to obey the laws of an "ecology of desire." In this ecological conception . . . the value of stored charge and thus potential discharge is effectively diminished if it is either insufficiently concentrated or insufficiently delayed.[90]

The notion of an energetic "ecology" of desire returns us to the persistent metaphor of the machine as an image of the conjunctions and rechannelings of energetic force. The diversity of economies that the mechanistic metaphor may signify—in the realm of the subjective, physical force, neural charge, and desire and in the arena of the objective, both consumption and production—calls for some synthetic theory. The figure of the machine has functioned as an analogue of the human body from the time of Descartes, whose *Discourse on Method* initiated an enduring association between the human body and automatons. But, as Georges Canguilhem has demonstrated, Descartes' association of man with machine is founded on a paradox. Since machines cannot create other machines, there is the need for some initiating intelligence, and this, Canguilhem argues, was provided by Descartes in the figure of god, in a divine teleology: "Thus, in positing mechanical equivalents for living things, Descartes banished teleology from the realm of human knowledge only to reinstate it in the (immediately forgotten) realm of divine knowledge."[91] The "soul" of the machine is thus located outside its mechanistic body. In the words of Descartes:

> This ought not seem strange to those who, cognizant of how many different automata or moving machines the ingenuity of men can devise, using only a very small number of parts, in comparison to the great multitude of bones, muscles, nerves, arteries, veins and all the other parts which are in the body of each animal, will consider this body like a machine that, having been made by the hand of God, is incomparably better ordered than any of those machines that can be invented by men.[92]

Descartes thus established a kind of regress: with automatons, man with his ingenious technological knowledge stands outside the machine as inventor and director, while in the human mechanism God occupies the place of motivating intelligence. What characterizes the modern machine, by contrast to Descartes' automaton, is an attempt to colonize the external soul—to bring the mind, and its economies of desire, within the scope of mechanical explanation. In short, the modern discourse of the machine, in its various economic, therapeutic, and aesthetic manifestations, seeks to invest the already mechanized body with a mechanized soul.

I believe that Duchamp's *Large Glass* is an allegory of this massive introjection of a mechanized mind within a body that had been refashioned through various innovative disciplinary technologies since the seventeenth century. As we have seen, Duchamp's mechanistic idiom exists within two parallel discourses: first, the capitalization of the rational that arose in tandem with Taylor's and Ford's transformations of the factory, and second, the rationalization of desire that characterized the explosion of consumption and the invention of sexology. It was not until dada that a poetry of the mechanized soul gained currency in avant-garde visual art—precisely in the figure of the machine that *does not work.* Jean Arp's description of one of Francis Picabia's 1919 machine images, *Alarm Clock,* demonstrates this poetry of breakdown:

> We found him very busy pulling a clock to pieces. . . . He attacked his alarm clock ruthlessly till he got to the spring which he pulled out triumphantly. He stopped working to greet us, then taking the wheels, the spring, the hands, and other secret parts of the clock, he immediately impressed them on paper. He connected these imprints together by lines and added to the drawing sentences full of wit.[93]

With great conceptual elegance, Picabia enacted the metaphor of the modern machine: he dissected the rational mechanism—the mechanical "body"—and thereby rendered it impotent,[94] but in the same gesture he imported its collapsed anatomy of wheels and gears into a different functional order, that of the mind. From his earliest machine portraits of 1915 in which an isolated mechanical element like a spark plug or a windshield is presented as a "psychological" rendering of the self, Picabia's mechanisms elided subjective identity with the metaphor of machinery. Perhaps this imbrication of the mechanical and the mental motivated him to dedicate his *La Fille née sans mère* (1918), a series of poems and machine-inspired drawings, to neurologists.[95] As William Camfield has concluded with regard to Picabia's machines: "They do not function in an ordinary manner because their contacts are psychological, not mechanical. . . . When viewed in this context, Picabia's machines do work."[96]

Camfield's remark, implying a transformation in the dada machine from a physical mechanics to a mechanics of the mind, offers an important clue. In *Alarm Clock* Picabia dismembered and remapped the organs of an ordinary alarm

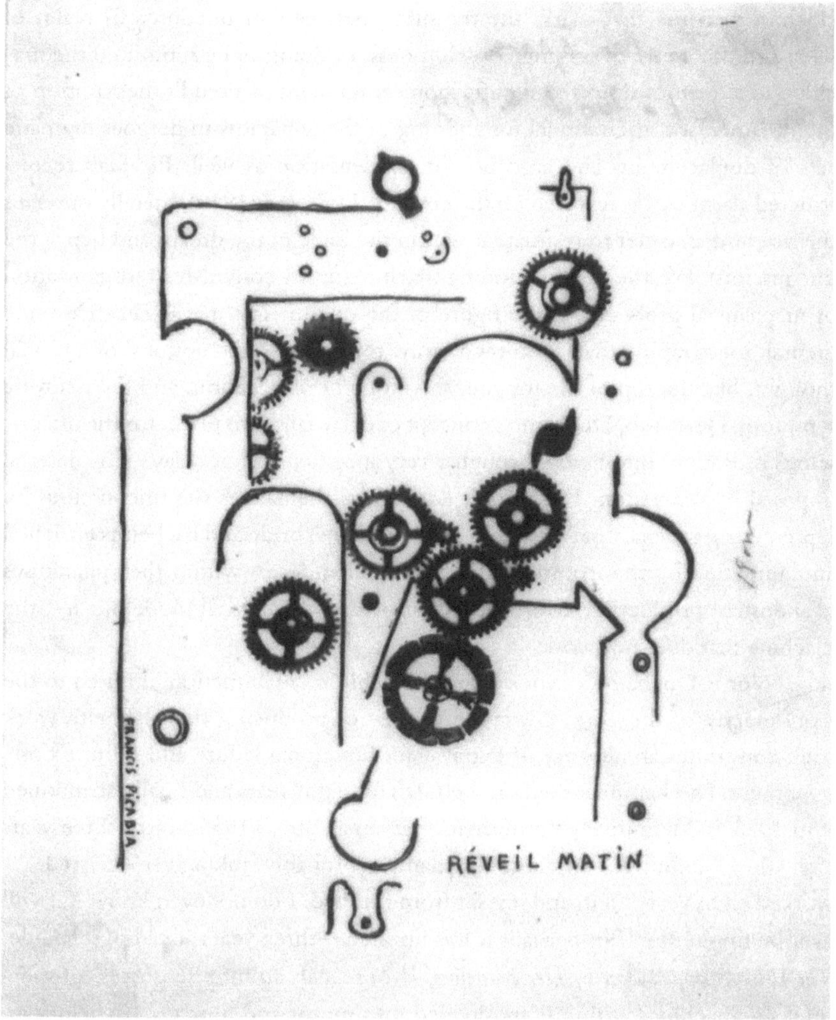

3.4 Francis Picabia. *Alarm Clock.* 1919. Pen and ink on paper, 13 × 9 ¾″. © 1990 Sotheby's, Inc. © 1997 Artists Rights Society (ARS), New York/ADAGP, Paris.

clock, a machine that marks the transition between an unconscious realm of sleep and the world of waking consciousness. In doing so he submitted the machine to a form of distorted signification reminiscent of Freud's theorization of the dream work: the rational functioning of the apparatus undergoes dramatic acts of displacement, and arguably, of condensation as well. Picabia's reconstructed alarm clock, featured on the cover of *Dada 4–5* (1919), literally unwraps the machine in order to resituate it within the logic of the dream and hence the unconscious. For the malfunctioning machine, in its convulsive reorganization of mechanical processes, is the figure of the unconscious par excellence—the mental topography that is known only through its disruptions of rational thought, like the slip of the tongue, the moment of negation, and the neurotic symptom. Here, too, Duchamp's concept of delay falls into place: for the unconscious is brought into being through a very specific form of delay—the deferral imposed by repression. Duchamp's *Large Glass* thematizes the unconscious by representing a scenario of frustrated desire between bride and bachelors enriched and amplified by the irruption of a consumerist desire within the apparatuses of industrial production. Moreover, he provided a structural model for it—the machine that does not work.

Nor is Duchamp's exploration of machinic "malfunction" limited to the iconography of the *Large Glass:* the process of producing this elaborate work itself constitutes an allegory of extravagant functional failure and infinite postponement. Duchamp worked on the *Glass* for eight years and finally abandoned it in 1923 as "definitively unfinished."[97] Even as late as 1956, thirty-three years after this "definitive" ending, Duchamp—probably jokingly—declared, "I worked eight years on it, and it is far from finished. I do not even know if it will ever be finished."[98] But perhaps it *was* finished—three years ahead of schedule. *The Bride Stripped Bare by Her Bachelors, Even* reveals an infinite process of splitting: the machines within it are divided into motor and fuel; the bachelors are kept apart from the bride; the commodities are insulated from possession "through the glass," and the machine complexes are divided from one another functionally. The trope of the modern machine, as I have argued, represents these various divisions, ultimately to incorporate them in a primary subjective split between a mechanized body and a mechanized soul. Perhaps his immersion in this poetry of division led Duchamp to realize that, alongside the machine, he had invented a much simpler metaphor for the divided subject of modernity: the membrane of glass itself.[99] This membrane is made visible—literally opaque—as a thing-in-itself in *Fresh Widow* of 1920 and *La Bagarre d'Austerlitz* of 1921, two small-scale freestanding windows whose transparency is obscured by leather squares in the former and whiting in the latter. As Duchamp declared to Harriet Janis in 1953: "I used the idea of the window to take a point of departure, as . . . I used a brush, or I used a form, a specific form of expression, the way oil paint is, a very specific term, specific conception. See, in other words, I could have made twenty windows with a different idea in each one, the windows being called 'my windows' the way you say 'my etchings.'"[100] As I have shown, Duchamp distinguished his *Large Glass* from conventional painting by proposing to call it a "'delay' instead of picture or painting; picture on glass becomes delay in glass." In his statement to Janis he suggested a second act of renaming: "I could have made twenty windows with a different idea in each one, the windows being called 'my windows' the way you say 'my etchings.'" The sequence of semantic displacements from "painting" to "delay" to "window" suggests that *Fresh Widow* succeeds the *Large Glass* in Duchamp's chain of metaphorical attenuations. The *Glass,* which had formerly eclipsed painting, is itself made obsolete by the literal, nearly readymade, metaphor of the window.[101]

Fresh Widow is a miniature model of a French window constructed according to Duchamp's specifications by a carpenter in New York. It is painted an odd shade of greenish-blue suggestive of tropical seas,[102] and its eight windowpanes are covered with black leather, which was "to be polished every morning like a pair of shoes, so that they shine like real panes."[103] This dazzling shine was to give the false impression of looking from outside into a perfectly dark room.[104] The window itself stands on a low sill with the inscription "Fresh Widow COPYRIGHT ROSE SELAVY 1920" and is distinguished by being the first work to be signed and conceived by Duchamp's feminine alter ego. Indeed, there is a strong formal resemblance between *Fresh Widow* and the series of photographs of a similarly proportioned two-paned window, veiled by a gauze

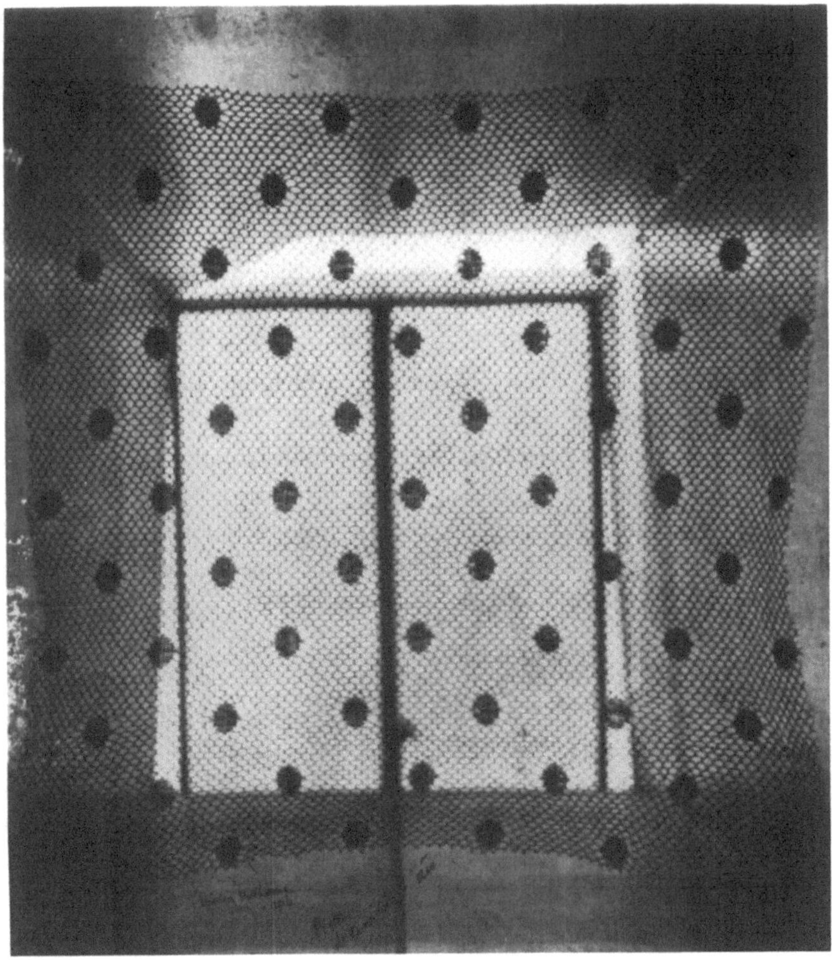

3.5 Marcel Duchamp. *Draft Piston*. 1914. Gelatin silver print, 23 ⅞ × 19 ⅝". Philadelphia Museum of Art: Gift of Mme. Marcel Duchamp. © 1997 Artists Rights Society (ARS), New York/ADAGP, Paris/Estate of Marcel Duchamp.

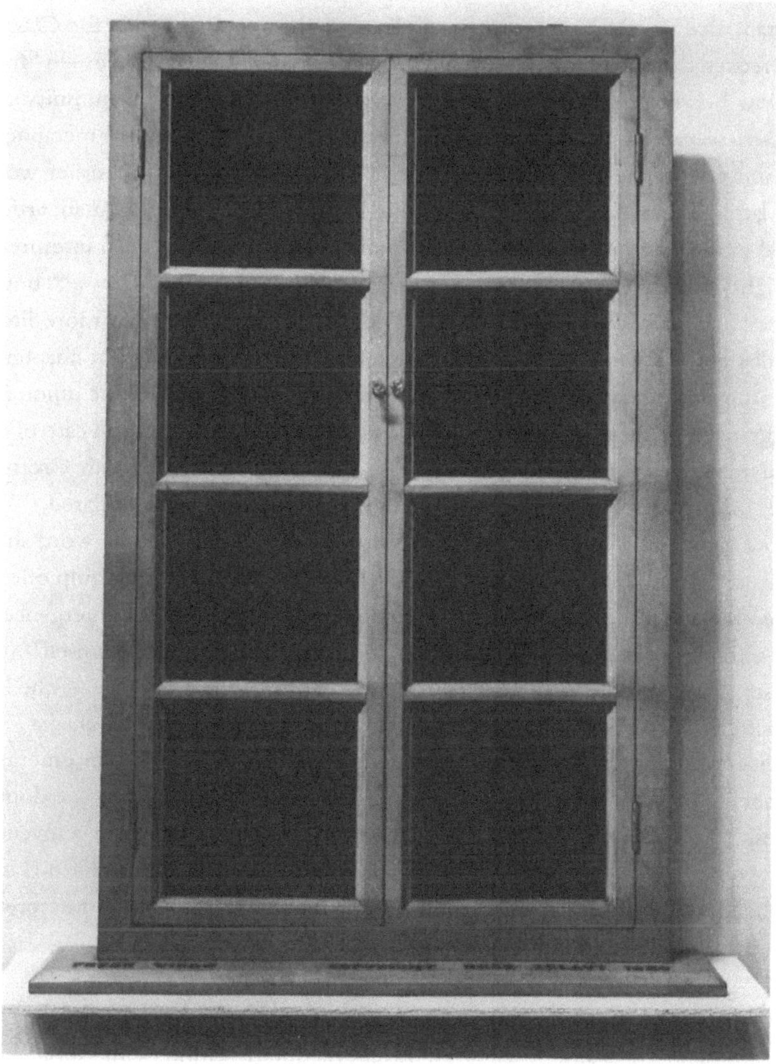

3.6 Marcel Duchamp. *Fresh Widow.* New York, 1920. Miniature French window, painted wood frame, and eight panes of glass covered with black leather, 30 ½ × 17 ⅝", on wood sill ¾ × 21 × 4". The Museum of Modern Art, New York. Katherine S. Dreier Bequest. Photograph © 1997 The Museum of Modern Art, New York. © 1997 Artists Rights Society (ARS), New York/ADAGP, Paris/Estate of Marcel Duchamp.

curtain, that was the basis for the *Draft Pistons* in the upper section of the *Glass*.[105] Moreover, the pun of the title, which projects the identity of a woman—a "fresh widow"—onto a "French window" makes the association of femininity and glass inescapable. These, however, are not the only links between the metaphorical universe of the *Large Glass* and that of *Fresh Widow.* As in the earlier work, the latter suggests a frustrated relationship between a man and a woman, articulated in the language of marriage. The pun "fresh widow" has been interpreted in light of castration anxiety and as a reference to French war widows,[106] but its association with Duchamp's "window" also suggests a richer and more literal oscillation between the artist's alternate selves. As I demonstrated in chapter 1, the language of marriage for Duchamp exceeded the bounds of erotic union and suggested a rigorous tie between ideas and things—a tie that, in the case of the readymade *Fountain,* he sought to break. In a letter written to Jean Crotti in 1921, the year following the construction of *Fresh Widow,* he declared, "You know very well that I have nothing to show—and that to me the word show [*exposer*] sounds like the word marriage [*épouser*]."[107] This amusing quip offers a profound insight into Rose Sélavy's "widowhood": for with her emergence—her exhibition/marriage—Marcel had "nothing to show for/of himself" (but Rose). What was carried on *within* the iconography of the *Large Glass*—the impossibility of connection between bachelors and bride—takes place *around Fresh Widow,* through the oscillation between Marcel and Rose, who, in emerging publicly, "killed" Marcel, thus making herself a widow. In 1920, she was doubly "fresh," being recently bereft of her "partner" and having just been reinvented as a woman. As in the *Large Glass,* this flickering between genders in *Fresh Widow* is elided with a contradiction within production. Molly Nesbit has interpreted this dynamic centering on Duchamp's gesture of copyrighting:

> The *Fresh Widow* is declared copyrighted by Duchamp's alias, Rose Sélavy. The claim to copyright brings the interrogation by the shop window to a different halt: Duchamp has claimed a copyright for a window that is not only plagiarized but by definition not eligible for copyright: the window is an industrial good in the eyes of the

> law; if suitably innovative it might be patented but never given the *droit d'auteur,* not even in America. The copyright was a bluff. But with it, Duchamp subjugated the culture of the patent in no uncertain terms: by means of that one word, he pulled the culture of the patent over into the culture of copyright, the traditional culture, the culture of artists.[108]

The untying of conventional gender roles in which Duchamp split into Marcel and Rose, is echoed by a second division: between physical capital, represented by the patent, and mental capital, signified by "the culture of the copyright . . . the culture of artists." As in the *Large Glass,* this division in production is elided with a destabilization of the commodity. For *Fresh Widow* occupies an undecidable territory between industrial tool and commodity. By virtue of its miniature size, it would seem to function as a scale model and therefore belong to the initial stages of production. It is equally possible that this small aperture could be for sale, but as an architectural element the window definitively belongs to neither the context of production nor of consumption, existing rather as a hybrid of both.

Fresh Widow reworks the multiple divisions—between male and female, production and consumption, mind and body—underlying Duchamp's elaborate metaphor of the machine. Instead of illustrating these myriad splittings through the invention of an arcane iconography as in the *Glass,* the little window *spatializes* them with great economy and simplicity. In place of the picaresque drama of bachelors and brides circulating through an impossible landscape of mechanisms, a single blocked glass—an object alternatively identified with production and consumption—functions as the pivot of two fictionalized selves, Rose and Marcel. It is as though *To Be Looked At (from the Other Side of the Glass) with One Eye, Close To, for Almost an Hour* of 1918, in which the viewer was split into two—s/he who "regards" and s/he who is looked at—had been darkened with leather shades, allowing the object and subject of the gaze to reside in the alternate persona of a single self. *Fresh Widow* is indeed the materialization of something that should by nature be invisible—a division that Duchamp might have called "infrathin," or the "passage" from virgin to bride (or bride to widow), or "'cuttage' in reserve."[109] Indeed, Duchamp associated his notion of infrathin with that of division, transparency, and "cuttage": "Reflection from a mirror—or glass— / flat/convex—infrathin **separation**—better / than screen, because it indicates / interval (taken in one sense) and / screen (taken in another sense)—separation / has the 2 senses male and female—."[110] This note brilliantly summarizes the significance of *Fresh Widow,* which is both interval and screen, male and female. Many commentators have noted that the French word for widow, *veuve,* is a colloquialism for the guillotine,[111] and that the widow/window is consequently an explicit instance of "'cuttage' in reserve."[112] The bloody promise of *Fresh Widow*—the divorce of head and body—is an uncanny transposition of an ideological beheading that separates physical capital from mental capital in the discourse of the modern machine. The little window taught Duchamp a profound lesson: he could invest the complexity of the *Large Glass* in an object with the seeming simplicity and opacity of the readymades, and this made it possible for him to abandon *The Bride Stripped Bare by Her Bachelors, Even.* Contrary to his own testimony, the *Glass* was really not "unfinished": *Fresh Widow* completed it (three years ahead of schedule). Nor was this "widow" simply an ending. She was also a beginning—the initial manifestation of Duchamp's work of the 1920s, which, like the infrathin, was nearly invisible and characterized by gestures of extraordinary modesty and significance.

4

The Self Readymade

> The readymade is the consequence of the refusal which made me say: There are so many people who make pictures with their hands, that one should end up not using the hand.[1]

> chess = a design on slate / that one erases, / the beauty of which / one can reproduce without the / intervention of the "hand"[2]

A photograph of Duchamp's New York studio, probably dating from 1918, shows the dusty disorder that, according to accounts of his friends, characterized the workroom of this otherwise impeccable figure. Cushions tossed on the floor, books and papers haphazardly subsiding on a desk, this is the chaos of the artist's workshop, where visual systems exist in fluid potential, not yet petrified into public form. Yet this photograph encompasses a juxtaposition that, like a manifesto, establishes the conditions of Duchamp's art from the 1920s onward. On the side wall, the horizontal grid of a chessboard has been tipped up and hung like a painting—the modernist abstraction par excellence—in order for Duchamp to produce the "erasable beauty" of chess matches carried out with absent opponents.[3] As his friend Henri-Pierre Roché recounted: "On the walls [were] large vertical chessboards on which matches by mail unfolded that he conducted

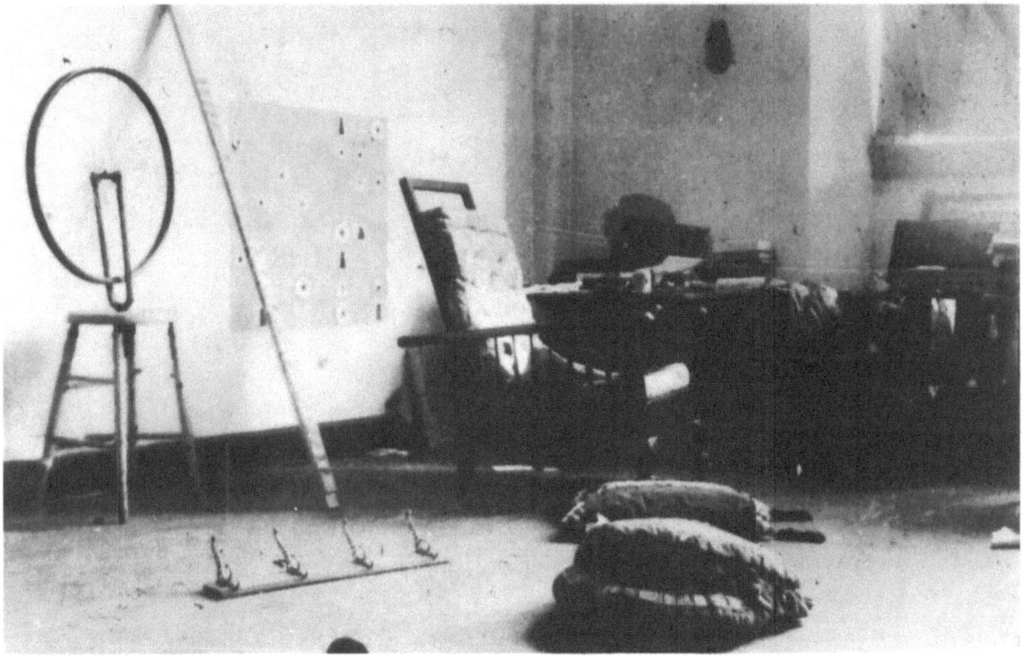

4.1 Marcel Duchamp. *Marcel Duchamp's Studio*. 1917. Photograph. © Succession Marcel Duchamp. © 1997 Artists Rights Society (ARS), New York/ADAGP, Paris/Estate of Marcel Duchamp.

against distant masters."[4] The simple but highly charged gesture of rotating a chessboard from the horizontal plane of the game to the vertical plane of painting disrupts that staple of Duchamp hagiography in which the artist abandons art in disgust sometime in the early 1920s in order to play chess full-time.[5] The rotated chessboard suggests that the relationship between chess and art was not necessarily one of displacement but rather of the transformation or transposition of painterly themes into a realm that obviates "the intervention of the hand." For an artist who considered the application of oil pigments a form of "olfactory masturbation," chess could function as a physically and conceptually hygienic painting machine. Duchamp explicitly established this possibility: "Actually, I believe that every chess player experiences a mixture of two aesthetic pleasures: first the abstract image akin to the poetic idea in writing, second the sensuous pleasure of ideographic execution of that image on the chessboards."[6] Moreover, in a letter written to Jean Crotti in 1920 Duchamp proposed a scheme to transform the chessboard into a shifting field of symbolic color strikingly reminiscent of Kandinsky's theory of color essences in *Concerning the Spiritual in Art:*

> Something else—I am about to launch on the market a new form of chess sets, the main features of which are as follows:
>
> The Queen is a combination of a Rook and of a Bishop—the Knight is the same as the one I had in South America. So is the Pawn. The King too.
>
> 2nd They will be colored like this.
>
> The white Queen will be light green.
>
> " black " " " dark "
>
> The Rooks will be blue, light and dark.
>
> The Bishops " " yellow, " " "
>
> The Knights, red, light and dark.
>
> White King and Black King
>
> White and Black Pawns
>
> *Please notice* that the Queen in her color is a combination of the Bishop and of the Rook (just as she is in her movements)—[7]

The interlocking spatial patterns of chess are allegorically intensified through color: the Queen, for instance, is both a visual and spatial combination of the bishop and the rook. Through this program Duchamp could produce a "painting" that was never twice the same, that perfectly responded to the imperatives of strategy and chance.

It would be an error to conclude that chess functioned exclusively for Duchamp as a metaphor for painting. The same 1918 photograph of his studio documents a second set of artistic transformations associated with the game. In the foreground, diagonally across from the hanging chessboard, is a coatrack bolted to the floor. Duchamp called this readymade of 1917 *Trébuchet,* "a chess term for a pawn placed so as to 'trip' an opponent's piece."[8] Indeed, in his 1932 book on chess, coauthored by Vitaly Halberstadt, Duchamp explicitly mentioned this type of trap.[9] In 1953 he described the installation of *Trébuchet* to Harriet Janis: "A real coat hanger that I wanted sometime to put on the wall and hang my things on but I never did come to that—so it was on the floor and I would kick it every minute, every time I went out—I got crazy about it and I said the Hell with it, if it wants to stay there and bore me, I'll nail it down . . . and then the association with the Readymade came and it was that."[10] If Duchamp's vertical chessboard realizes a painterly ideal of "erasable beauty," *Trébuchet* initiated a second aesthetic order in which the manoeuvres of the game spill out into everyday space, where not merely an inanimate surrogate like a chess piece is tripped up, but the artist himself. If Duchamp put himself in the position of the "piece" rather than the player, inadvertently tripped by a "pawn" of his own placing, this was not the first instance in which chess provided a means of self-identification. Such an association was already fundamental in his cubism.[11] While women—sisters, virgins, and brides—are represented in the cubist paintings of 1911 and 1912 as fields of immensurable carnality imperfectly formalized by immanent systems of measurement, men tend to be captured inside the agonistic space of the chessboard. In Duchamp's studies and paintings of chess players dating from 1911 male figures are represented as stylized profiles—as though they themselves were pieces being played, an impression confirmed by his frequent practice of extending the grid of the game board behind and beside the central figures and placing chessmen not only before them where the board should be but all around them, as though they were the principal objects in a game that had escaped its gridded precincts and colonized the entire world.[12] This is precisely what *Trébuchet* accomplished six years later in the space of the studio: the migration of the game, in the guise of a trap, into the realm of everyday life. Chess therefore meets art in two directions—through its colonization of the plane of painting, and by its projection outward into the realm of the readymade. It not only occupies these two spaces but unites them like a hinge.

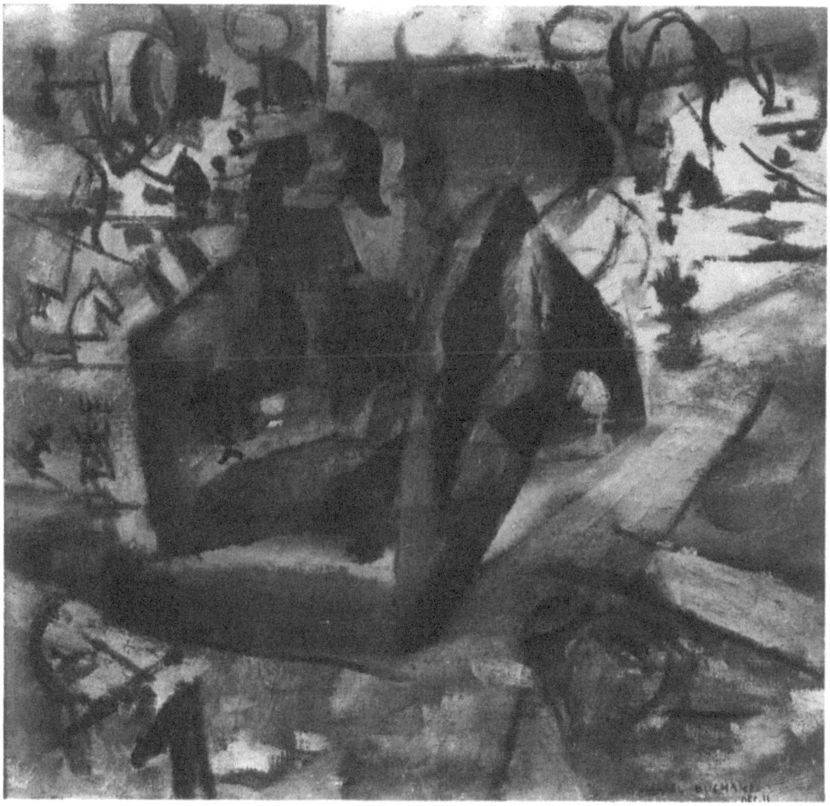

4.2 Marcel Duchamp. *The Chess Players*. Neuilly, 1911. Oil on canvas, 42 ½ × 39 ¾″. Musée national d'art moderne, Paris. © 1997 Artists Rights Society (ARS), New York/ ADAGP, Paris/Estate of Marcel Duchamp.

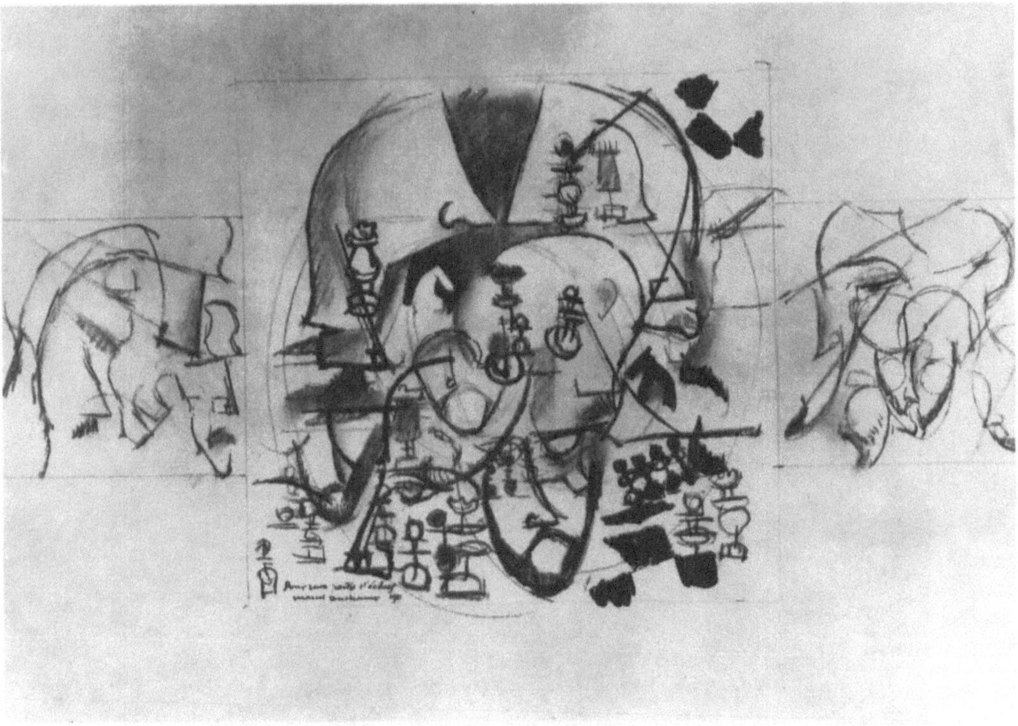

4.3 Marcel Duchamp. *Study for The Chess Players* or *For a Game of Chess*. Neuilly, 1911. Charcoal and India ink on paper, 17 11/16 × 24 3/16″. Succession Marcel Duchamp. © 1997 Artists Rights Society (ARS), New York/ADAGP, Paris/Estate of Marcel Duchamp.

For Duchamp chess was not a renunciation of art but rather a means of rethinking its terms. To Truman Capote he declared: "And why . . . isn't my chess playing an art activity? A chess game is very plastic. You construct it. It's mechanical sculpture and with chess one creates beautiful problems and that beauty is made with the head and hands."[13] And to Pierre Cabanne: "A game of chess is a visual and plastic thing, and if it isn't geometric in the static sense of the word, it is mechanical, since it moves; it's a drawing, it's a mechanical reality."[14] In the previous chapter I argued that *Fresh Widow,* as a literalization and spatialization of an act of division or cutting, is the successor to the mechanical iconography of the *Large Glass*. Duchamp's emphasis on chess, which emerged at around the same time as *Fresh Widow,* constitutes a second transformation of his discourse of mechanization—centering not on the machine's fundamental capacity to divide but rather on its status as an economy of movement or force. Duchamp's "discovery" of chess—and by this I mean not his initiation into the game but rather his adoption of its terms as an aesthetic idiom—solved the problem that he introduced in 1913 with the construction of the *Bicycle Wheel.* For despite his preoccupation with movement or "passage," *Bicycle Wheel* is the only kinetic object that he produced until the *Rotary Glass Plates (Precision Optics)* of 1920. Duchamp sought not to simulate motion as the futurists' had but rather to diagram it, to capture it within a grid of measurement.[15] Indeed, in his cubist painting he accomplished the inverse of what he praised in chess. If chess "isn't geometric in the static sense of the word," but "it is mechanical, since it moves," his cubist masterworks as well as the *Large Glass* immobilize movement and the machine: the dynamism they introduce is indeed *geometric in the static sense of the word.*[16] Duchamp was fascinated by movement, but he was equally aware of the immense difficulty in representing it without falling into what he called "urban impressionism."[17] *Bicycle Wheel* is the emblem of this difficulty, and its presence between the tipped chessboard on the wall and *Trébuchet* nailed into the floor in the studio photograph of 1918 uncannily completes the discursive field that we might call "Duchampian chess." For the conceptual elegance of chess—and of the optical machines Duchamp created in the twenties and thirties—lies in the deployment of an aesthetic dynamism that has none of the simulationist literalness of futurist paintings. With chess the static readymade is restaged as a series of interactions even more complex than those evoked in the *Glass.* The game provided Duchamp with a systemic model of mechanical movement, which unlike either the *Large Glass* or *Fresh Widow* is virtually invisible as an art object, or at least "erasable." Chess is the model of the readymade put into action, both within the painterly plane of the chessboard and in the world of everyday life. The game's capacity to demonstrate the reversibility of these diverse spaces—those of the canvas and of the "world"—is encoded in the modest photograph of Duchamp's New York studio.[18]

Even if it were true that Duchamp gave up art for chess during the 1920s,[19] such a renunciation could only be tautological because for him the game was a serious continuation of his artistic preoccupations. The fact is, Duchamp *never did give up art*—he continued to produce works whose scarcity and physical modesty have led many of his commentators to accept, and thus to disseminate, the myth of its abandonment. But acknowledging this oversight should not lead us to invert the false dichotomy of art and chess by devaluing the second term. The game was no mere idle pastime for the artist, a smoke screen that could block the scrutiny of the art world.[20] Rather, as I have demonstrated, chess, like the machine before it, provided Duchamp with a productive conceptual and aesthetic model that was uniquely capable of synthesizing the "spatial realism" or literalness of the readymades and the systemic complexity of the *Large Glass*. The question, then, is not so much why Duchamp gave up art in the face of chess but rather how he could invent an art that would equal the conceptual beauty and elegance of the game. The difficulty of this challenge, I believe, accounts in part for both Duchamp's limited production in the 1920s and for the striking originality of the works that he did create during this period.

One of the strangest of these—and one unique in Duchamp's production—is the assemblage titled *Why Not Sneeze Rose Sélavy?* of 1921, which was originally commissioned by Katherine Dreier's sister Dorothea. The work consists of a small bird cage filled with 152 marble cubes,[21] a cuttlebone, four wooden perches, and a thermometer. The bottom of the cage is inscribed with the text, "Why Not Sneeze Rose Sélavy?" Noting the similarity between the aleatory accumulation of marble units in this object and the jumble of cubes that forms the foreground of Duchamp's 1925 poster for the French Chess Championship in Nice,[22] Hubert Damisch has suggested that the contents of *Why Not Sneeze?* might be considered a collapsed or dimensionally transposed chessboard. He even stipulates that the number of cubes that would occur in a three-dimensional chessboard space ($8 \times 8 \times 8 = 512$) is a numerical anagram of the 152 cubed marbles in the cage.[23] Indeed, Damisch's suggestion of a link between *Why Not Sneeze?* and chess is given further plausibility in the full text of the note I quoted at the outset of this chapter:

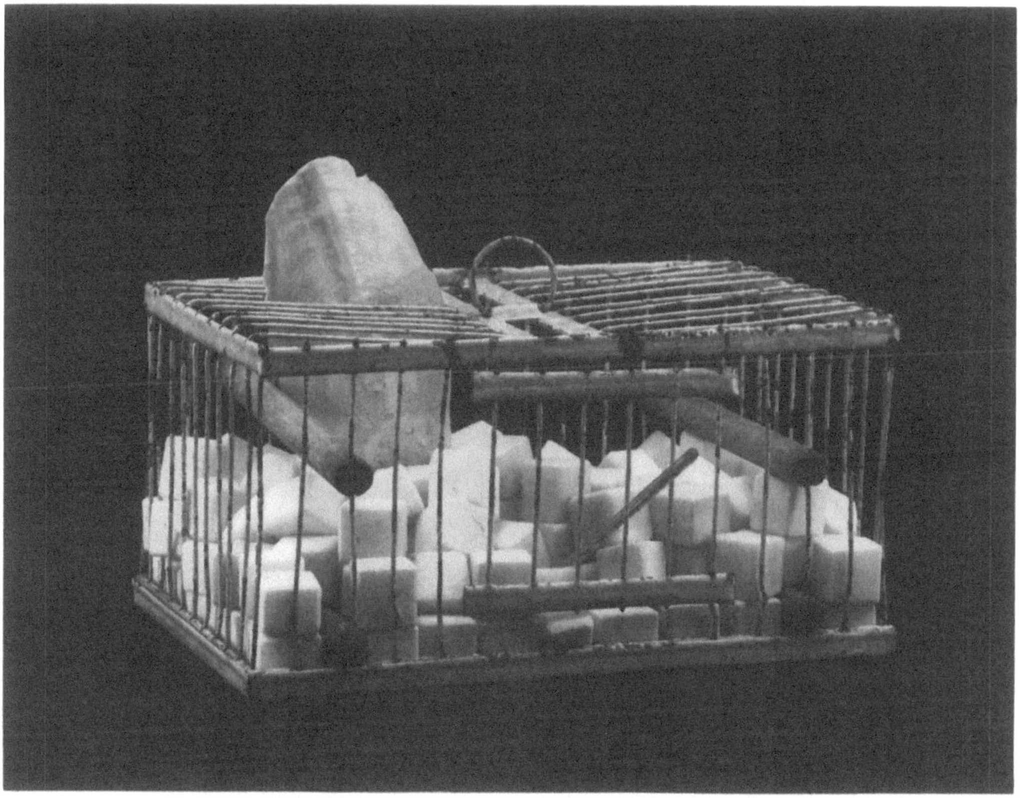

4.4 Marcel Duchamp. *Why Not Sneeze Rose Sélavy?* New York, 1921. Painted metal bird cage, marble cubes, thermometer, and cuttlebone, 4 ½ × 8 ⅝ × 6 ⅜". Philadelphia Museum of Art: The Louise and Walter Arensberg Collection. Photo by Graydon Wood, 1994. © 1997 Artists Rights Society (ARS), New York/ADAGP, Paris/Estate of Marcel Duchamp.

temperature, / "color" of touch
linear time or "duration"
chess = a design on slate / that one erases, / the beauty of which /
one can reproduce without the / intervention of the "hand."[24]

This text, in which the art-historically opposed terms of opticality and tactility collapse through an analogy between color and temperature, is consistent with Duchamp's penchant for transposing sensory data from one grid of measurement to another, from one dimension to another.[25] According to this text, the thermometer is a painting machine whose "colors" are inaccessible to the eye—consisting instead of gradations of warmth. In a 1954 letter to André Breton, Duchamp made this structural parallelism even more explicit: "I have in any event at my disposition the *thermometer* of chess, which registers quite precisely my deviations from a line of thought strictly 'syllogistic.'"[26]

Despite Duchamp's metaphorical description of chess as a psychic thermometer, the significance of *Why Not Sneeze?* is not exhausted by its multiple allusions to the game. As I have shown, the spatial intricacies of chess produced a topological dimension within Duchamp's work that characterized many of his readymade practices of the twenties. In *Fresh Widow,* for instance, an imploded opposition between inside and out, here and there, functions as a pivot between Duchamp and his "widow," Rose Sélavy. Like the miniature window, the little bird cage transforms the failed eroticism of the *Large Glass* into an ensemble of readymades. There is explicit evidence in Duchamp's notes for a strong iconographic connection between *The Bride Stripped Bare by Her Bachelors, Even* and *Why Not Sneeze Rose Sélavy?* In one text from the *Green Box* he suggested that a "cage" was the alternative to glass as the environment for the bride: "Put the whole bride under a glass case, or into a transparent cage." And in another: the bride's "pulse needle in addition to its vibratory mvt. is mounted on a wandering leash. It has the liberty of caged animals."[27] Moreover, Duchamp explicitly related the bride to a meteorological device enclosed within a cage in a note of 1913:

IN THE PENDU; FEMELLE—AND THE BLOSSOMING BAROMETER.

> The filament substance might lengthen or shorten itself in response to an *atmospheric pressure* organized by the wasp. (filament substance *extremely sensitive* to differences of artificial atmospheric pressure controlled by the wasp).
>
> —Isolated cage—containing the filament subst. in which would take place—the storms and the fine weathers of the wasp.[28]

If the caged thermometer suggests the figure of Duchamp's bride—an allusion only strengthened through the time-honored, if misogynist association of birds with women—the bachelors are present, too. They enter as a pile of marble cubes: a collapsed figure of the chessboard, coded as masculine. But the identification between these marble "blocks" and the bachelors of the *Large Glass* need not be routed through chess: one of the their many metaphorical identities, as stated in Duchamp's notes, was as a "firm ground . . . the masonry base of the bachelor machine."[29] The marble "bricks" are an aleatory formation of the "masonry base of the bachelor machine," an identity that—if we recall the association between window and women established in *Fresh Widow*—emerges in the brick base of one side of the glass in *La Bagarre d'Austerlitz,* a work produced in the same year as *Why Not Sneeze?*

The bird cage thus spatializes the erotic economy of the *Large Glass,* in which combinations of readymade elements displace narrative structure altogether. Duchamp retroactively confirmed the close association between these two works in his *Boîte-en-Valise* of 1935–41, a carefully constructed retrospective "exhibition" composed of reproductions ingeniously folding out of a small suitcase. In this work, a small cut-out photograph of *Why Not Sneeze?,* propped on a special plaster base to suggest three-dimensionality, is positioned directly in front of the central reproduction of the *Glass.* The smaller, ostensibly offhand work, seems to spill out of the great masterpiece in a vivid demonstration of derivation. Nor is the resemblance between the two works limited to the bird cage's metaphorical transposition of bride and bachelors. This work, like its predecessor, implies an onanistic impasse that, as in *Fresh Widow,* is encoded in the title. As an explosive and ejaculatory convulsion of the body a sneeze is easy to sexualize, and Duchamp did so explicitly in one of his notes: "utilization / apparatus to \ record / collect and / transform all the little external manifestations / of (man's) energy (in excess or lost) / like / for example . . . spitting or of blood, vomittings, ejaculation, sneezing.[30]

If the question, "Why not sneeze?" might otherwise be phrased as "Why not come?" the cage acquires a nuance consistent with the "frigidity" of the marble.[31] For according to Duchamp, these instances of bodily release have nothing to do with volition but rather dramatize the split between semiautonomous body and an ineffectual mind:

> First of all there's the dissociational gap between the idea of sneezing and the idea of . . . 'Why not sneeze?' because, after all, you don't sneeze at will; you usually sneeze in spite of your will. So the answer to the question, Why not sneeze? is simply that you can't sneeze *at will!* And then there's the literary side, if I may call it that . . . but 'literary' is such a stupid word . . . it doesn't mean anything . . . but at any rate there's the marble with its coldness, and this meant that you can even say you're cold, because of the marble, and all the associations are permissible.[32]

Following the associations suggested by this statement, *Why Not Sneeze?* constitutes a fascinating footnote to the erotic standoff of the *Glass.* Duchamp implied that the sneeze—and by association, sexual consummation—cannot be willed, and therefore the failure of bride and bachelors to accomplish "coition through the glass" may be attributed not to an absence of desire but rather to the inexorable force of an unconscious will that transforms erotic partners from volitional "players" into unconscious "pieces" being played.

Why Not Sneeze Rose Sélavy? is a complex combination of readymade elements, but for precisely that reason, it is not nearly so conceptually economical as *Fresh Widow,* which similarly transforms the terms and conflicts of the *Large Glass.* The former work, however, produces a topological space—the space of the cage or miniaturized room. It was not until 1927 that Duchamp found the opportunity to synthesize the figure of division-in-itself that *Fresh Widow* introduced and the topological promise of chess, as elaborated in *Why Not Sneeze?* He did so in his studio at 11 rue Larrey in Paris, where he had a door installed at the corner of his workroom that fit two doorways: the bathroom on one side, and the bedroom on the other. If both *Fresh Widow* and *La Bagarre d'Austerlitz,* not to mention the *Large Glass* and *To Be Looked At,* create a division within space in which a here—"this side of the window"—is separated from a there—"the far side of the window"—the door at rue Larrey is the paradoxical elision of equivalently opposing terms: open and closed. Yet when the studio door is closed, it is also always open, and when it is not closed it opens onto two doorways.[33] Charged with negotiating access between the space of mental activity and those dual sites of carnal sensuality, the bedroom and the bathroom, this door—which is also always an aperture—simultaneously embodies and undermines the notion of division.[34]

The topographical force of the door lies in its capacity for movement: its paradox of belonging to two places at once. As I have argued, such transformation, or passage, from one state to another was central to Duchamp's earlier art. But in his cubism, as well as the *Large Glass,* movement could only be represented through transitional moments of stasis. In *Bride* and *Network of Stoppages* a system of measurement emerges from and is projected onto the body of a woman, and in the *Large Glass* the circulation of illuminating gas or the blossoming of the bride is frozen into a diagram. As I have shown, these immobilizations carry a wide range of erotic and social implications, including the onanistic standoff between man and woman, the alienation of the commodity, and the oscillation between mental and physical economies of affect or force. But in all of these works, only the figure of stabilization—the image itself—is visible while the movement of the represented objects must necessarily remain virtual. The converse is true in the door at rue Larrey: here motion is literal, and its immobilization is virtual. In its hingelike shifts the door may open and close, but each

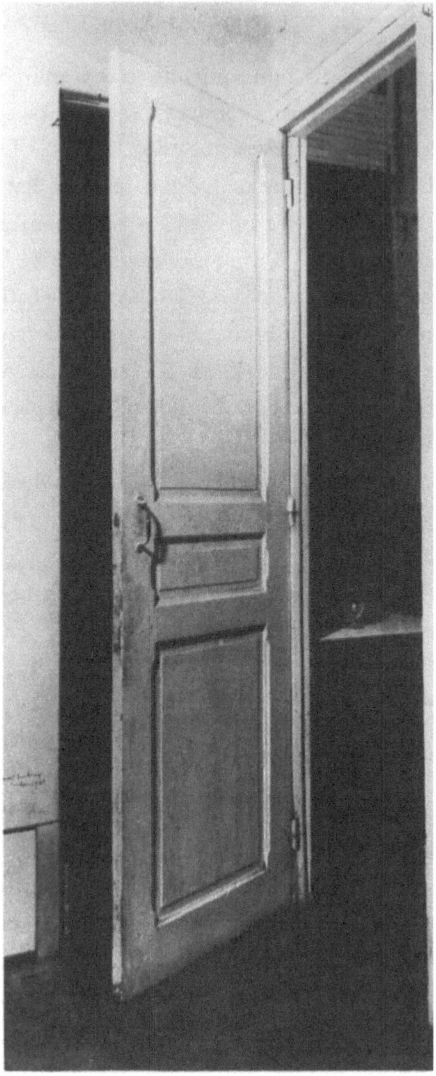

4.5 Marcel Duchamp. *Door, 11 rue Larrey.* Paris, 1927. Wooden door made by a carpenter following Duchamp's specifications, 86 ⅝ × 24 11/16". Photo Arturo Schwarz Collection, Milan. Photo: S.A.D.E. archives. © 1997 Artists Rights Society (ARS), New York/ADAGP, Paris/Estate of Marcel Duchamp.

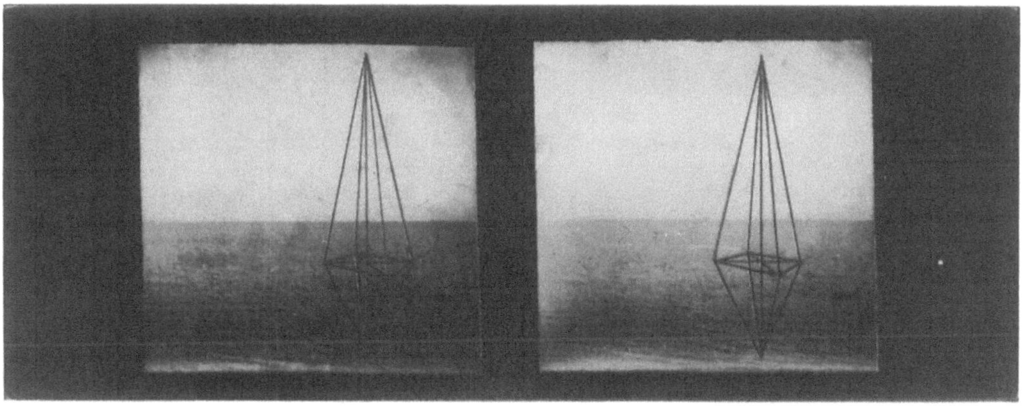

4.6 Marcel Duchamp. *Handmade Stereopticon Slide.* c. 1918–19. Cut and pasted stereopticon slide, and pencil on black paper surfaced cardboard, 2 ⅝ × 6 ¾″. The Museum of Modern Art, New York. Katherine S. Dreier Bequest. Photograph © 1997 The Museum of Modern Art, New York. © 1997 Artists Rights Society (ARS), New York/ADAGP, Paris/Estate of Marcel Duchamp.

move is contradicted: every opening is also a closing, and vice versa—movement is initiated only to be circumscribed.

The door's contradiction parallels the other significant elision of opposing terms that characterizes Duchamp's art of the 1920s: his optical "research." For Duchamp's various optical machines, beginning with the *Rotary Glass Plates (Precision Optics)* of 1920 and continuing through the *Rotary Demisphere* of 1925 and *Anémic Cinéma* of 1926, produce alternating illusions of convexity and concavity. These spinning spiral patterns produce an erotic, pulsatile imbrication of opposing volumes, created entirely by the eye.[35] But these contradictory illusions of convexity and concavity cancel out both on account of their sequential alternation and because they are founded in the flatness of a spinning, two-dimensional drawing. In fact, the optical paradox of these apparatuses was already embedded in the very simple work *Hand Stereoscopy* of 1918–19, composed of two nearly identical photographs in which a polygonal volume is superimposed upon a seascape. As in the door at rue Larrey, this work transforms planar surfaces into a

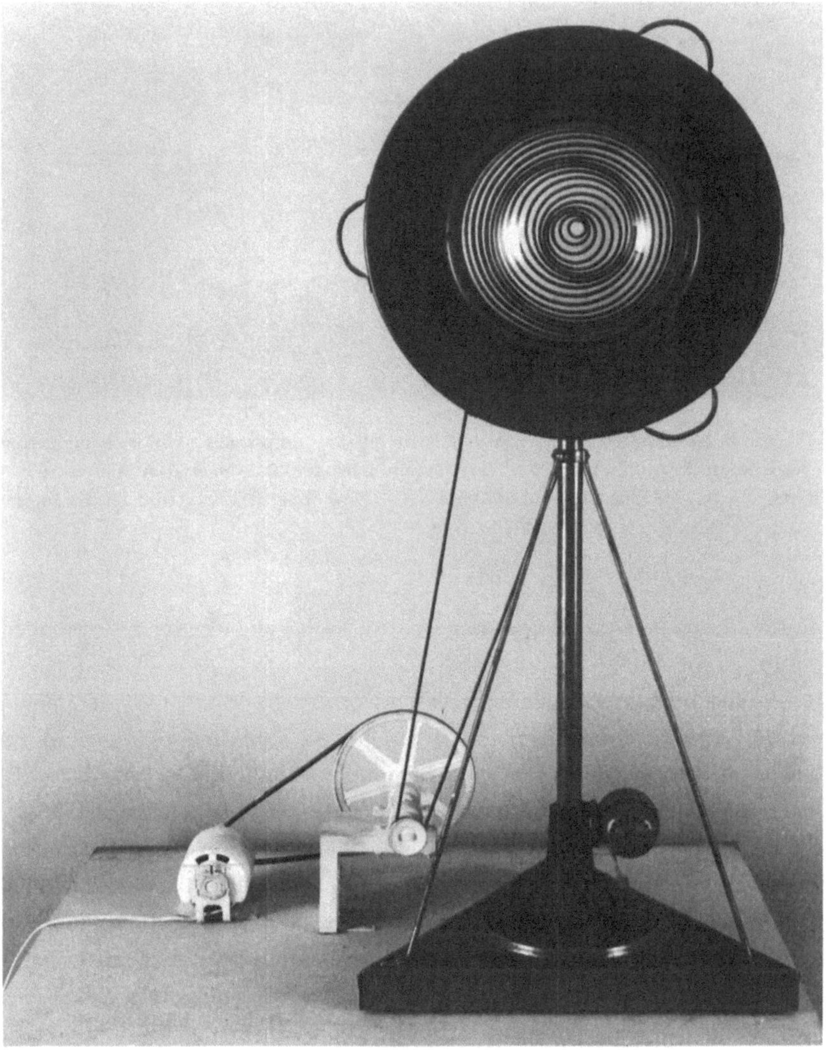

4.7 Marcel Duchamp. *Rotary Demisphere (Precision Optics)*. Paris, 1925. Motor-driven construction: painted wood demisphere, fitted on black velvet disk, copper collar with plexiglass dome, motor, pulley, and metal stand, 58 ½ × 25 ¼ × 24″. The Museum of Modern Art, New York. Gift of Mrs. William Sisler and Edward James Fund. Photograph © 1997 The Museum of Modern Art, New York. © 1997 Artists Rights Society (ARS), New York/ADAGP, Paris/Estate of Marcel Duchamp.

three-dimensional space: flat objects (photographs or doors will do equally well) are mentally synthesized to produce a third dimension.

Like *Fresh Widow* Duchamp's door wipes away the iconography of bride and bachelors that had played across the surface of the *Large Glass* in order to reveal an underlying structure of spatial opposition. Nine years earlier *To Be Looked At* had prefigured the door's structural paradox. As its title suggests, this study for the *Large Glass* is to be looked *at* like a screen, but it also explicitly instructs the viewer to look *through* it from behind like an aperture. In the door, which elaborates an analogous contradiction of transparency and opacity, or open and closed, Duchamp attenuated this earlier paradox—equally characteristic of the *Large Glass*—to near invisibility. By embedding the work seamlessly in the environment of his studio, he answered a question that he posed to himself fourteen years earlier in 1913: "Can one make works which are not works of 'art?'"[36] If the readymades of the teens—undoubtedly the first attempt to solve this conundrum—were produced from an encounter between a commodity and its inscription, the door and related works of the twenties emerged from a different species of encounter. Here the readymade is understood not so much in terms of objects as in relationship to *environments.* The door like *Trébuchet* functions as a trap or the strategem in a game: it forms a situation in which ordinary life is convulsively transformed by an unforeseen paradox. Readymades like *In Advance of the Broken Arm* or *Fountain* provoked questions about the nature of the art *object,* but the door presents a more insidious riddle by disrupting the entire mise-en-scène of everyday life. It is true that like the miniature cage of *Why Not Sneeze?,* which cannot be entered by the viewer, the door was a controlled experiment, accessible only to the artist and his guests. But despite their privacy these works answered one of the fundamental challenges posed by chess within Duchamp's art: how to invent a readymade practice that is both topographical and kinetic.

The topography of the game board is only one aspect of chess as a model for art making. The intersubjective nature of the game brought Duchamp's notion of the readymade as *rendezvous* to fruition. For unlike his readymades of the teens, which mark an encounter between a thing and the artist's textual inscription of it, chess involves the meeting of two *players* within an arena of readymade rules. Such a meeting, characterized by the same sort of immobilization as the bride's liaison with the bachelors in the *Large Glass,* is elaborated in Duchamp and Halberstadt's arcane chess treatise, *L'Opposition et les cases conjuguées sont reconciliées.*[37] In one sense, *L'Opposition et les cases conjuguées* is an indulgently specialized book, whose subject, in Duchamp's words, is "end-game problems of possible games but so rare as to be nearly Utopian."[38] Precisely this utopian quality, however, brings the metaphorical dimension of the book into focus. Opposition and *cases conjuguées,* or "sister squares" as it is translated in English, refer to two related types of impasse at the end of a chess match, where the "principal domains" of possible safe moves for each king mirror one another, locking them into a seemingly fruitless symmetry of parallel maneuvers. This rare end game exemplifies within chess the virtual immobilization of the door at rue Larrey: movement is possible but ultimately pointless in that each move made by one king may be canceled through a parallel move by the other. The important point in our context is not to fathom the highly arcane intricacies of the chess moves but rather to recognize how Duchamp and Halberstadt's concept of "heterodox oppositions" establishes a figure of immobilized reversibility between two subjective positions, two players: "Now we have already remarked that each square of the White principal domain is on the same diagonal as its sister in the Black principal domain: this circumstance makes it possible to superimpose the White principal domain on the black principal domain by folding. The hinge will be [a] diagonal."[39] The authors suggest a seismic eruption within the horizontal topology of the chessboard: folding it over itself, like a sheet of paper, so that the lateral motions of the pieces are superimposed. Two principal domains, originally separated from one another on the gridded playing field suddenly—from a different point of view, or *dimension*—demonstrate a hidden symmetry.[40]

The door at rue Larrey, like the arcane end games of *L'Opposition et les cases conjuguées,* is what Duchamp would have called a "hinge-picture." Unlike a conventional cubist painting or even the *Large Glass,* it remains invisible unless acted upon. Someone must open a door or perceive the symmetry of white and

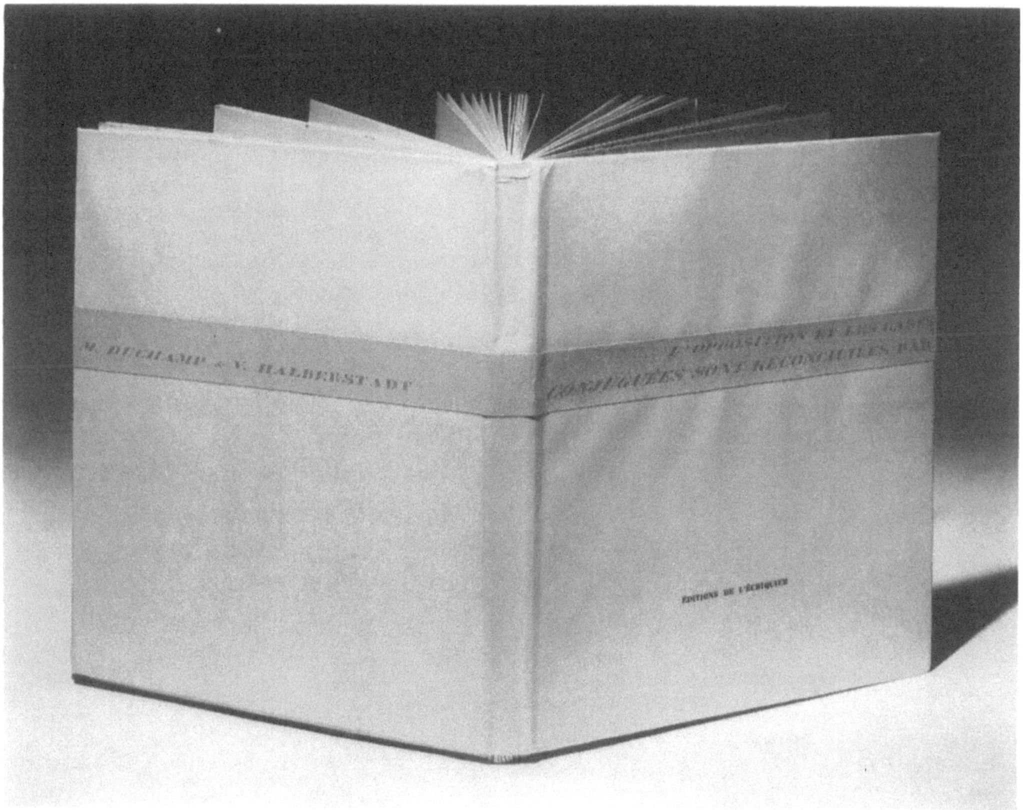

4.8 Marcel Duchamp and Vitaly Halberstadt. *L'Opposition et les cases conjuguées sont réconciliées* (*Opposition and Sister Squares Are Reconciled*). 1932. Book, 11 × 10 ½". © Succession Marcel Duchamp. © 1997 Artists Rights Society (ARS), New York/ADAGP, Paris/Estate of Marcel Duchamp.

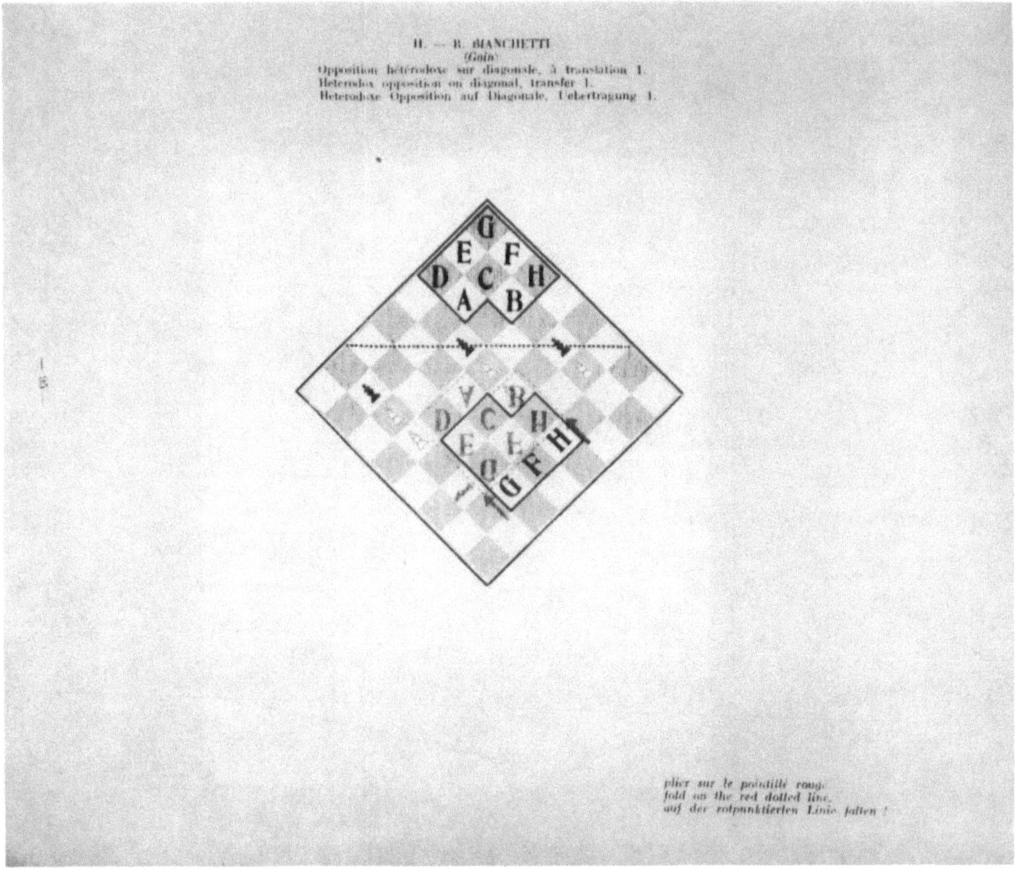

4.9 Marcel Duchamp and Vitaly Halberstadt. *L'Opposition et les cases conjuguées sont réconciliées* (*Opposition and Sister Squares Are Reconciled*). 1932. Detail (page 95), 11 × 10 ½″. © Succession Marcel Duchamp. © 1997 Artists Rights Society (ARS), New York/ADAGP, Paris/Estate of Marcel Duchamp.

black king—these foldings require a "player" or an "inhabitant." The hinge is therefore both a point of dimensional transfer and a site of subjective encounter. As Hubert Damisch has argued, such encounters may allegorize the unconscious. Building from the linguistic work of Emile Benveniste and the psychoanalytic theories of Jacques Lacan, in which the self is defined through differentiations from an other in language—an other introjected within the subject as *unconscious*—Damisch describes games that, like chess, are played with two players, in psychoanalytic terms. In successive moves each player redefines the conditions of the other's mobility—each alternately becomes the projection or embodiment of the other's unconscious:

> In the case of strategic games, the unconscious is the strategy of the other. Duchamp's aspiration—to introduce chance into chess—makes sense as a project only in playing with the bi-polar structure that is the condition of the game: chance here being nothing but the given name of the unconscious and, through it, of the trickery which is at the base of all surprise as it is of all thought.[41]

What Damisch calls Duchamp's dream of introducing chance into the chess match is actually one half of a bilateral relationship between chess and roulette. Schwarz summarizes the terms of this metaphorical association:

> From Monte Carlo, where he was experimenting with the roulette system that was to prompt him to issue the *Monte Carlo Bond,* he wrote to Jacques Doucet [January 16, 1925], "I would like to force roulette to become a game of chess." When I told Duchamp that I did not fully grasp the relationship between chess and gambling, since the former involves the mind while the latter involves chance, he replied: "In both cases it is a fight between two human beings, and by introducing more chance in chess and reducing the chance factor in gambling, the two activities could meet somehow."[42]

For Damisch, "the two activities" meet in the unconscious. In fact following Duchamp's suggestion of converse quotients of chance and rationality in chess and roulette, Damisch argues that through the strategy of a martingale, chance itself arises as a second "player"—as an Other (opponent): "And what is a martingale if not a strategy for an a priori definition of a series of moves based on a combination of a probabilistic sort, but one intended to counteract chance, to trick it, catching it up in its own laws, to treat it finally as an opponent, and roulette as a two-party game, one that obeys an actual geometry?"[43] Damisch's treatment of game theory produces a reversible notion of the unconscious: each player is alternately the embodiment of volition, for him/herself, and the figure of the unconscious for his/her opponent. The hinge between spatial dimensions is also a hinge between psychic positions. If the door in rue Larrey operates through a logic of actual movement and virtual arrest, chess, and particularly the endgame impasse explored in *L'Opposition et les cases conjuguées,* is the model for a permanent alternation between the *player* and the *piece-being-played.*

Although chess and roulette do indeed "meet somehow" through their converse relationship to chance and the mind, Duchamp had a greater stake in forcing "roulette to become a game of chess" than simply improving his odds of winning in Monte Carlo. If, as Damisch asserts, a chess match may allegorize the unconscious as an intersubjective encounter between a player and his or her other (player), in roulette the confrontation with the other-as-chance is carried out within an economy of financial speculation. When Damisch asserts that the application of a martingale causes chance to operate "as an opponent, and roulette as a two-party game," he assigns the aleatory spins of the wheel the position of "second player"—the place of the unconscious. Indeed, as we have seen, in the *Monte Carlo Bond* the work of the unconscious (its erection of oedipal structure) aligns with chance-as-money: the self (Marcel Duchamp) is projected as a family (Marcel, Rrose, and the "demistock"), and, in turn, the family is organized as a corporation—employee (Marcel), chairman of the board (Rrose), and dividend (demistock). The Oedipal process is imagined in terms of corporate structure. Nor is this concept of the unconscious as a quasi-corporate entity exceptional in Duchamp's art of the 1920s. More often than not when figurative representations appear in this decade—as in Rrose Sélavy's *Belle Haleine, Eau de Voilette* of 1921, *Wanted: $2,000 Reward* of 1923, and *Monte Carlo Bond* of 1924—they arise at the point of a transaction, at the hinge between buyer and thing-to-be-bought. This is the case in a little-discussed magazine ad for an Archipenko exhibition at the Société Anonyme in 1921, which, although presented anonymously, is generally attributed to Duchamp.[44] Beside an illustration of Archipenko's relief sculpture *Woman Standing* (1920) is the headline "Archie Pen Co." and a text that includes the following pitch: "For having invented the circle, Columbus, as everyone knows, was tried and sentenced to death. Today an ARCHIE PEN draws automatically a line of accurate length such as, for instance, the hypothenuse of a possible triangle in which the length of the other two sides is given arithmetically. It thinks for you." Even more striking than Duchamp's atomization of Archipenko's name into the homophonic Archie Pen Co. is his declaration that the pen "thinks for you." The pen—and *Woman Standing,* with its sharply pointed abstraction of the figure's legs does look uncannily like the nib of a fountain pen—is transformed from a subordinate instrument meant to execute the writer's or designer's will into the very site of his or her controlling volition. Human intervention is only necessary as a dumb motive force: to set the pen in motion since "it thinks for you." Not only is the artist's self *incorporated* as the Archie Pen Co., a chilling oscillation is established between the human subject and the commodity: each alternatively occupying the positions of volitional "player" and a passive "piece-being-played."[45]

For Duchamp, then, *incorporation* signified a double logic: on the one hand, the artist's metamorphosis into a corporate entity[46] and on the other a related transformation of the self through an introjection of the aleatory forces of the market. This would seem Duchamp's point when he proposed charging people to breathe: "Establish a society in which the individual has to pay for the air he breathes (air meters; imprisonment and rarefied air, in case of non-payment simple asphyxiation if necessary (cut off the air)."[47] As this sinister proposal demonstrates, Duchamp fantasized a form of colonization by financial markets that would reach deep within the individual body to those biological functions fundamental to life. In fact the image of the self as "breather" has a

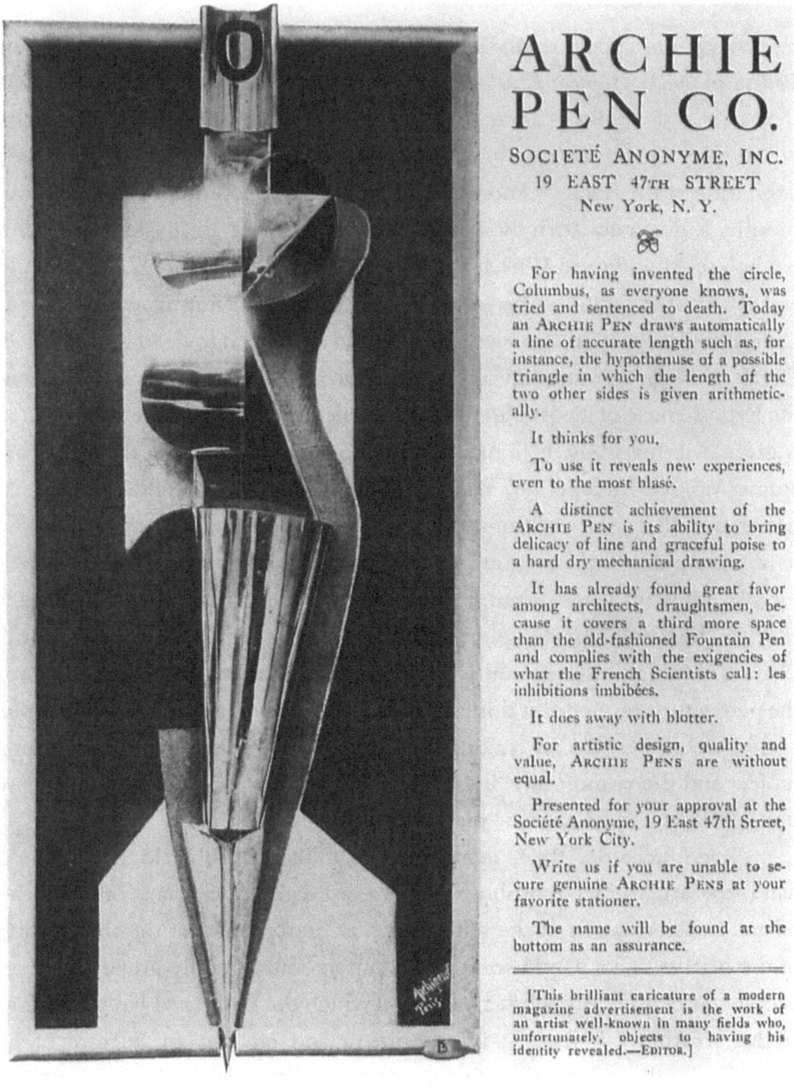

4.10 Attributed to Marcel Duchamp. "Archie Pen Co.," advertisement from *The Arts* 1, no. 3 (February–March 1921). Philadelphia Museum of Art: The Louise and Walter Arensberg Archives. © 1997 Artists Rights Society (ARS), New York/ADAGP, Paris/ Estate of Marcel Duchamp.

significant history in his art. There is, for instance, the readymade *50 cc of Paris Air,* which Duchamp brought for the Arensbergs as a gift on his return to New York in 1919. While ostensibly nothing more than the perfect souvenir from Paris for a "couple that has everything," this object—a pharmacist's ampoule emptied of its contents, filled with air, and labeled "Serum Physiologique"—suggests that air itself is a kind of medicine requiring purchase. The *Large Glass* itself is full of "breathers." Not only are the malic molds—the bachelors' most explicit surrogates—constructed like lungs through which circulate "illuminating gas," breathing or "ventilation" is a fundamental function of the bride.[48] This is perhaps clearest in the three "draft pistons" that open up within the bride's "milky way." As I described in chapter 1, these pistons derive from drafts of air: Duchamp transposed their contours from a series of photographs of a gauzy curtain blown before an open window. The draft pistons not only serve as apertures letting air—*drafts*—into the carnal topography of the bride, like mouths, they emit language: "the commands of the pendu femelle."[49]

As in so many of Duchamp's works after he left the *Glass* "definitively unfinished," what was once associated with narrative iconography—the breathing of the machine—was transposed onto an ensemble of readymades. This process of attenuation is embodied in a work of 1921 titled *Belle Haleine, Eau de Voilette,* consisting of a boxed readymade perfume bottle fitted with a picture of Rrose Sélavy and inscribed with her stylized initials as well as her two "homes," New York and Paris. Nancy Ring has demonstrated that during the 1920s the American cosmetics industry exploited celebrity endorsements through the presence of advertising photographs similar to Rrose's picture on the bottle, as well as the borrowed sophistication of French names for products. She concludes, "When translated literally as 'Beautiful Breath' [Belle Haleine], the name is somewhat comical in the manner of American cosmetics companies' uses of French, but it nonetheless carries delicate connotations of an impalpable sweetness."[50] The "somewhat comical" name has a greater significance than its echo of American advertising: it is the successor to the draft pistons and the *50 cc of Paris Air.* It is beautiful *breath,* bottled up for sale and fitted with a double simulation of the self of the artist: Duchamp as photograph and Duchamp as

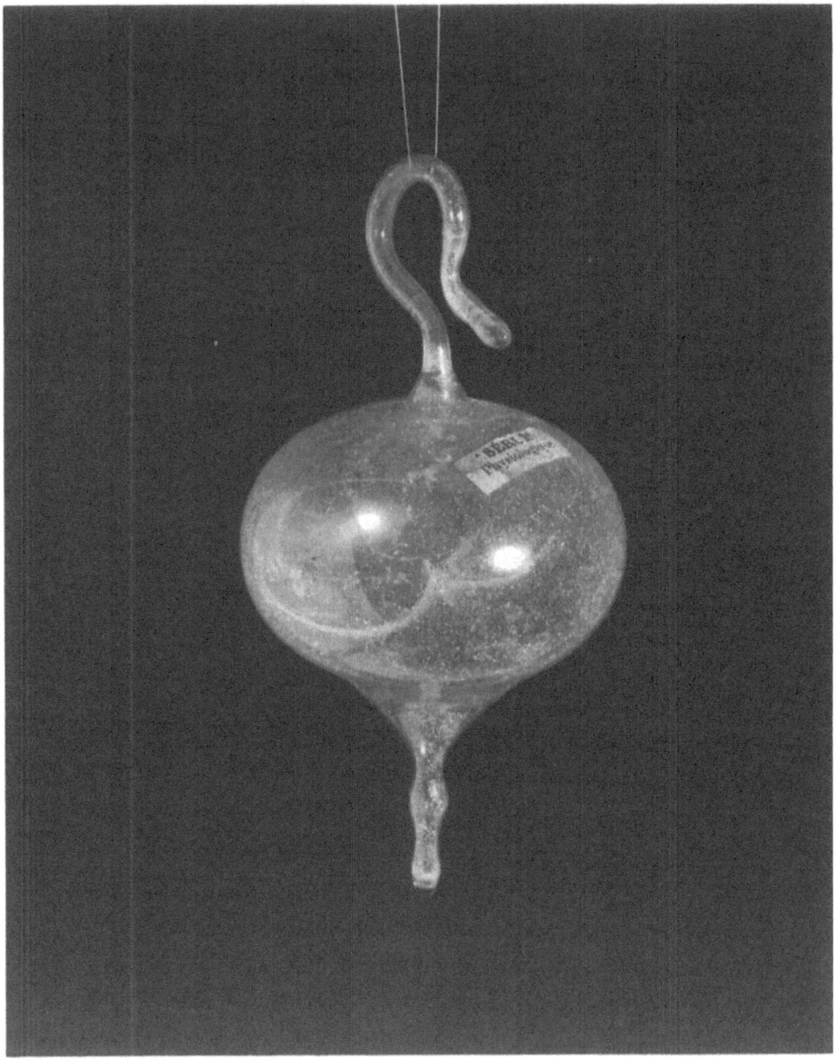

4.11 Marcel Duchamp. *50 cc of Paris Air.* Paris, December 1919. Glass ampoule (broken and mended), 5 ¼″ in height. Philadelphia Museum of Art: The Louise and Walter Arensberg Collection. Photo by Graydon Wood, 1993. © 1997 Artists Rights Society (ARS), New York/ADAGP, Paris/Estate of Marcel Duchamp.

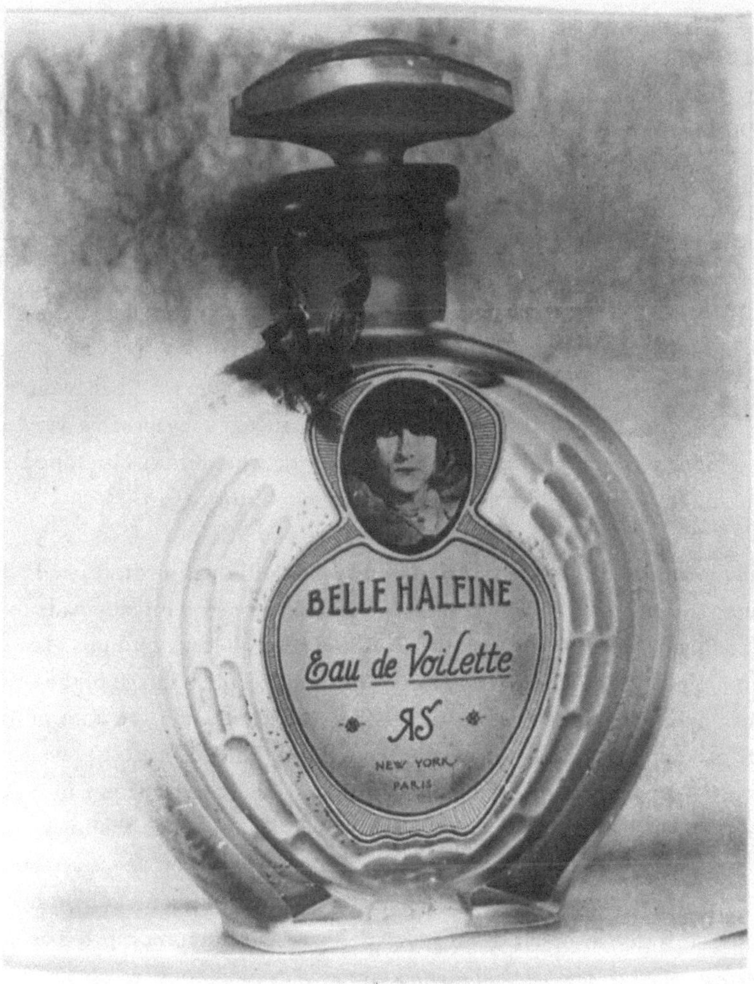

4.12 Man Ray. *Perfume Bottle for Belle Haleine, Eau de Voilette* [photograph of a work by Duchamp]. 1921. Gelatin silver print (stamped postcard), 4 ½ × 3 ⅝″. Philadelphia Museum of Art: Purchased: Alice Newton Osborne Fund and funds contributed by Ann and Donald McPhail upon the occasion of the 100th birthday of Marcel Duchamp. © 1997 Artists Rights Society (ARS), New York/ADAGP/Man Ray Trust, Paris.

woman. After all, Duchamp's note for a "hilarious picture" in the *Green Box* suggested "put[ting] the whole bride under a glass case, or into a transparent cage"[51]—like a bottle of perfume packaged in a box. Like *Why Not Sneeze?, Belle Haleine* is a transposition of the bride, a different kind of painting machine. As Duchamp wrote to Jean Crotti in 1952, he considered painting nothing more than an ephemeral perfume:

> American museums want at any price *to teach* modern art to young students who believe in a "chemical formula."
>
> All that produces only the vulgarization and complete disappearance of the *original fragrance.*
>
> This does not deny what I was saying above, for I believe in the original fragrance, but like all fragrances, it evaporates very quickly (some weeks, some years at most); what remains is a dried nut, classified by historians in the chapter "history of art."[52]

Even more dramatically than *Fresh Widow,* which, although a constructed object, is often considered a readymade, *Belle Haleine* presents the readymade as self. Not only does the bottled "breath" of Rrose Sélavy—packaged in a glass body surmounted by a photographed face—offer an objectified image of the subject, Duchamp's metaphorical association between perfume and the aura of an art work accomplished a secondary process of reification of the artist as well as the artwork—a process already underway through his transformation into Rrose Sélavy. In Duchamp's "figurative" works of the 1920s, where the image of the body returns only as a photograph of the artist in masquerade (as a woman, a criminal, or a faun) and therefore, already transformed into something other than himself, it is not so much the readymade that is anthropomorphized as *the self that is encountered readymade.*[53] This encounter, or "rendezvous" to use Duchamp's own term, brings the "other player" posited by Damisch—in roulette or the financial exchanges of the commodity marketplace represented by chance-as-money—directly into the self, introjected as a proper unconscious. This intersubjective model of the unconscious founded in the logic of the game exceeds

Freudian theories and introduces a notion closer to those developed in the 1960s by thinkers like Michel Foucault and Louis Althusser. The type of unconscious projected by *Belle Haleine,* "Archie Pen Co.," and the *Monte Carlo Bond* is what Foucault would call discourse, or Althusser, ideology. It is the *material* unconscious, a set of social conditions that determine what can and cannot be said or what can and cannot be believed at a particular historical moment.

At virtually the same time that Duchamp was developing his psychic idiom of a self caught in the process of commodification, André Breton was preparing his first manifesto of surrealism, published in 1924. Notwithstanding their mutual respect and the several collaborative ventures they undertook together, no two versions of the psychic mechanism could be more divergent than Breton's and Duchamp's. And this, perhaps, is why the latter never allowed himself to be officially associated with the surrealist movement even though he participated in many of its activities. For Breton, the unconscious and the strategies of automatism in writing, painting, and *objets trouvés* developed to gain access to it, held the promise of psychic liberation and revolution, whereas for Duchamp, the unconscious was the locus of constraint, repetition, and commodification. Perhaps nothing demonstrates this opposition so vividly as Breton's famous encounter with found objects in *L'Amour fou.* He and Alberto Giacometti each found the solution to a problem or the answer to a wish in their uncanny encounters with objects in the Paris flea market. Giacometti recognized in a sinister helmet precisely the form he has been seeking to complete his unresolved sculpture of a standing woman, while Breton discovered in a wooden spoon shaped like a shoe the embodiment of a phrase—"cinderella ash-tray"—that had preoccupied him for some time. Breton compared these marvelous encounters to the fulfillments offered by dreams: "*The finding of an object serves here exactly the same purpose as the dream, in the sense that it frees the individual from paralyzing affective scruples, comforts him and makes him understand that the obstacle he might have thought unsurmountable is cleared.*"[54] It is hard to imagine a concept of the readymade further removed from Duchamp's conceptual projects of the twenties. While Breton invoked a world in which the psyche is *projected* outward to transform reality into the fulfillment of a dream, Duchamp represented the converse operation: the world, and particularly the exigencies of commodity exchange, is *introjected* by the subject. If for Breton, the unconscious turns inside out, for Duchamp its mechanism brings the outside in. In *Compulsive Beauty* Hal Foster has described Breton's relationship to this dynamic:

> In short, the question of the constraints of the conscious mind obscured the more important question of the constraints of the *un*conscious mind. In many ways the fact that Bretonian surrealism confused decentering with liberation, psychic disturbance with social revolt, made for the aporia around which it swirled. . . . For automatism revealed a compulsive mechanism that threatened a literal *désagrégation* of the subject, and in doing so it pointed to a different unconscious from the one projected by Bretonian surrealism—an unconscious not unitary or liberatory at all but primally conflicted, instinctually repetitive.[55]

Drawing heavily on Freud's 1920 text *Beyond the Pleasure Principle,* Foster argues that Breton's liberatory concept of the unconscious was constantly disrupted by the uncanny return within surrealist artworks of what Freud identified as the death drive. Opposing, or perhaps even subsuming the forces of Eros, central to Breton's surrealism, was what Freud posited as a second instinctual force, the death drive, characterized by compulsive repetition and the binding of mental energy. According to Foster, the compulsive repetition of the death drive returns within the surrealists' predominantly celebratory imagery through their fascination with uncanny forms of doubling such as automatons, objective chance, and other marvelous encounters. In what we might call Duchamp's "surrealism"[56] there is no such misrecognition of psychic constraint as liberation: from the start his version of the unconscious was characterized by repetition and repression. Duchamp's art—both on the level of the body and of the mind—began as, and continued to be, a poetry of immobilization.

In *Beyond the Pleasure Principle* Freud made a statement every bit as radical as his conclusion twenty years earlier that dreams functioned as the fulfillments of wishes. He proclaimed: "*It seems, then, that an instinct is an urge inherent in organic life to restore an earlier state of things* which the living entity has been obliged to abandon under the pressure of external disturbing forces; that is, it is a kind of organic elasticity, or, to put it another way, the expression of the inertia inherent in organic life."[57] While this theory was initially linked to the death drive, or the instinctual tendency of living organisms to return to their inorganic origins, Freud ultimately proposed placing sexual instincts under the same authority. He speculated that these, too, return the subject to an earlier primordial, hermaphroditic state by reunifying now-distinct male and female germ cells. Freud's text is remarkable for several reasons and in recent years has spawned a fascinating array of commentaries.[58] I would like to emphasize, however, the radically tautological nature that he attributed to the unconscious, leading to the notorious and still astounding declaration that "*the aim of all life is death.*"[59] Human life according to Freud is no more than a circuitous path back to its starting point, a compulsive act of replication or reproduction or, according to the terms of Duchamp's art, an endless picaresque conjugation of machines leading to nothing but onanistic equilibrium or a regime of infinite spins of the roulette wheel whose ultimate result is to "break even." Indeed, Duchamp's primary works of the thirties (the *Green Box* of 1934 and the *Boîte-en-Valise* of 1935–41) perform such a compulsive self-reproduction with virtually no detour.

One of the most frequent explanations that Duchamp gave for abandoning painting was his desire to avoid repeating himself. For instance, in 1945 when Denis de Rougemont asked whether Duchamp had explicitly decided to give up painting after the triumph of the *Nude Descending a Staircase* at the Armory show, Duchamp replied:

> Not at all! . . . I didn't give up by attitude. I didn't decide anything at all! I am simply waiting for ideas . . . I had thirty-three ideas, I painted thirty-three pictures. I don't want to copy myself like all the others. You know, to be a painter is to copy and multiply the few ideas one has had now and then. . . . That's what makes a painter. . . . Do you think they like that, and enjoy painting fifty times, a hundred times the same thing? Not at all, they are not even producing paintings but cheques.[60]

Despite this disdain for copying oneself, Duchamp spent great portions of his life doing exactly that. Not only are the *Green Box* and the *Boîte-en-Valise* entirely composed of elaborate reproductions of the artist's textual and visual work, even the *Large Glass,* the most "innovative" object in his oeuvre was, according to his own testimony, an act of reproduction: "It was more recopying, copying some sketches that I'd done on glass already, so there was no creativeness there, no invention any more, it was just a translation of a thing already done, to my mind at least, onto glass."[61] Indeed, this 1961 statement is no mere retrospective revision: as the texts from the *Green Box* as well as Duchamp's drawings make clear, the *Large Glass* was conceptualized quite rapidly during the mid-teens, while its painstaking execution on glass absorbed several years of work. This contradiction between Duchamp's explicit revulsion to "copying himself" and the irrefutable evidence that "copying" was one of his preferred aesthetic strategies seems irreconcilable unless we recall the double meaning of the word *copy.* Duchamp had a horror of *repeating* himself, which is quite different from faithfully *reproducing* his own conceptions. The artist who makes the "same" painting fifty or one hundred times is doing so not as an explicit act of reproduction but rather with a presumption of originality, and it is this false innovation that Duchamp paradoxically wished to avoid through his own perfectly tautological acts of reproduction. As he stated, the execution of the *Glass*—which, we should remember, is contemporaneous with the development of the readymade—is a re-presenting of something *already done.* This concept of the readymade as an act rather than a thing is implicit in its original theorization as the product of a rendezvous between object and artist, which is constituted as an artwork through an *act* of inscription. Only in the activity of the 1920s, however, did the readymade emerge as a specifically *mental* object—in chess as a painting machine; in the optical machines, *Fresh Widow,* and the door at rue Larrey as the spatialization of negation; and in the return of the figure as a commodified or readymade self in *Belle Haleine,* "Archie Pen Co.," and the *Monte Carlo Bond.*

Perhaps the most radical and emphatic expression of the unconscious as a readymade in Duchamp's oeuvre occurs in the uncanny process of reproduction that constitutes the *Green Box* and the *Boîte-en-Valise.* In chapter 2 I described

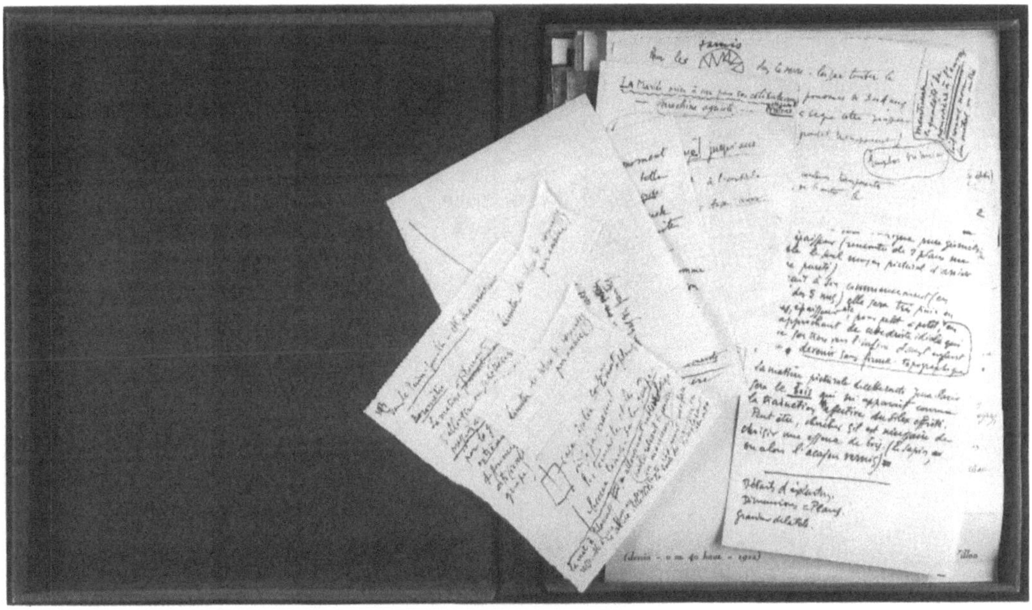

4.13 Marcel Duchamp. *The Bride Stripped Bare by Her Bachelors, Even (The Green Box).* 1934. One color plate and ninety-three facsimiles of manuscript notes, drawings, and photographs, contained in a green flocked cardboard box, 13 1/16 × 11 × 1″. Philadelphia Museum of Art: The Louise and Walter Arensberg Archives. © 1997 Artists Rights Society (ARS), New York/ADAGP, Paris/Marcel Duchamp Estate.

the artist's painstaking efforts to faithfully re-create the irregular scraps of paper and various ink colors of his original notes for the *Large Glass.* In the *Boîte,* which was produced as an edition of three hundred over several years,[62] a collection of sixty-nine reproductions of Duchamp's oeuvre is presented partly in an unfolding armature and partly in special folders housed in valises and later simply boxes. Between 1935 and 1940 Duchamp produced the images that would be included in the edition, but instead of using advanced means of color reproduction available at the time to represent his paintings and works on glass he purposely chose the outdated method of collotype printing with *pochoir,* a process

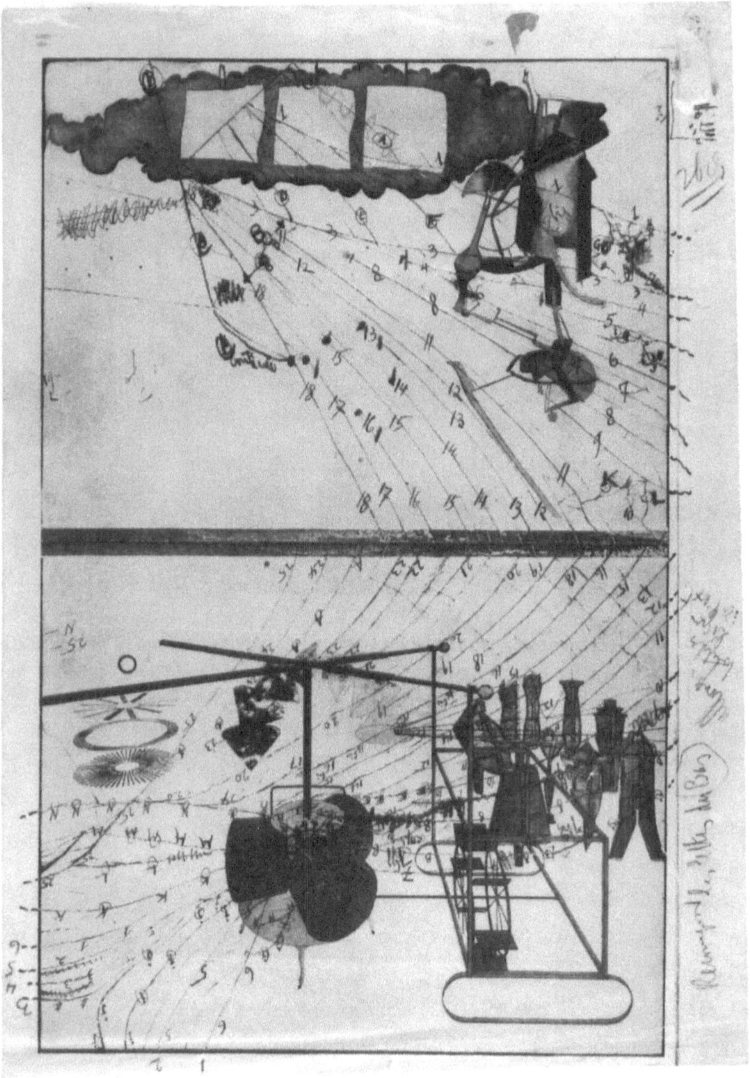

4.14 Marcel Duchamp. Proof print of the *Large Glass* (reversed) with cracks marked in red ink. No date. Photographic reproduction, cut with hand additions in red and black ink, blue crayon, and graphite, 15 ¼ × 10 7⁄16″. © Succession Marcel Duchamp. © 1997 Artists Rights Society (ARS), New York/ADAGP, Paris/Marcel Duchamp Estate.

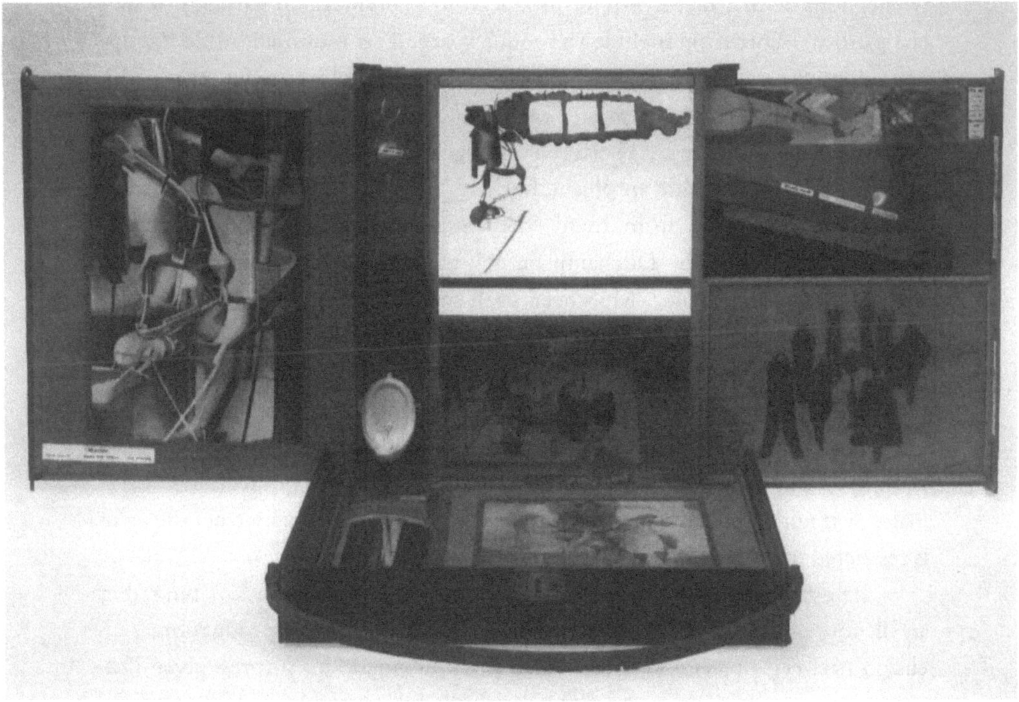

4.15 Marcel Duchamp. *Boîte-en-Valise*. 1941. Leather valise containing miniature replicas, photographs, and color reproductions of works by Duchamp, 16 × 15 × 4″. Philadelphia Museum of Art: The Louise and Walter Arensberg Archives. © 1997 Artists Rights Society (ARS), New York/ADAGP, Paris/Estate of Marcel Duchamp.

of hand coloring using stencils. An average of thirty different stencils was required for each proof, all of which were colored by Duchamp himself, often, since he was living in Paris at the time, in elaborate consultation with the American owners of his paintings. These proofs, or *coloriages originaux,* resulted, according to Ecke Bonk, "in 'authorized' new versions of his most important paintings; and in the cases of *Mariée* and *Nu descendant un escalier* No. 2 the reproductions had been signed and notarized like stock certificates."[63] In the twenty-four deluxe *Boîtes-en-valise* produced first—typically for friends or special patrons—Duchamp included a unique work of art mounted inside the upper lid of the valise. In at least eleven of these deluxe editions one of his hand-colored proofs served as an "original." The *coloriages originaux* therefore established an infinite regress between original and reproduction: they are indisputably copies of a unique art object, but with regard to the series of three hundred copies produced from them, they are "original"—a status explicitly conferred upon them by Duchamp himself through their inclusion as unique works in the deluxe *Boîtes*. Moreover, each successive copy, even though executed by the craftsmen of a printing house rather than the artist himself, shares with an original work of art the process of applying pigment by hand onto a surface. This disruption of technologies of reproduction through the "return" of the artist's manual touch must have motivated Duchamp to choose the *pochoir* technique. But if copying is transformed into the production of successive "originals," it is not thereby redeemed. Rather the converse is equally true: the artist is restricted to performing a compulsive series of repetitions.

The *Boîte-en-valise* is therefore no simple retrospective-in-a-box but rather an allegory of the self caught in the compulsive repetition of reproduction. This elision between object and self—which should come as no surprise given Duchamp's preoccupations in the 1920s—is brilliantly exemplified by the official title of the *Boîte* inscribed just inside each deluxe valise: *de ou par Marcel Duchamp ou Rrose Sélavy*. As is so often the case with Duchamp, this title not merely describes but embodies the work that it names. For not only is the relationship between subject and object—reproducer and thing being reproduced—disrupted through the aporia of *de ou par,* the subject is further split through its division into *Marcel Duchamp ou Rrose Sélavy.* Superficially it may seem that the purpose of the *Boîte-en-valise* is to shore up Duchamp's artistic identity through a coherent summary of his oeuvre, but as an elaborate performance of compulsive repetition—the same form of repetition that Freud associated with the unconscious instinctual drives of death *and* Eros—Duchamp represented a self that is alternately organic and inorganic, masculine and feminine. The act of copying both *constitutes and destroys* the self, just as the choice of a readymade in 1915 had performed the commodity's successive states of deterritorialization and reterritorialization within the marketplace. But by the 1920s, and especially in his reproductive arts of the 1930s, Duchamp no longer solicited encounters with readymades. His interest had migrated from things to actions and from machines to selves—he had begun to realize that the artist's gesture was as hopelessly circumscribed as a snow shovel "in advance of the broken arm." He had found himself—*readymade.*[64]

Conclusion

With his *Boîte-en-Valise* Marcel Duchamp completed the metaphorical labor begun in *The Bride Stripped Bare by Her Bachelors, Even.* In the latter work the trope of the machine functioned as a switching station between a body submitted to the rationalizations of Taylorism and a mind subjected to psychic techniques of mechanization. Duchamp's modernity—in fact, modernity *tout court*—must be conceived not as an epic of disciplined bodies or of colonized minds but rather as the chiasmatic intersection of these two epistemological imperatives. The *Boîte* encapsulates this duality perfectly: the artist as brain worker elides with the artist as manual laborer—both producing the same aesthetic forms. The *Boîte* is both the capitalist's briefcase and the workman's toolbox. Nor is this the only lesson of Duchamp's miniature retrospective: it signals a transposition, spanning some thirty years, from the readymade as *matter* caught in the commodity's cycle of sublimation and desublimation to the readymade as a model of the self constituted by a compulsion to repeat or reproduce itself. A shift from Duchamp's cubist idiom of the body to a thematics of the unconscious paralleling and to some extent negating Breton's more liberatory surrealism has been the subject of *Infinite Regress.* My ambition in tracing this history is to dislodge the readymade from the crude and reductive discourses of reification that have characterized much of its postwar critical reception.

If Duchamp's readymade strategies may be understood as constituting models of the self, then we must reconsider their relationship to "reification." Simply put, if the subject is already an object[1]—characterized by its interpellation into existing identities—then how can it undergo a process of *objectification?* This redundancy is brilliantly unveiled through Duchamp's strategies of self-appropriation—a redundancy that calls into question an entire tradition of postwar art criticism greatly influenced by Peter Bürger's theory of the neo-avant-garde.[2] Bürger seized upon Duchamp's readymades in his *Theory of the Avant-Garde* as the perfect illustration of "modernism-as-commodification." But as Benjamin Buchloh has pointed out in a slightly different context with regard to Bürger's argument,[3] by positing a "reified" subject, one presumes some originary form of selfhood untouched by the pressures and exigencies of the marketplace. I believe that such a subject does not and cannot exist in modernism. I have sought to demonstrate that for Duchamp the readymade did not constitute a teleology of reification but rather an infinite regress of transactual encounters in which the object-as-self and later the self-as-object are submitted to a quantification that is ultimately temporary and provisional, always itself falling back into materiality. This transactual notion of the readymade, exemplified by works like *Tzanck Check* of 1919 and the *Monte Carlo Bond* of 1924, functions as a model of subjectivity produced and reproduced in the repetitions of unconscious compulsion. In light of this revised view of the readymade, Bürger's theory of the neo-avant-garde is woefully inadequate. Commodification does not occur "once and for all" but rather constitutes a single moment within a relay of identifications between subjects and objects—a moment infinitely repeated within the transactual field of the marketplace.

Such an enriched notion of Duchamp's most epistemologically significant artistic strategy as an intersubjective and interobjective process, characterized both by alienation *and* desire, allows us to consider his postwar legacy in a new light. If, as I believe, the Duchampian readymade represents the modern (and postmodern) self as a subject constituted in relation to its desire for and identification with commodities, then the postwar artistic practices that are regularly condemned as "neo-avant-garde" respond to Duchamp's legacy in ways that have been radically misunderstood. When Jasper Johns made a bronze sculpture simulating two ordinary ale cans in 1960 or Robert Gober laboriously constructed a series of three urinals in 1988 rather than simply choosing such objects as Duchamp might have done, they were not merely aestheticizing the radical or originary readymade gestures of 1913–15. These "postmodern" artists were building on Duchamp's most sophisticated understanding of the readymade as defined in the *Boîte-en-Valise* of 1935–41, not on his early formulation of the problematic in works like *In Advance of the Broken Arm* of 1915 or even *Fountain* of 1917. Johns and Gober as well as a multitude of others ranging from Robert Rauschenberg to Sherrie Levine project the texture of their own labor—and desire—into the commodities that surround them, just as Duchamp in his *Boîte* represented his own oeuvre—his own self—caught in an endless economy of reproduction. Like the older artist to whom they are indebted, postwar practitioners of appropriation have *found themselves readymade,* and like Duchamp, they have chosen to explore this fertile position as a central condition of modern art and modern life.

Notes

Introduction

1. For Duchamp as alchemist see Arturo Schwarz, *The Complete Works of Marcel Duchamp* (New York: Harry N. Abrams, 1970). For Duchamp's relationship to fourth-dimensional mathematics see Linda Dalrymple Henderson, "Marcel Duchamp and the New Geometries," in *The Fourth Dimension and Non-Euclidean Geometry in Modern Art* (Princeton: Princeton University Press, 1983), 117–63. For the most prominent account of the readymade and institutional critique, see Thierry de Duve, *Pictorial Nominalism: On Marcel Duchamp's Passage from Painting to the Readymade,* trans. Dana Polan (Minneapolis: University of Minnesota Press, 1991). For Duchamp's relationship to gender, see Amelia Jones, *Postmodernism and the En-Gendering of Marcel Duchamp* (Cambridge: Cambridge University Press, 1994).

2. For the relationship between carnality and optics in Duchamp's art, see Rosalind Krauss, "Where's Poppa?" in *The Definitively Unfinished Marcel Duchamp,* ed. Thierry de Duve (Halifax: Nova Scotia College of Art and Design; Cambridge: MIT Press, 1993), 433–62. For the relationship between painting and the readymade see de Duve, *Pictorial Nominalism,* and for discussions of gender see Jones, *Postmodernism and the En-Gendering of Marcel Duchamp.*

3. For a discussion of this critical debate see David Joselit, "Duchamp's Legacy," review of *Postmodernism and the En-Gendering of Marcel Duchamp* by Amelia Jones, *Art in America* 82, no. 9 (September 1994): 35–37.

4. See Rosalind Krauss, "The Motivation of the Sign" and Yve-Alain Bois, "The Semiology of Cubism," in William Rubin, ed., *Picasso and Braque: A Symposium* (New York: The Museum of Modern Art, 1992), 261–86; 169–208.

5. I use the term *simulated readymades* to refer to objects that seem to be industrially produced but are in actuality either handmade by Duchamp or constructed by others according to his specifications.

1 Mensuration *en abyme:* Marcel Duchamp's Cubism

1. Michel Sanouillet and Elmer Peterson, eds., *The Writings of Marcel Duchamp* (New York: Da Capo Press, 1973), 44–45.

2. The *Large Glass* was produced between 1915 and 1923, but notes and drawings for the work date from as early as 1913.

3. For my extensive discussion of the gendered iconography of *The Bride Stripped Bare by Her Bachelors, Even* see chapter 3.

4. These are among the many bachelor surrogates in the lower region of the *Large Glass*. Duchamp characterized them as a "cemetery of uniforms or liveries."

5. Rosalind Krauss, "The Motivation of the Sign," in *Picasso and Braque: A Symposium,* ed. William Rubin (New York: The Museum of Modern Art, 1992), 271.

6. See Yve-Alain Bois, "The Semiology of Cubism," in Rubin, *Picasso and Braque: A Symposium,* 169–208; as well as Yve-Alain Bois, "Kahnweiler's Lesson," in *Painting as Model* (Cambridge: MIT Press, 1990), 65–97; and Rosalind Krauss, "In the Name of Picasso," in *The Originality of the Avant-Garde and Other Modernist Myths* (Cambridge: MIT Press, 1985), 23–40.

7. While I am concerned to draw a distinction in emphasis between the cubism of Picasso and that of Duchamp, it is important to remark that to a greater extent than Krauss acknowledges, semiosis is incomplete and *in process* in Picasso's analytic cubism. Bois' account in "The Semiology of Cubism" is more alert to this condition. Moreover in his later, or synthetic, cubism

Picasso made a few works composed of fields of fractured body parts, reminiscent of Duchamp's cubism.

8. Jean-François Lyotard, *Libidinal Economy,* trans. Iain Hamilton Grant (Bloomington: Indiana University Press, 1993), 2–3.

9. Ibid., 14.

10. *Libidinal Economy* is a controversial book that Lyotard himself was prone to excoriate in later years. Its importance—and the source of its uneasy reception—derives in part from its ambitious effort to rethink Marx in terms of Freud, to assess the possibility of criticality in the face of libidinal formations that undo stable theoretical categories and concepts. At many points in the text Lyotard's awareness of the polymorphous field of libidinal investments completely disrupts the possibility of efficacious critique.

Duchamp stands at precisely this juncture of the libidinal and the critical—in fact I hope to demonstrate how this unstable relationship plays out through his successive transformations of the readymade. Thus, while acknowledging that *Libidinal Economy* is an eccentric book in an eccentric oeuvre, I feel it is an effective tool in describing this particular dynamic in Duchamp's art.

For an excellent description of the historiographic position of *Libidinal Economy,* see Iain Hamilton Grant's introduction, ibid., xvii–xxxiv.

11. Sanouillet and Peterson, eds., *The Writings of Marcel Duchamp,* 36.

12. Two obvious examples of this are the *Large Glass* itself, which Duchamp often associated with the bride (in spite of its bachelor component), and *Fresh Widow* of 1920. I will elaborate below on the relationship between them and the draft pistons.

13. Pierre Cabanne, *Dialogues with Marcel Duchamp,* trans. Ron Padgett (New York: Da Capo Press, 1979), 43.

14. Jonathan Crary has made a similar observation in "The Passage from Virgin to Bride," *Arts Magazine* 51, no. 1 (January 1977): 96–99: "This is what we see in *The Passage:* an intensive time in which logic breaks down and in which the individual, as a separate whole body, is

dissolved. Distinctions between subject and object, between causes and effects, become meaningless." (98).

15. Crary's observations are again pertinent: "Volumes suddenly become voids, planes modulate into lines, and lines disintegrate into dots. Distinctions between figure and ground, between surface and depth, are impossible to make." Ibid., 96.

16. Bois, "The Semiology of Cubism," 182, 184.

17. Sanouillet and Peterson, eds., *The Writings of Marcel Duchamp,* 22.

18. Ibid., 31.

19. Jean Clair, *Marcel Duchamp ou le grand fictif; essai de mythanalyse du grand verre* (Paris: Editions Galilée, 1975), 88–89. My translation.

20. Klaus Theweleit, *Male Fantasies: Volume 1: Women, Floods, Bodies, History,* trans. Stephen Conway, in collaboration with Erica Carter and Chris Turner (Minneapolis: University of Minnesota Press, 1987), 244.

21. Ferdinand de Saussure, *Course in General Linguistics,* ed. Charles Bally and Albert Sechehaye with the collaboration of Albert Riedlinger, trans. Roy Harris (La Salle, Ill.: Open Court, 1983), 113.

22. Ibid., 117.

23. Karl Marx, *Capital: A Critique of Political Economy,* vol. 1, *The Process of Capitalist Production,* ed. Frederick Engels, trans. Samuel Moore and Edward Aveling (New York: International Publishers, 1967), 71.

24. Ibid., 85.

25. Marx invested the commodity with body and soul, just as Duchamp anthropomorphized the falling string in the *3 Standard Stoppages* and the illuminating gas in the *Large Glass.*

26. Georg Simmel, *The Philosophy of Money,* ed. David Frisby, trans. Tom Bottomore and David Frisby (London: Routledge, 1990), 376–77.

27. T. J. Clark, *The Painting of Modern Life: Paris in the Art of Manet and His Followers* (New York: Alfred A. Knopf, 1984), 118. Clark also draws upon Simmel's theories of prostitution and currency (102, 144).

28. Ibid., 102.

29. Ibid., 92.

30. Clark notes a dynamic in *Olympia* between collapse of the body and its restructuring through rigid outlines, which I have pointed out in Duchamp's *Network of Stoppages.* Ibid., 134–35.

31. I am referring here to the "milky way" in Duchamp's *Large Glass.*

32. Charles Baudelaire, "The Painter of Modern Life," in *The Painter of Modern Life and Other Essays,* trans. and ed. Jonathan Mayne (New York: Da Capo Press, 1964), 29–38.

33. A similar argument might be made with regard to Cézanne's monumental paintings of bathers dating from 1894 to 1906. In these works the body of the nude seems to comply with the order of the pictorial system rather than that of human anatomy.

34. See Abigail Solomon-Godeau, "Going Native," *Art in America* 77, no. 7 (July 1989): 118. For the best discussion of the complex discursive context and gender politics of *Spirit of the Dead Watching* in both Tahiti and Paris see Griselda Pollock, *Avant-Garde Gambits; 1888–1893: Gender and the Color of History* (New York: Thames and Hudson, 1992).

35. As I will argue below, according to structural anthropology such an exchange of women as gifts is homologous with commodity exchange.

36. For a different account of the dispersal or distortion of the modernist nude, See Yve-Alain Bois' discussion of the relationship between color and line in Matisse's painting. Yve-Alain Bois, "Matisse and 'Arche-drawing,'" in *Painting as Model,* 3–63.

37. For a discussion of the visual prominence of the war wounded in France see Kenneth E. Silver, "*Fluctuat nec mergitur*," in *Esprit de Corps; The Art of the Parisian Avant-Garde and the First World War, 1914–1925* (Princeton: Princeton University Press, 1989), 186–218.

38. Guillaume Apollinaire, "Duchamp," in *Marcel Duchamp in Perspective,* ed. Joseph Masheck (Englewood Cliffs, N.J.: Prentice-Hall, 1974), 26. Apollinaire's declaration here is clearly hyperbolic, and one could make a case for the persistence of the nude in cubism. There is, for instance, Henri Le Fauconnier's *Abundance* (1910–11) and, more significantly, Robert Delaunay's *The City of Paris* (1912). But in each of these instances my central point holds: the illusion of carnality is liquidated into a regularized field of notation. In Delaunay's painting the bodies of the three graces seem interwoven with the fabric of the Parisian cityscape.

39. Cabanne, *Dialogues with Marcel Duchamp,* 24–26.

40. Ibid., 28.

41. Ibid., 29.

42. Ibid., 33.

43. Ibid., 28–29.

44. In spite of this question about Duchamp's literal knowledge of Picasso's work of this period, I think it remains valid to compare them within the discourse of the nude that I have been trying to sketch. Whether Duchamp's cubism was a self-conscious challenge to Picasso's and Braque's (which he does seem to imply in his statements about *Dulcinea* and *Yvonne and Magdeleine Torn in Tatters*) is less important than his invention of an alternate cubist discourse. No matter how he arrived at his cubist paintings, Duchamp presented a different means of transforming the body into the semiotic. I believe that an attempt to outline the discursive field of painterly strategies available to artists interested in the same or similar problems—in this case, those that may be grouped under the term *cubism*—is more productive than a simplistic recounting of direct influence.

45. For an analysis of the fundamental role that metaphor and metonymy play in language, see Roman Jakobson, "Two Aspects of Language and Two Types of Aphasic Disturbances," in

Fundamentals of Language, 2nd ed. (The Hague: Mouton, 1971), 69–96; and Roland Barthes, "Syntagm and System," in *Elements of Semiology,* trans. Annette Lavers and Colin Smith (New York: The Noonday Press, Farrar, Straus and Giroux, 1968), 58–88.

46. Cabanne, *Dialogues with Marcel Duchamp,* 29.

47. Ibid., 34.

48. Ibid., 35.

49. This was the central metaphor in Etienne-Jules Marey, *Animal Mechanism; A Treatise on Terrestrial and Aerial Locomotion* (London: Henry S. King & Co., 1874), especially 1–4.

50. He wrote: "Science has before it two obstacles that hinder its progress: first the defectiveness of our senses for discovering truths, and next the insufficiency of language for expressing and transmitting those that we have acquired." E[tienne]-J[ules] Marey, *La Méthode Graphique dans les Sciences Expérimentales et Principalement en Physiologie et en Médecine* (Paris: G. Masson, 1878), i (my translation).

51. Ibid., iii. My translation.

52. François Dagognet, *Etienne-Jules Marey: A Passion for the Trace,* trans. Robert Galeta with Jeanine Herman (New York: Zone Books, 1992), 62.

53. Ibid., 43.

54. Ibid., 149.

55. Anne D'Harnoncourt and Kynaston McShine, eds., *Marcel Duchamp* (New York: Museum of Modern Art; Philadelphia: Philadelphia Museum of Art, 1973), 263.

56. Simmel, *The Philosophy of Money,* 370–84.

57. Claude Lévi-Strauss, *The Elementary Structures of Kinship,* trans. James Harle Bell, John Richard von Sturmer, and Rodney Needham (Boston: Beacon Press, 1969), 24.

58. Ibid., 51.

59. Ibid., 65.

60. Ibid., 493.

61. Ibid., 496.

62. Luce Irigaray, "Women on the Market," in *This Sex Which Is Not One,* trans. Catherine Porter (Ithaca: Cornell University Press, 1985), 176.

63. Ibid., 177.

64. Ibid., 186.

65. William Camfield asserts, "Norton was one of only a handful of Duchamp's friends with insider knowledge about the Richard Mutt case, and I submit that her article reflects not only the conversation within that group of friends but the concepts generated and accepted by Duchamp himself." William A. Camfield, *Marcel Duchamp Fountain* (Houston: The Menil Collection, Houston Fine Art Press, 1989), 39.

66. Louise Norton, "Buddha of the Bathroom," *The Blind Man,* no. 2 (May 1917): unpaginated.

67. Marx's notion of the commodity as a Maritornes should be recalled here.

68. Saussure is very much aware of the unstable boundary between (phonic) substance and semiotic form. He went so far as to declare, "A language thus has this curious and striking feature. It has no immediately perceptible entities. And yet one cannot doubt that they exist, or that the interplay of these units is what constitutes linguistic structure" (105).

Saussure addressed this dilemma by drawing an explicit distinction between substance and form. *Form* is precisely the alliance of matter and thought, as distinct from "a transformation of thoughts into matter [or] a transformation of sounds into ideas" (111). He wrote, "Linguistics, then, operates along this margin, where sound and thought meet. *The contact between them gives rise to a form, not a substance*" (111). In other words, the semiotic exists in a dimension apart from but nonetheless dependent on the flows of substance: a realm of form—the signifier—that conjoins matter and idea. He is closer then than one might think to Lyotard's notion of the tensor. The difference is one of degree; for while Lyotard seeks to retain the pulsional mayhem of the sign, Saussure sees such a prospect as a disastrous error: "In other words, *the language itself is a form, not a substance.*. The importance of this truth cannot be overemphasized. For all our mistakes of terminology, all our incorrect ways of designating things belonging to the language originate in our unwittingly supposing that we are dealing with a substance when we deal with linguistic phenomena" (120). It is not so much that Saussure refuses to acknowledge the dependence of the sign on matter as that he believes this relationship to be beyond rather than within the semiotic system. Saussure, *Court in General Linguistics.*

69. Barthes, *Elements of Semiology,* 65.

70. Sanouillet and Peterson, eds., *The Writings of Marcel Duchamp,* 96.

71. This argument parallels Marx's genealogy of the commodity, which includes a stage preceding the institution of a universal equivalent—gold or money—in which every commodity may act as a mirror of another commodity's value. By projecting such a "primitive" form of the commodity, Duchamp once again emphasized its tendency to "regress." Marx, *Capital,* vol. 1, 47–83.

72. Jean Clair, "Marcel Duchamp et la tradition des Perspecteurs," in *Marcel Duchamp abécédaire,* ed. Jean Clair with the collaboration of Ulfe Linde (Paris: Musée National d'Art Moderne, Centre National d'Art et de Culture Georges Pompidou, 1977), 153. Translation mine.

73. Sanouillet and Peterson, eds., *The Writings of Marcel Duchamp,* 33.

74. Ibid., 72.

75. This is according to Schwarz, *The Complete Works of Marcel Duchamp,* 471.

76. Sanouillet and Peterson, eds., *The Writings of Marcel Duchamp,* 80.

77. Ibid., 31–32.

78. The resemblance between the receding "line" of color samples and the segment divided into colors would seem to make this conclusion more plausible. After all, the former is a kind of three-dimensional line built up of overlapping sheets of color.

79. Sanouillet and Peterson, eds., *The Writings of Marcel Duchamp,* 29.

80. Ibid., 95.

81. Ibid., 71.

82. Schwarz, *The Complete Works of Marcel Duchamp,* 461.

83. Ibid., 471.

84. Ibid., 471.

85. Rosalind Krauss has called attention to this title in relation to the indexical nature of the work: "Given the role of the indexical sign within this particular painting, its title should not surprise us. *Tu m'* is simply 'you' / 'me'—the two personal pronouns which, in being shifters, are themselves a species of index." I want to place greater emphasis on how the phrase reproduces *within language* the interplay of mensurability and immensurability between bodies that I have traced in this chapter. Rosalind E. Krauss, "Notes on the Index: Part 1," in *The Originality of the Avant-Garde and Other Modernist Myths,* 199.

2 Between Reification and Regression: Readymades and Words

1. Michel Sanouillet and Elmer Peterson, eds., *The Writings of Marcel Duchamp* (New York: Da Capo Press, 1973), 32.

2. The two most prestigious and influential accounts of Duchamp's displacement of traditional practices of art by the commodity are those of Peter Bürger and Thierry de Duve. Bürger argues that as a form of institutional critique that demonstrates the commodity status of artworks, the readymade "negates the category of individual production" implying that art founded on a belief in individuality—like painting and even the preponderance of avant-garde

abstraction—is consequently obsolete. See Peter Bürger, *Theory of the Avant-Garde,* trans. Michael Shaw (Minneapolis: University of Minnesota Press, 1984), 47–54.

De Duve's argument is more subtle and ultimately more productive. He argues that with Duchamp's readymades, and particularly *Fountain* (1917), the traditional form of aesthetic judgement—"Is it beautiful?"—is transposed from the specific to the generic in the question, "Is it art?" Rather than proclaiming the death of painting, the readymade signals a new aesthetic order in which the judgment of an object's status as art is fundamental. See Thierry de Duve, *Kant after Duchamp* (Cambridge: MIT Press, 1996).

3. One of the striking contradictions of the reception of Duchamp's art is the simultaneous association of his work with theoretical accounts of the "death of the author" (due to his choice of readymade objects that avoid decisions founded in personal taste) and the tendency to attribute to him massive powers of critique via the readymade's supposed capacity to "unveil" the logic of commodity capitalism (which anyway was hardly veiled for any culturally alert intellectual at the time or since).

4. On the desublimation of language in Duchamp's art of the teens, particularly as it relates to the poetic and cryptographic projects of Walter Arensberg, see Molly Nesbit and Naomi Sawelson-Gorse, "Concept of Nothing: New Notes by Marcel Duchamp and Walter Arensberg," in Martha Buskirk and Mignon Nixon, eds., *The Duchamp Effect: Essays, Interviews, Round Table* (Cambridge: MIT Press, 1996), 131–75.

5. Sanouillet and Peterson, *The Writings of Marcel Duchamp,* 31–32.

6. This text was originally published in the little magazine *Rogue* in October 1916 under the title "THE, Eye Test, Not a 'Nude Descending a Staircase.'" It is therefore interesting to note that Duchamp saw this textual exercise as a response—perhaps even a rebuttal—of the painting for which he had become notorious in New York, the *Nude Descending a Staircase.* The title also introduces opticality—an "eye test" as a function not of image but of language.

7. Arturo Schwarz, *The Complete Works of Marcel Duchamp* (New York: Harry N. Abrams, 1970), 457.

8. As has been often remarked, such language games are indebted in part to Duchamp's interest in Raymond Roussel. For Roussel's own explanation of his literary method first posthumously

published in 1935, see Raymond Roussel, *Comment j'ai écrit certains de mes livres* (Paris: Jean-Jacques Pauvert Editeur, 1963); and for a sustained critical analysis of this system see Michel Foucault, *Death and the Labyrinth: The World of Raymond Roussel,* trans. Charles Ruas (Berkeley: University of California Press, 1987).

9. Roman Jakobson, "Two Aspects of Language and Two Types of Aphasic Disturbances," in *Fundamentals of Language,* 2nd ed. (The Hague: Mouton, 1971), 82–83.

10. *In Advance of the Broken Arm,* contemporary to *"The"* (both of 1915), was the first of Duchamp's works to be explicitly called a "readymade."

11. "Once there is a world postal system, signifiers have standardized prices that mock all meaning. Once there are telegrams and postcards, style is no longer the man, but an economy of signs." Friedrich A. Kittler, *Discourse Networks 1800/1900,* trans. Michael Metteer with Chris Cullens (Stanford: Stanford University Press, 1990), 191.

12. Sanouillet and Peterson, *The Writings of Marcel Duchamp,* 31.

13. Anne D'Harnoncourt and Kynaston McShine, eds., *Marcel Duchamp* (New York: Museum of Modern Art; Philadelphia: Philadelphia Museum of Art, 1973), 280.

14. In the text fragment "Condition of a Language," which I quoted earlier, Duchamp wrote "Compose a schematic sign designating each of these words. (this sign can be composed with the standard stops)." Sanouillet and Peterson, *The Writings of Marcel Duchamp,* 31.

15. Schwarz, *The Complete Works of Marcel Duchamp,* 462.

16. They are nearly, but not quite, squares.

17. See my discussion of *Tu m'* in chapter 1.

18. Schwarz, *The Complete Works of Marcel Duchamp,* 462.

19. Note Duchamp's own suggestion that the language of the inscriptions in *With Hidden Noise* is analogous to an advertising language. As he stated in the description quoted above: "On the

brass plaques I wrote three short sentences in which letters were occasionally missing *like in a neon sign when one letter is not lit and makes the word unintelligible*" [my emphasis]. D'Harnoncourt and McShine, *Marcel Duchamp,* 280.

20. The seventeen photographs were mounted on a total of fifteen matboards because three notes pertaining to the *3 Standard Stoppages* were mounted on the same board. For an English translation of the notes included in *The 1914 Box,* see Sanouillet and Peterson, *The Writings of Marcel Duchamp,* 22–25.

21. Schwarz, *The Complete Works of Marcel Duchamp,* 584.

22. This quote is from a 1954 interview with Michel Sanouillet cited in Craig E. Adcock, *Marcel Duchamp's Notes from the Large Glass: An N-Dimensional Analysis* (Ann Arbor: UMI Research Press, 1983), 9.

23. It should be recalled in the context of *The 1914 Box* that in "Specifications for 'Readymades'" Duchamp wrote, "*The important thing then is just* this matter of timing, this snapshot effect."

24. Sanouillet and Peterson, *The Writings of Marcel Duchamp,* 26.

25. For an interesting discussion of the "made" as artistic technique versus the "found" as immanent originality within the artist, vis-à-vis the work of Cézanne and the impressionists, see Richard Shiff, *Cézanne and the End of Impressionism: A Study of the Theory, Technique and Critical Evaluation of Modern Art* (Chicago: University of Chicago Press, 1984).

In an interview with Katharine Kuh, Duchamp suggested a biological and psychological dimension of the readymade that once again suggests the ready*found:* "So man can never expect to start from scratch; he must start from ready-made things like even his own mother and father." The readymade is here linked to what I have identified as the readyfound: a matrix of psychological (and genetic) givens determined, in part, by one's parents. If each person may be understood as ready*made* by others—including but not limited to one's children—then others, like one's parents, are ready*found* by oneself. Katharine Kuh, *The Artist's Voice: Talks with Seventeen Artists* (New York: Harper & Row, 1960), 90.

26. Sanouillet and Peterson, *The Writings of Marcel Duchamp,* 23.

27. This note clearly makes a statement about war and its own brutal "deferment" of the body into parts. For my purposes, however, I am setting aside this important dimension of its meaning.

28. This argument is made most forcefully by Thierry de Duve, whose work I discuss below. For a different account of the readymade as a displacement of painting see Dalia Judovitz, *Unpacking Duchamp: Art in Transit* (Berkeley: University of California Press, 1995).

29. Aside from Duchamp's signature and the inscription of time and/or date, the phrases written onto readymades are typically only indirectly related or completely irrelevant to the function of the original commodity. "In Advance of the Broken Arm," appended to a snow shovel in 1915, might lend itself to a coherent narrative, but the inscription of a steel dog comb in 1916 with the phrase *3 ou 4 gouttes de hauteur n'ont rien à faire avec la sauvagerie* [3 or 4 drops of height have nothing to do with savagery] seems intended to create a massive divergence between the meaning of the words and the function of the object.

30. Schwarz, *The Complete Works of Marcel Duchamp,* 463.

31. Ibid., 463. Linde is referring to the Bride in the *Large Glass.*

32. See my discussion of the bride's inscription(s) in chapter 1. The relevant passages in Duchamp's notes from *The Green Box* are in Sanouillet and Peterson, *The Writings of Marcel Duchamp,* 36–38.

33. It is also consistent with my reading in chapter 1 of cubist paintings like *Bride* (1912) and *The Passage from Virgin to Bride* (1912) as demonstrations of the passage of a "great ephemeral skin" or libidinal field of the body into a proto-linguistic signifying system.

34. See Molly Nesbit, "The Rat's Ass," *October,* no. 56 (Spring 1991): 18.

35. Schwarz, *The Complete Works of Marcel Duchamp,* 477.

36. Thierry de Duve, *Pictorial Nominalism: On Marcel Duchamp's Passage from Painting to the Readymade,* trans. Dana Polan (Minneapolis: University of Minnesota Press, 1991), 18.

The nominalist transformation within modern art in which aesthetic questions become judgments as to whether a particular object is an *art* object is explored at length in de Duve's *Kant after Duchamp*. Since my project here is to assess the nature of the transition between Duchamp's painting and his readymades, I have chosen to focus on de Duve's earlier text, *Pictorial Nominalism*. Unlike *Kant after Duchamp*, this book directly engages the metaphors of Duchamp's cubism.

37. De Duve actually traces the much earlier invention of the tube of paint in the eighteenth and nineteenth centuries: "Although tin or copper tubes were already in use in England at the end of the 18th century for the preservation of watercolor, it was only around 1830–40 that tubes of oil paints began to be available on the market." He links the development of plein-air painting in the nineteenth century to the availability of such paint tubes and emphasizes their significance with regard to the antiretinal pointillism of Seurat. See Thierry de Duve, "The Readymade and the Tube of Paint," *Artforum* 24, no. 9 (May 1986): 115–16.

38. De Duve, *Pictorial Nominalism*, 159.

39. In a highly original argument de Duve suggests that Duchamp's stay in Munich in the summer of 1912—during which he produced both the *Bride* and *The Passage from Virgin to Bride*—could have made him aware of the "secession" model of the Central European avant-gardes. As opposed to the dynamic of rejection in Parisian advanced art, embodied in the opposition of the official Salon to the Salon des Indépendants or the Salon d'Automne, advanced artists in Vienna, Berlin, and Munich operated through secession. De Duve asserts that this latter model accomplishes a simultaneous divorce from and continuation of a "dead" or academic tradition. De Duve, *Pictorial Nominalism*, 96–118.

40. Ibid., 34.

41. Ibid., 68.

42. De Duve makes much of the fact that the letter *i* is all that distinguishes the virgin from the phallus: "Witness how the thematic subject matter of the canvas—its signified—is sustained by and referred to the emergence of the subject in the Lacanian sense, the *I* as signifier. The small *i* to be added to *verge* (penis) to produce *vierge* (virgin) signals the irruption of this other, capital *I* that, as Jean Suquet says, 'we might as well get from the Greeks. Let us pay homage to the

phallus. What better key could open up a fairy tale whose heroes are a Bride and her bachelors?'" Ibid., 41.

43. "It is this self-referential folding over of the successfully passed test onto the tested condition that authorizes the reduction of the plurality of the readymades to the singular of *the readymade* and establishes its paradigmatic value for art in general: *the readymade* is simultaneously the operation that reduces the work of art to its enunciative function and the 'result' of this operation, a work of art reduced to the statement 'this is art,' exemplified by Duchamp's readymades." De Duve, *Kant after Duchamp,* 389.

44. My insistence on Duchamp's strategy of "materializing" language and commodities clearly opposes the critical traditions that have sought to see Duchamp in a mystical light, either through alchemy, as in the work of Arturo Schwarz, or in four-dimensional mathematics.

45. This fascination with the vertigo of difference is exemplified by Duchamp's "infrathin," which he described by example. According to de Duve, "The infra-thin separation is working at its maximum when it distinguishes the same from the same, when it is an indifferent difference, or a differential identity: 'The difference (dimensional) between 2 mass-produced objects [from the same mold] is an infra thin when the maximum (?) precision is obtained.'" De Duve, *Pictorial Nominalism,* 160.

46. See Gilles Deleuze and Félix Guattari, *Anti-Oedipus: Capitalism and Schizophrenia,* trans. Robert Hurley, Mark Seem, and Helen R. Lane (Minneapolis: University of Minnesota Press, 1983).

47. For a reading of this work that includes interesting biographical information on Tzanck see Peter Read, "The *Tzanck Check* and Related Works by Marcel Duchamp," in *Marcel Duchamp, Artist of the Century,* ed. Rudolf Kuenzli and Francis M. Naumann (Cambridge: MIT Press, 1990), 95–105.

48. The venerable psychoanalytic trope in which the loss of teeth is associated with castration need hardly be mentioned here.

49. Jean-François Lyotard, *Libidinal Economy,* trans. Iain Hamilton Grant (Bloomington: Indiana University Press, 1993), 138.

50. The following discussion of the *Monte Carlo Bond* is derived from my "Marcel Duchamp's *Monte Carlo Bond* Machine," *October*, no. 59 (Winter 1992): 8–26. In that text I discuss Rrose Sélavy's position in a broader discourse of femininity and the machine in the early and mid-1920s.

51. Robert Lebel, *Marcel Duchamp* (New York: Grove Press, 1959), 50. Written on the bond note is the following statement: "Remboursables au pair en trois ans par tirages artificiels à partir du ler Mars 1925" [Redeemable at par in three years by artificial drawings beginning the 1st of March 1925]. *Tirage* may refer to printing and also the drawing *of a check*. Hence, the association between art and money established in *Tzanck Check* is echoed here.

52. Sanouillet and Peterson, *The Writings of Marcel Duchamp,* 185.

53. Ibid., 187.

54. Ibid., 187.

55. Lebel, *Marcel Duchamp,* 50.

56. Raymond Roussel, *Impressions of Africa,* trans. Lindy Foord and Rayner Heppenstall (New York: Riverrun Press, 1983), 144.

57. Ibid., 148.

58. Foucault, *Death and the Labyrinth,* 14.

59. Pierre Klossowski, "Nietzsche's Experience of the Eternal Return," in *The New Nietzsche,* ed. David B. Allison (Cambridge: MIT Press, 1985), 111.

60. Rrose Sélavy's calling card included two "professional" affiliations or areas of expertise. Above her name, the card read, "Precision Oculism," and below, "Complete Line of Whiskers and Kicks." Sanouillet and Peterson, *The Writings of Marcel Duchamp,* 105.

61. This text was first published in *Littérature* in 1922. Sanouillet and Peterson, *The Writings of Marcel Duchamp,* 105. The translation is Elmer Peterson's.

62. Deleuze and Guattari, *Anti-Oedipus,* 246.

63. Ibid., 116.

64. Thierry de Duve, "Marcel Duchamp or The *Phynancier* of Modern Life," *October,* no. 52 (Spring 1990): 68–69.

65. Deleuze and Guattari, *Anti-Oedipus,* 20.

66. Annette Michelson, "'Anémic Cinéma' Reflections on an Emblematic Work," *Artforum* 12, no. 2 (October 1973): 69.

67. Note that within the readymades and assisted readymade projects of the teens and twenties strategies of fragmentation of the body (i.e., the *Tzanck Check*) coexist with instances of its multiplication, as in the *Monte Carlo Bond.* This duality is analogous to what I described in chapter 1 as a metaphoric fragmentation in *Yvonne and Magdeleine Torn in Tatters* (1911) versus a metonymic multiplication of the body in *Dulcinea* (1911). As I have argued in various other ways, this demonstrates a structural continuity between Duchamp's cubism and his readymade explorations: his continuing interest in fragmentation and multiplication is transposed from its roots in the feminine body to the realm of deterritorialized financial flows.

68. Deleuze and Guattari, *Anti-Oedipus,* 264.

69. For two recent studies that explore Duchamp's adoption of Rrose Sélavy as a challenge to traditional codes of masculinity, see Nancy Ring, *New York Dada and the Crisis of Masculinity: Man Ray, Francis Picabia, and Marcel Duchamp in the United States, 1913–1921* (Ann Arbor: UMI Dissertation Services, 1993); and Amelia Jones, *Postmodernism and the En-Gendering of Marcel Duchamp* (Cambridge: Cambridge University Press, 1994).

70. This was a familiar trope in Duchamp's works of the early twenties. For instance a little-discussed work, *Vous pour moi?* of 1922 inscribes the reflexive text "Vous pour moi?" (echoing the intersubjective collision implied in the title *Tu m'*) on a series of luggage tags with the name of Rrose Sélavy and her address on Broadway in New York. The mobility implied in travel is transported to the identity of the subject him/herself.

71. Louis Althusser explicitly links the act of interpellation that calls a subject into being with police surveillance: "I shall then suggest that ideology 'acts' or 'functions' in such a way that it 'recruits' subjects among the individuals (it recruits them all), or 'transforms' the individuals into subjects (it transforms them all) by that very precise operation which I have called *interpellation* or hailing, and which can be imagined along the lines of the most commonplace everyday police (or other) hailing: 'Hey, you there!'" Louis Althusser, "Ideology and Ideological State Apparatuses (Notes towards an Investigation)," in *Lenin and Philosophy,* trans. Ben Brewster (New York: Monthly Review Press, 1971), 174.

72. Sanouillet and Peterson, *The Writings of Marcel Duchamp,* 187.

73. It is no coincidence that the unified image of the body returns at this moment in Duchamp's work only via the photograph, the simulationist medium par excellence.

74. These quotes are from the passage cited at length above. Lyotard, *Libidinal Economy,* 138.

3 Modern Machines: From the Virgin to the Widow

1. Michel Sanouillet and Elmer Peterson, eds., *The Writings of Marcel Duchamp* (New York: Da Capo Press, 1973), 160.

2. According to Arturo Schwarz, Duchamp did not remember asking this question at the 1912 Salon de la Locomotion Aérienne in Paris, but it has been quoted widely. See Arturo Schwarz, *The Complete Works of Marcel Duchamp* (New York: Harry N. Abrams, 1970), 595–96.

3. There have been many extended studies of Duchamp's *Large Glass.* Among the most prominent are: Craig Adcock, *Marcel Duchamp's Notes from the "Large Glass": An N-Dimensional Analysis* (Ann Arbor: UMI Research Press, 1983); Jean Clair, *Marcel Duchamp ou le grand fictif* (Paris: Editions Galilée, 1975); John Golding, *Marcel Duchamp: The Bride Stripped Bare by Her Bachelors, Even* (New York: The Viking Press, 1972); Octavio Paz, *Appearance Stripped Bare,* trans. Rachel Phillips and Donald Gardner (New York: Arcade Publishing, 1978); Arturo Schwarz, *The Complete Works of Marcel Duchamp;* and Jean Suquet, *Miroir de la mariée* (Paris: Flammarion, 1974).

4. Jean Suquet, "Possible," trans. Tamara Blanken and Thierry de Duve; revised by Dennis Young in *The Definitively Unfinished Marcel Duchamp,* ed. Thierry de Duve (Halifax: The Nova Scotia College of Art and Design; Cambridge: MIT Press, 1993), 86.

5. Nonetheless, since important elements in the *Glass* such as the illuminating gas and the waterfall are invisible, they are only accessible through Duchamp's words.

6. Sanouillet and Peterson, *The Writings of Marcel Duchamp,* 51.

7. Ibid., 53.

8. Ibid., 50.

9. Ibid., 68.

10. Ibid., 56–57.

11. Ibid., 51. Duchamp mentions only eight molds in this text; he would later add an additional one.

12. *Marcel Duchamp, Notes,* trans. and ed. Paul Matisse (Boston: G. K. Hall, 1983), note 142 (recto), unpaginated.

13. Ibid., note 143 (recto), unpaginated.

14. Sanouillet and Peterson, *The Writings of Marcel Duchamp,* 57.

15. Matisse, *Marcel Duchamp, Notes,* note 134, unpaginated.

16. This preoccupation was of course paralleled by his interest in molds, another means of representing an absent dimensionality.

17. Jean Clair, "Marcel Duchamp et la tradition des perspecteurs," in *Marcel Duchamp abécédaire,* ed. Jean Clair with the collaboration of Ulfe Linde (Paris: Musée National d'Art Moderne, Centre National d'Art et de Culture Georges Pompidou, 1977), 154. My translation.

18. Jacques Lacan, *The Four Fundamental Concepts of Psycho-Analysis,* ed. Jacques-Alain Miller, trans. Alan Sheridan (New York: W. W. Norton), 86–87.

19. Ibid., 89.

20. It is fascinating to note here that one of Duchamp's texts in the 1914 box seems an almost exact anticipation of Sartre's and Lacan's definition of the gaze: "One can look at [see] seeing; / one can't hear hearing." Sanouillet and Peterson, *The Writings of Marcel Duchamp,* 23.

There is a second important instance of "Sartrean looking" related to the *Large Glass.* According to the instructions in the title of the 1918 work on glass *To Be Looked At (from the Other Side of the Glass) with One Eye, Close To, for Almost an Hour),* a study for the upper-right quadrant of the bachelor machine, the viewer is to stand "behind" the object, peering through a lens into the room in which it is installed (currently, a gallery in the Museum of Modern Art). The viewer, therefore, becomes a spectacle: as in Lacan's formulation, s/he is seen (by other museum visitors) seeing. For a discussion of this, see Rosalind Krauss, "The Blink of an Eye," in *The States of "Theory": History, Art, and Critical Discourse,* ed. David Carroll (New York: Columbia University Press, 1990), 178–79.

21. Lacan, *The Four Fundamental Concepts of Psycho-Analysis,* 83.

22. Ibid., 87–88.

23. Sanouillet and Peterson, *The Writings of Marcel Duchamp,* 65.

24. Ibid., 35.

25. Ibid., 65.

26. The Wilson-Lincoln illusion and its combination of optical illusion and anamorphosis anticipates the pulsing eroticism of Duchamp's rotary reliefs of the 1920s and '30s. See Rosalind E. Krauss, *The Optical Unconscious* (Cambridge: MIT Press, 1993), 95–146.

27. Lacan, *The Four Fundamental Concepts of Psycho-Analysis,* 80–81.

28. Jean Clair writes, "We examine the constituent parts of that small glass, with its transparency, measurements and functional intent—always remembering the instruction of the title to

apply one eye closely to it (which is not unreminiscent of the perspective instrument called a *portillon,* a stylus placed upright in the center of a graduated dial, with a lens at its tip)." Jean Clair, "Duchamp and the Classical Perspectivists," *Artforum* 16, no. 7 (March 1978): 44.

29. Matisse, *Marcel Duchamp, Notes,* note 129, unpaginated.

30. I am purposely rendering the viewer masculine here.

31. Sanouillet and Peterson, *The Writings of Marcel Duchamp,* 39.

32. Ibid., 45.

33. Ibid., 30.

34. Ibid., 42.

35. Ibid.

36. Ibid.

37. Ibid., 43.

38. Ibid.

39. Ibid., 44.

40. Ibid.

41. In an argument that theoretically amplifies Duchamp's invention of a *cinematic* blossoming for the bride, Annette Michelson has suggested that film is rooted in fetishistically analyzing the feminine body and then reconstituting it synthetically: "We will want once more to note that assiduous, relentless impulse which claims the female body as the site of an analytic, mapping upon its landscape a poetics and an epistemology with all the perverse detail and somber ceremony of fetishism. And may we not then begin to think that body in its cinematic relations somewhat differently? Not as the mere object of a cinematic *iconography* of repression and

desire—as catalogued by now in the extensive literature on dominant narrative in its major genres of melodrama, *film noir,* and so on—but rather as the fantasmatic ground of cinema itself.

"We will then wish to consider once again, and somewhat differently, those acts of magic perpetrated upon the female subject, as by Edison and Méliès in the films of the primitive period (1900–1906), for the mutilations, reconstitutions, levitations, and transformations performed upon her body are to be read not, as has been suggested, as instances of male envy of the female procreative function. We may rather understand them as the obsessive reenactment of that proleptic movement between analysis and synthesis which will accelerate and crystallize around the female body in an ultimate, fantasmatic mode of representation *as* cinema." Annette Michelson, "On the Eve of the Future: The Reasonable Facsimile and the Philosophical Toy," *October,* no. 29 (Summer 1984): 19–20.

42. Sanouillet and Peterson, *The Writings of Marcel Duchamp,* 45.

43. Ibid., 36.

44. Ibid., 38.

45. Ibid., 31–32.

46. Ibid., 51.

47. Henry Ford, *My Life and Work,* in collaboration with Samuel Crowther (Garden City, N.Y.: Doubleday, Page, 1923), 46, 280.

48. Ibid., 80.

49. Sigmund Freud, "Project for a Scientific Psychology," in *The Origins of Psycho-Analysis: Letters to Wilhelm Fleiss, Drafts and Notes: 1887–1902,* ed. Marie Bonaparte, Anna Freud, and Ernst Kris, trans. Eric Mosbacher and James Strachey (New York: Basic Books, 1954), 426.

50. In an important article Charles Maier argues that rationalization and scientific management held the promise during the 1920s of overcoming class conflict by bringing about a society of unprecedented abundance: "What the Americanist vision seemed to promise through its brash teachings of productivity, expertise and optimalization was an escape from having to accept

class confrontation and social division. Albeit for very different reasons, all the enthusiasts of scientific management and technological overhaul were seeking to deny the necessary existence of the pre-war model of ideological conflict and to validate a new image of class relationships." C. S. Maier, "Between Taylorism and Technocracy," *Journal of Contemporary History* 5, no. 2 (1970): 29.

Jeffrey Herf calls attention to how technology was made to serve a conservative folk mythology in interwar Germany, which, in a very different way from that postulated by Maier, also masked class differences in favor of a shared ethnic or national identity: "The accomplishment of the reactionary modernists within the conservative revolution was to have made a virtue out of the necessity of embracing technics by shifting technology out of the sphere of *Zivilisation* and into that of *Kultur.* By so doing, they could embrace technology without adopting a rationalist world view in politics and culture." Jeffrey Herf, *Reactionary Modernism: Technology, Culture, and Politics in Weimar and the Third Reich* (Cambridge: Cambridge University Press, 1984), 40.

51. François Guéry and Didier Deleule, *Le Corps productif* (Paris: Mame, 1972), 6. My translation.

52. Frederick Winslow Taylor, *The Principles of Scientific Management* (New York: Harper & Brothers, 1911), 38.

53. Didier Deleule, "The Living Machine: Psychology as Organology," trans. Randall Cherry in *Incorporations; Zone 6,* ed. Jonathan Crary and Sanford Kwinter (New York: Zone Books, 1992), 208.

54. Guéry and Deleule, *Le Corps productif,* 7. My translation.

55. For the best discussion of the science of work and its relationship to thermodynamic metaphors see Anson Rabinbach, *The Human Motor: Energy, Fatigue, and the Origins of Modernity* (Berkeley: University of California Press, 1992). Rabinbach traces the emergence of the concept of "labor power" from the mid-nineteenth century to the early twentieth century and demonstrates the relationship between the energetic economy of work that was rationally codified in the late nineteenth century and the first two laws of thermodynamics. The potential held out by the first law of thermodynamics, the conservation of energy, discovered by Hermann von Helmholtz in 1847, was the optimistic belief in an almost unlimited system of pro-

duction. However, the second law of thermodynamics, the discovery of entropy by Rudolf Clausius at around the same time, suggested the problem of fatigue, which "became the most apparent and distinctive sign of the external limits of body and mind, the most reliable indicator of the need to conserve and restrict the waste and misuse of the body's unique capital—its labor power" (6).

56. Deleule declares, "In other words, consciousness is the result of a subtraction. Anything that cannot be attributed to the automaton-machine is attributed, quite simply, to consciousness." Consciousness and individual will cause problems on the factory floor. Again, Deleule specifies, "language widens the gap separating man and machine, and, moreover, language is at once indispensable and superfluous. Although it is the most basic means of communicating or acknowledging a sensation, it continually insinuates itself into man's every attempt to evaluate his relation with the world, inevitably introducing mistakes, misjudgments." Deleule, "The Living Machine: Psychology as Organology," 213, 210. Here we have a fascinating repositioning through the optic of class of Lacan's (or any bourgeois psychoanalyst's) conviction that language is the locus of the unconscious. If the middle- or upper-class analysand's speech is considered the key to unraveling his or her pathology, the worker's very possession of speech causes problems in his or her proper mechanistic functioning.

57. Michel Foucault seems to have this in mind when he describes the function of the discourse of sexuality—of which psychoanalysis, of course, is a major component—for the bourgeoisie: "The primary concern was not repression of the sex of the classes to be exploited, but rather the body, vigor, longevity, progeniture, and descent of the classes that 'ruled.' This was the purpose for which the deployment of sexuality was first established, as a new distribution of pleasures, discourses, truths, and powers; it has to be seen as the self-affirmation of one class rather than the enslavement of another: a defense, a protection, a strengthening, and an exaltation that were eventually extended to others—at the cost of different transformations—as a means of social control and political subjugation." Michel Foucault, *The History of Sexuality,* vol. 1: *An Introduction,* trans. Robert Hurley (New York: Vintage Books, 1980), 123.

58. Deleule, "The Living Machine: Psychology as Organology," 210.

59. Tom Lutz, *American Nervousness, 1903: An Anecdotal History* (Ithaca: Cornell University Press, 1991), 6.

60. George M. Beard, *American Nervousness: Its Causes and Consequences* (New York: Putnam's, 1881), 9.

61. Ibid., 98–99.

62. A[chille-Adrien] Proust and Gilbert Ballet, *The Treatment of Neurasthenia,* trans. Peter Campbell Smith (London: Henry Kimpton, 1902), 7.

63. Rabinbach writes, "If at the outset, neurasthenia was identified by Beard and his European followers as the inability of mind and body to resist the onrushing stimuli of modernity, Ribot and Bücher attempted to find a social purpose in our natural propensity to resist inordinate expenditures of energy. In *misonéisme* energy conservation is no longer threatened by fatigue but is accelerated by it. In Ribot's theory, in Janet's psychology, and in the debates over primitive inertia, the allegedly pathological resistance of savages and neurasthenics to modernity was balanced by the normalizing function of fatigue—the response that enables society to restore depleted energy." Rabinbach, *The Human Motor,* 177.

64. Lutz, *American Nervousness,* 25.

65. Matisse, *Marcel Duchamp, Notes,* note 135, unpaginated.

66. As I have tried to demonstrate, such a connection between finance, psychic identity, and the machine was at the heart of Duchamp's *Monte Carlo Bond* of 1924. See my "Marcel Duchamp's *Monte Carlo Bond* Machine," *October,* no. 59 (Winter 1992): 8–26; as well as my discussion of this work in chapter 2.

67. Sanouillet and Peterson, *The Writings of Marcel Duchamp,* 74.

68. Robert Lebel, *Marcel Duchamp* (New York: Grove Press, 1959), 68.

69. Schwarz, *The Complete Works of Marcel Duchamp,* 125.

70. "Marcel Duchamp, Vite," interview by Jean Schuster in *le surréalisme, même* (Paris), no. 2 (Spring 1957): 144. My translation.

71. Schwarz, *The Complete Works of Marcel Duchamp,* 138, n. 140.

72. Ibid., 144. My translation.

73. Lebel, *Marcel Duchamp,* 31. It is also relevant to remember that Duchamp imagined one of the malic molds as a department-store delivery boy.

74. Sanouillet and Peterson, *The Writings of Marcel Duchamp,* 76.

75. Katharine Kuh, "Marcel Duchamp," in *The Artist's Voice: Talks with Seventeen Artists* (New York: Harper & Row, 1960), 83.

76. For a discussion of how Max Ernst transformed such a catalogue spread of commodities, see Rosalind Krauss, "The Master's Bedroom," *Representations,* no. 28 (Fall 1989): 55–76.

77. Emile Zola, *The Ladies' Paradise,* intro. by Kristin Ross (Berkeley: University of California Press, 1992), 27.

78. Rosalind H. Williams, *Dream Worlds: Mass Consumption in Late Nineteenth-Century France* (Berkeley: University of California Press, 1982), 95. For a discussion of the department store as a new cultural form see also Michael B. Miller, *The Bon Marché: Bourgeois Culture and the Department Store 1869–1920* (Princeton: Princeton University Press, 1981).

79. For a discussion of Zola's gendered descriptions of the shopping experience see Rachel Bowlby, "'Traffic in Her Desires': Zola's *Au Bonheur des Dames,*" in *Just Looking: Consumer Desire in Dreiser, Gissing and Zola* (New York: Methuen, 1985), 66–82.

80. Zola, *The Ladies' Paradise,* 70.

81. Ibid., 97.

82. "And so the shaft went on with its meal for half an hour, gulping men down more or less greedily according to the depth of the level they were bound for; but it never stopped, for the hunger of this gigantic maw could swallow up a whole people." Emile Zola, *Germinal,* trans. Leonard Tancock (London: Penguin Books, 1954), 40.

83. Zola, *The Ladies' Paradise,* 280.

84. Ibid., 214.

85. Sanouillet and Peterson, *The Writings of Marcel Duchamp,* 26.

86. Birken asserts that in place of classical economic theory of the seventeenth through the nineteenth centuries in which production—in both agriculture and manufacturing—was thought to be an inexhaustible source of wealth, marginalist economists in the United States and Europe during the late nineteenth century replaced the notions of labor and need with the concepts of consumption and desire, thereby allowing consumption to displace production as the motivating force of economic activity: "In the last quarter of the nineteenth century, the marginalists thus replaced the contradictions of political economy with a coherent and surprisingly uniform theory of value. According to the new theory, value was neither the objective result of social labor nor of social need for products, but was simply attached to objects by the subjective desire of consumers" (32). Whereas property—whether a feudal estate or one's personal labor power—had been the basis of political identity through the time of Marx, "in the course of the twentieth century, desire ha[d] begun to replace property as the symbolic badge of individualism" (12). The so-called marginalist economists reversed classical attempts to link the value of things to either their utility or to the labor necessary for their production: "Commodities themselves were not so much material goods as desired objects. Anything (material or not) that was desired was potentially a commodity" (28–29). See Lawrence Birken, *Consuming Desire: Sexual Science and the Emergence of a Culture of Abundance, 1871–1914* (Ithaca: Cornell University Press, 1988).

87. Guéry and Deleule, *Le Corps productif,* 15, 16. My translation.

88. Birken, *Consuming Desire,* 29.

89. Duchamp's specifications for readymades also include the concept of delay: he wrote, "by planning for a moment to come (on such a day, such a date such a minute), '*to inscribe* a readymade'—The readymade can later be looked for.—(with all kinds of delays)." Thus, Duchamp's conception of the readymade as a commodity submitted to a process of delay parallels the program of the *Large Glass.* Sanouillet and Peterson, *The Writings of Marcel Duchamp,* 32.

90. Birken, *Consuming Desire,* 83.

91. Georges Canguilhem, "René Descartes," in *A Vital Rationalist: Selected Writings,* ed. François Delaporte, trans. Arthur Goldhammer (New York: Zone Books, 1994), 235.

92. René Descartes, "Discourse on Method," in *Discourse on Method and Meditations on First Philosophy,* 3rd ed., trans. Donald A. Cress (Indianapolis: Hackett, 1993), 32.

93. William A. Camfield, *Francis Picabia* (Princeton: Princeton University Press, 1979), 119. This statement was drawn from Arp's preface for a 1950 exhibition of Picabia's art at the Rose Fried Gallery in New York.

94. It is interesting to note in passing that the Cartesian automaton was closely linked to clock mechanisms. It would be nice to believe, although it seems impossible to prove, that this may have, in part, motivated Picabia's choice of a clock.

95. "La fille née sans mère c'est la machine. Tous les dessins sont mécaniques et représentent des machines imaginaires. Le livre . . . est dédié aux médecins noeurologues." P. A. Benoit, *A propos des "Poèmes de la fille née sans mère"* (Alès: n.p., 1958), unpaginated. Picabia was undergoing neurological treatment at the time he wrote this book, published in 1918.

96. Camfield, *Francis Picabia,* 90.

97. "As for the *Large Glass,* he worked on it until his next trip to Europe in February 1923 when he considered it definitively unfinished." Lebel, *Marcel Duchamp,* 49.

98. Sanouillet and Peterson, *The Writings of Marcel Duchamp,* 127.

99. It is clear that Duchamp had grown weary of the *Glass,* and perhaps *Fresh Widow* and *La Bagarre d'Austerlitz* helped him to justify quitting: "[The *Glass*] held me until 1923, the only thing I was interested in, and I even regret not finishing it, but it became so monotonous, it was a transcription, and toward the end there was no invention. So it just fizzled out." Pierre Cabanne, *Dialogues with Marcel Duchamp,* trans. Ron Padgett (New York: Da Capo Press, 1971), 65.

100. D'Harnoncourt and McShine, *Marcel Duchamp,* 295.

101. Such a supposition is given further credence in Arturo Schwarz's discussion of *Fresh Widow:* "Duchamp told the author: 'Instead of being considered a painter, I would have liked, on this occasion, to be thought of as a *fenêtrier*! The latter word, which is an untranslatable neologism, should convey the idea of a 'windower'—*not* a window maker, but rather a person concerned with the possible developments a window might undergo. Answering a question put to him by Serge Stauffer, Duchamp wrote that he was led by 'the idea (always) to make something which could not be called a picture (in this case 'make windows').'" Schwarz, *The Complete Works of Marcel Duchamp,* 480.

102. There is a persistent suggestion of kitsch surrounding this strange color.

103. "D'être cirés tous les matins comme une paire de chaussures, de sorte qu'ils reluisent comme de vrais carreaux." Quoted in Jean Clair, *Marcel Duchamp, catalogue raisonné* (Paris: Musée National d'Art Moderne, 1977), 98.

104. Schwarz, *The Complete Works of Marcel Duchamp,* 479.

105. As the ciphers for the Bride's commandments, these draft pistons were a particularly important aspect of her anatomy. See my discussion of this element in chapter 1.

106. For a discussion of castration see Schwarz's account in *The Complete Works of Marcel Duchamp,* 480. Molly Nesbit declares that *Fresh Widow* "makes a joke at the expense of the French war widow." Molly Nesbit, "Ready-Made Originals," *October,* no. 37 (Summer 1986): 63.

107. Francis M. Naumann, "Affectueusement, Marcel: Ten Letters from Marcel Duchamp to Suzanne Duchamp and Jean Crotti," *Archives of American Art Journal* 22, no. 4 (1982): 15. Duchamp was responding to Crotti's invitation to show at the Salon Dada.

108. Nesbit, "Ready-Made Originals," 63. While Nesbit's analysis of Duchamp's use of copyright is brilliant, I disagree with her conclusion that "art became the only way for [Duchamp] to escape the tyranny of the shop window" (64). As I have shown, Duchamp did not share the simplistic and moralistic belief that commodification should be overcome (as though this were possible) that motivates so many cultural critics today. Over half a century ago Duchamp recog-

nized the complex and contradictory relationship between eroticism, production, and consumption and sought to chart this epistemological field. I believe that he would have felt it impossible—and not even interesting—to transcend the "tyranny of the shop window," which as I have shown was also the tyranny of erotic isolation.

109. This expression comes from a text in the *Green Box:* "Razor blades which cut well and razor blades which no longer cut / The first have 'cuttage' in reserve / —Use this 'cuttage' or 'cuttation.'" Sanouillet and Peterson, *The Writings of Marcel Duchamp,* 31.

110. Matisse, *Marcel Duchamp, Notes,* note 9, unpaginated.

111. See, for example, Michel Butor, "Reproduction interdite," *Critique,* no. 334 (March 1975): 273; and Schwarz, *The Complete Works of Marcel Duchamp,* 480.

112. Indeed, his theorization of the infrathin brought all of these elements together: "Cutting (*noun*)—cutting (*adj.*) (guillotine, razor blades / sliding— / Drying—gluing / viscosity— (/ breakage. / Burning / melting (in liquids with sugar for ex.) / Porosity—imbibition (blotting paper) Permeability / to water and air / (leather) / Pushing-in (nails, planting an arrow) / rubbing scratching— / adjusting registering—." Matisse, *Marcel Duchamp, Notes,* note 26 (verso), unpaginated.

The association of the infrathin with polishing—the leather of *Fresh Widow* was to be polished every day—which appears in this note indirectly in reference to "rubbing" is made explicit in note 27: "Filing—polishing— / the infra thin file— / sandpaper—emery cloth / rubbing down lacquer / often these operations reach / the infrathin—"

4 THE SELF READYMADE

1. Marcel Duchamp, interview with Otto Hahn, *L'Express,* July 23, 1964, quoted in Jennifer Gough-Cooper and Jacques Caumont, eds., "Ephemerides on and about Marcel Duchamp and Rrose Sélavy 1887–1968," in *Marcel Duchamp,* ed. Pontus Hulten (Milan: Bompiani, 1993), unpaginated [entry for July 23, 1964].

2. *Marcel Duchamp, Notes,* ed. and trans. Paul Matisse (Boston: G. K. Hall, 1983), note 273, unpaginated.

3. Building on Leo Steinberg's notion of the "flatbed," Rosalind Krauss has emphasized the modern and postmodern opposition between the horizontal plane of the body and the vertical space of opticality. Traditionally, the rotation of a horizontal object (such as Jackson Pollock's drip paintings, produced on the floor, or Andy Warhol's "piss paintings") into the vertical constitutes them as art objects. According to this argument, Duchamp the arch antiretinalist played with the entry of chess into retinality, or perhaps more accurately, he imported the "erasable beauty" of chess into painting as a model *counter* to pure retinality. Rosalind E. Krauss, *The Optical Unconscious* (Cambridge: MIT Press, 1993), 243–329.

4. Henri-Pierre Roché, *Victor (Marcel Duchamp)* (Paris: Centre National d'Art et de Culture Georges Pompidou, Musée National d'Art Moderne, 1977), 66. My translation.

5. It is perhaps relevant that in his later years Duchamp repeatedly and cheerfully denied that he ever formally renounced painting.

6. Marcel Duchamp, address to the New York State Chess Association, August 30, 1952, quoted in Gough-Cooper and Caumont, "Ephemerides," unpaginated [entry for August 30, 1952].

7. Francis M. Naumann, "Affectueusement, Marcel: Ten Letters from Marcel Duchamp to Suzanne Duchamp and Jean Crotti," *Archives of American Art Journal* 22, no. 4 (1982): 14.

8. Anne D'Harnoncourt and Kynaston McShine, eds., *Marcel Duchamp* (New York: Museum of Modern Art; Philadelphia: Philadelphia Museum of Art, 1973), 283.

9. Marcel Duchamp and Vitaly Halberstadt, *L'Opposition et les cases conjuguées sont reconciliées* (Paris: Editions de L'Echiquier, 1932), 9.

10. D'Harnoncourt and McShine, *Marcel Duchamp,* 283.

11. In the brilliant article "La Défense Duchamp," Hubert Damisch does call attention to the intersubjective nature of Duchamp's cubist studies and paintings of men—probably himself and his brothers—playing chess. I will return to his treatment of this issue, but for the moment I am placing a slightly different emphasis on the confrontations Duchamp represents. Hubert

Damisch, "La Défense Duchamp," in *Marcel Duchamp: tradition de la rupture ou rupture de la tradition?,* ed. Jean Clair (Paris: Union Générale d'éditions, 1979), 90–91; trans. Rosalind Krauss as "The Duchamp Defense," *October,* no. 10 (Fall 1979).

12. By 1910 Duchamp had helped produce a board game called *petits chevaux* based on the steeplechase course at Auteuil. He had painted the cloth and designed some of the game pieces, in the form of horses and jockies. One is inscribed, "GAMBIT; Ecurie: Marcel." Gough-Cooper and Caumont, "Ephemerides," unpaginated [entry for April 9, 1910].

13. Marcel Duchamp, interview by Truman Capote in Richard Avedon, *Observations* (New York: Simon and Schuster, 1959), 55.

14. Pierre Cabanne, *Dialogues with Marcel Duchamp,* trans. Ron Padgett (New York: Da Capo Press, 1987), 18.

15. See my discussion of Duchamp's cubism in chapter 1.

16. In a 1960 interview Duchamp made the following remark about the *Nude Descending a Staircase:* "The idea of a nude descending a staircase came from the fact that I had seen photographs called "chronophotographs" in *L'Illustration.* At that time there were a lot of experiments, photographs repeating each movement, and giving the diagram of movement. You could argue that doesn't give any idea at all of movement. Indeed it doesn't, but it describes it. After all a picture is a diagram of an idea." Gough-Cooper and Caumont, "Ephemerides," unpaginated [entry for December 30, 1960].

17. "The Futurists, for me, are urban Impressionists who make impressions of the city rather than of the countryside." The impressionists were the epitome of what Duchamp considered "pure retinality," the displacement of thought by impression. Cabanne, *Dialogues with Marcel Duchamp,* 35.

18. In 1919 in a letter to the Arensbergs, Duchamp declared: "I feel I am quite ready to become a chess maniac. Everything around me takes the shape of the Knight or the Queen, and the exterior world has no other interest for me other than its transformation to winning or losing positions." Gough-Cooper and Caumont, "Ephemerides," unpaginated [entry for June 20, 1919].

19. Duchamp was indeed a serious player. He took part in his first chess tournament in 1923, where he ranked third, and continued to play throughout his life, although less competitively as the years went on. Beginning in 1937 he wrote an occasional chess column for the Paris newspaper *Ce Soir* until publication was suspended on account of the war. For a thorough account of Duchamp's career in chess see Arturo Schwarz, "Precision Play—An Aspect of the Beauty of Precision," in *The Complete Works of Marcel Duchamp* (New York: Harry N. Abrams, 1970), 57–75.

20. Duchamp, while not abandoning art, did often assert his desire to leave behind the art world. Like so many of his convictions, however, this one was contradictory in practice. He was active throughout the 1920s in various curatorial and even speculative schemes, such as his partnership with Katherine Dreier in the Société Anonyme (founded in 1920) and his purchase and sale of large numbers of works by Brancusi and Picabia.

But from the 1920s onward Duchamp's marked tendency to produce art in semisecrecy increased, to the point that his final work, the *Etant Donnés* produced between 1946 and 1966, was only posthumously revealed and known previously only to a tiny number of Duchamp's intimate circle.

21. There is some doubt, according to the conservation records of the Philadelphia Museum of Art, whether there are 152 or 153 marble cubes in *Why Not Sneeze?*.

22. According to Schwarz, the design of cubes in the poster was derived in the following way: "Duchamp photographed a number of building blocks which he threw into a net bag to form an 'accumulation.' An enlargement was made of this photo, eliminating all details except the chance configuration of the blocks in the net. This enlargement was then used as a basis for the final drawing, in which the cubes were colored light-pink and black." Schwarz, *The Complete Works of Marcel Duchamp,* 493.

23. Damisch, "The Duchamp Defense," 27.

24. Matisse, *Marcel Duchamp, Notes,* note 273, unpaginated.

25. The work is characterized by an infinite regress of sensory shifts. As Schwarz and others have remarked, based on Duchamp's own comments, the marble at first looks like a pile of insubstantial sugar cubes, so that when one picks it up s/he is surprised by the great weight of

the object. Moreover, while the sugar cubes might imply warmth, the marble is quite cold. Schwarz, *The Complete Works of Marcel Duchamp,* 487.

Ecke Bonk adds the further interpretation that these marble cubes were "used in kettles to prevent deposits of lime scale by their motions in the boiling water." This association with great heat would also contradict the "cold" of the marble. Ecke Bonk, *Marcel Duchamp: The Box in a Valise; de ou par Marcel Duchamp ou Rrose Sélavy; Inventory of an Edition,* trans. David Britt (New York: Rizzoli, 1989), 223, note 1.

26. Gough-Cooper and Caumont, "Ephemerides," unpaginated [entry for October 4, 1954].

27. *The Writings of Marcel Duchamp,* ed. Michel Sanouillet and Elmer Peterson (New York: Da Capo Press, 1973), 30, 45. In a collage of 1925, *Nous nous cajolions,* which juxtaposes a crude line drawing of a lion's cage beside which stands a woman with a young boy, the text "NOUS NOUS CAJOLIONS," and a photograph of mens' room graffiti, the elements of sexuality and a caged woman (the title is homophonic with the expression "Nanny's lion cage") are explicitly linked. The (virginal) nanny combines with the (bacheloresque) graffiti in an opposition reminiscent of the terms of the *Large Glass.*

28. Ibid., 48. The thermometer has a long history of association with femininity. For a fascinating treatment of this subject, see Terry Castle, "The Female Thermometer," *Representations,* no. 17 (Winter 1987): 1–27.

Moreover, there might be a more personal reference in the inclusion of the thermometer in *Why Not Sneeze?,* which may account for the explicit distaste that both Dorothea and Katherine Dreier manifested for the work. In 1920, only a year before the small cage was constructed, Man Ray, who had no particular affection for Dreier, made a rather cruel object portrait of her titled *Catherine Barometer,* which Ruth Bohan describes: "Measuring over four feet from top to bottom and constructed out of a variety of miscellaneous materials, including a washboard and a clump of steel wool, Man Ray's object represents a satirical parody of an actual barometer. It is also laced with explicit sexual overtones. Advising the spectator to 'shake well before using,' an action that would cause the mercury in a true barometer to rise rapidly. Man Ray's object obviously seeks to play on Dreier's name—a rising barometer indicating 'dryer' weather conditions. On the other hand, an agitated barometer causes the mercury to spill completely out the top of the tube, in unmistakable orgasmic fashion, rendering the barometer totally useless." Ruth L. Bohan, "Katherine Sophie Dreier and New York Dada," *Arts Magazine* 51, no. 9 (May 1977): 100.

29. Sanouillet and Peterson, *The Writings of Marcel Duchamp,* 39.

30. Matisse, *Marcel Duchamp, Notes,* note 176, unpaginated.

31. The suggestion of sexual allusion continues in the cuttlebone itself, which is meant to be "pecked" by birds.

32. Schwarz, *The Complete Works of Marcel Duchamp,* 487.

33. When the door is suspended between doorways the simultaneous opposition between open and closed is refigured as a simultaneous dichotomy of two spatially discrete states of openness: "open here" and "open there."

34. Brian O'Doherty has shown that spatial paradox also characterizes Duchamp's important exhibition designs. In the Exhibition of Surrealism at the Galerie Beaux-Arts in Paris in 1938, Duchamp reversed ceiling and floor by hanging bags of coal on the ceiling and installing a chandelierlike brazier in the middle of the floor. In his installation *Mile of String* for the 1942 exhibition "First Papers of Surrealism" in New York, Duchamp similarly confounded presence and absence by filling the presumed void of the room with a tangle of string, thus transforming emptiness into a palpable thing. Brian O'Doherty, "Inside the White Cube: Part III Context as Content," *Artforum* 15, no. 5 (November 1976): 39–40.

35. For the best discussion of Duchamp's optical machines, see Krauss, *The Optical Unconscious,* 95–146.

36. Sanouillet and Peterson, *The Writings of Marcel Duchamp,* 74.

37. *L'Opposition et les cases conjuguées sont reconciliées* is an extraordinary sculptural object whose conventional book form incorporates a series of spatial foldings and unfoldings, which literally begin at the beginning—with the covers themselves. On the front cover, the title is justified to the right and is set on two lines, the bottom of which fills its entire width. But as in the title *La Mariée mise à nu par ses celibataires, même* there is a supplemental word: *L'Opposition et les cases conjuguées sont reonciliées par.* The mystery of this hanging *par* is easier to unravel than that of the *même:* it indicates the names of the authors printed, justified to the left, on the back cover,

giving the impression that the title's text should continue unbroken across the open end of the book. Like the studio door with two doorways or the optical illusion of two contradictory spiral volumes, this book has two spines: one binding its pages, and the other "virtual" spine binding its title to its authors. Two opposing rotations are thus solicited from the reader holding *L'Opposition et les case conjuguées* in his or her hand: the conventional gesture of opening the front cover in order to read its text is short-circuited by the imperative to follow the hanging *par* and turn the book over in order to continue reading the text of its title.

My argument is confirmed by a unique version of *L'Opposition et les cases conjuguées* (1932) that was in the collection of the late Mme. Duchamp. This book is bound in leather and decorated with chessboard patterns justified to the right of the front cover and to the left of the back cover. Although this design does not produce an accurate image of a chessboard along the "virtual" spine of the open end of the book, it does create a mirror effect from front to back (the mirror was one of Duchamp's favorite images of dimensional transfer). This unique object is bound by a leather loop inscribed with the title, but unlike the printed title of the edition, this title loop is broken from front to back between the "c" and "i"—the precise midpoint—of the word *reconciliées* in what can hardly be anything else than another Duchampian pun on the perpetual process of joining and breaking apart. It literally creates a split within *reconciliation*.

The spatialization of the book through the separation of its "internal" text from its physical envelope was not a new trope for Duchamp. As early as 1919 he gave instructions to his sister Suzanne and her husband Jean Crotti to make an "unhappy readymade" as a kind of wedding present in which a geometry book was to be hung on the balcony outside their apartment. Duchamp remarked to Pierre Cabanne: "The wind had to go through the book, choose its own problems, turn and tear out the pages." D'Harnoncourt and McShine, *Marcel Duchamp*, 288–89.

In 1922 Duchamp designed a "book" of texts by the art critic Henry McBride for the Société Anonyme. Titled *Some French Moderns Says McBride*, this object included various articles printed in successively larger type organized in a ring binder. But instead of printing the name of each text on the tabs of the dividers inserted in the ring binder, each carried one letter of the title, "Some French Moderns Says McBride," causing an atomization and spatialization of the title paralleling that of the turning pages of the book. Duchamp's long-term relationship with Mary Reynolds undoubtedly led him to think even more explicitly of books as objects. In 1935 he designed a bookbinding for *Ubu Roi* by Alfred Jarry, executed by Reynolds, in which, as in *L'Opposition et les cases conjuguées sont reconciliées*, the covers had to be flattened out in order for the title to be legible: A large abstract *U* is superimposed on each the front and back covers and a *B* forms a spine, so that the opened book reads "UBU." Incidentally, the author's name is also on the back cover, and *Roi* is indicated only by a royal emblem within the *u* on the front.

In spite of these fascinating works, Duchamp was clearly more interested in "boxes" than books, where his texts were not restricted by a rigid order or binding. In fact, the first and final manuscripts of *L'Opposition et les cases conjuguées,* as well as several notes, diagrams, and other materials relating to it were combined in a box with the label of the Paris department store Old England. He attempted this kind of dissociative effect even in more conventional book designs.

A second level of dissociation, between what Duchamp might have called the appearance and the apparition (signifying somewhat idiosyncratically the optical or sensory image of a thing versus its "mold" or geometric model), is conveyed by the type for the covers of *L'Opposition.* It was generated by a photograph of the shadows cast by zinc stencils. See Gough-Cooper and Caumont, "Ephemerides," unpaginated [entry for September 8, 1931].

38. D'Harnoncourt and McShine, *Marcel Duchamp,* 302.

39. Duchamp and Halberstadt, *L'Opposition et les cases conjuguées,* 21.

40. Nor were Duchamp and Halberstadt satisfied simply to imply this operation of the hinge. *L'Opposition et les cases conjuguées* is illustrated with "8 diagrams on transparent paper which, folded over on the hinge indicated by a red dotted line, show the mechanism of superposition of the White principal domain on the Black principal domain" (91). The rotation signaled by the binding of the book's cover is thus played out within the book itself, some of whose pages are meant to be folded upon one another in a parallel instance of rotation.

41. Damisch, "The Duchamp Defense," 25.

42. Schwarz, *The Complete Works of Marcel Duchamp,* 60.

43. Damisch, "The Duchamp Defense," 19.

44. The ad is presented anonymously in *The Arts* (February–March 1921) with the following attribution: "[this brilliant caricature of a modern magazine advertisement is the work of an

artist well-known in many fields who, unfortunately, objects to having his identity revealed.—Editor.]." Ruth Bohan and Francis Naumann both attribute this work to Duchamp, and it seems unlikely given his intense involvement with the Société Anonyme at this time that it could have been by anyone else. See Bohan, "Katherine Sophie Dreier and New York Dada," 98; and Francis M. Naumann, *New York Dada 1915–23* (New York: Harry N. Abrams, 1994), 160–61.

The very name of the Société Anonyme, founded in 1920 as the first "museum" of contemporary art in the United States by Katherine Dreier, Man Ray, and Duchamp, projects the logic of reification beyond the individual artwork or artist and onto their institutional networks. *Société anonyme* is the French term for "incorporated," which was ironically doubled when the collaborators added the English synonym to the official title of the organization: Société Anonyme, Incorporated. This redundancy suggests the degree to which Duchamp played with the practice of art as a corporate entity, an Archie Pen Co. or a *société anonyme.*

Man Ray suggested the name Société Anonyme, and as he was not fluent in French at this time, it is unclear whether he understood its colloquial meaning. Duchamp, however, loved the joke and wholeheartedly endorsed it. Bohan, "Katherine Sophie Dreier and New York Dada," 98.

Duchamp emphasized the irony of this French-English redundancy in the collection of writings by the art critic Henry McBride that he designed for the Société Anonyme, *Some French Moderns Says McBride* (1922) (see note 37). The articles are reprinted and placed in a loose-leaf notebook organized with dividers. From the front, the translucent plastic tabs of these dividers each hold groups of letters that spell out the title of the book from top to bottom. As one turns the pages, however, a different legend is spelled out on the back of the tabs: "Société Anonyme Incorporated."

45. The fact that the image of the "pen" derives from a woman's body projects a parallel alternation between gender identities consistent with Duchamp's contemporaneous adoption of Rrose Sélavy as an alter ego.

46. Despite Duchamp's often vituperative condemnations of the commodification of art and his current postmodern reputation as the fountainhead of artistic practices that criticize or even condemn the museum and gallery system, his attitude toward the art market was not one of simple renunciation. Indeed he was highly sensitive to the relationship between an artist's career and financial speculation. In a 1952 letter to Jean Crotti he declared: "Artists of all times are like the gamblers of Monte Carlo, and this *blind* lottery allows some to succeed and ruins

others. In my opinion neither the winners nor the losers are worth worrying about. It's a good personal *deal* for the winner and a bad one for the loser. . . . Everything happens through pure luck. Artists who during their life time have known how to make their shoddy goods appreciated are excellent travelling salesman, but nothing guarantees the immortality of their work." Naumann, "Affectuesement, Marcel," 16–17. Despite his assertion that an artist's reputation may rise and fall like the fortunes of a gambler at roulette, Duchamp was not content to allow chance to rule his own career or those of his close friends. In working assiduously to shape the two foremost collections of his work, the Arensbergs' and Katherine Dreier's, he devoted enormous energy to making this "*blind* lottery" more like a game of chess. He was ultimately so successful in this venture that far from simply breaking even, as he had in his speculations at the roulette table in Monte Carlo, he earned the enormous dividend of a comprehensive presentation of his oeuvre in a major American museum. Duchamp understood that the museum and the art market were not about to disappear and that in order to accomplish anything an artist must take the exigencies of this institutional network into account. He realized that no one is offered a *choice* of whether to "buy in" to modernity or not—everyone is in it already.

47. Sanouillet and Peterson, *The Writings of Marcel Duchamp,* 31.

In interviews toward the end of his life, he often referred to himself as a "breather." In 1954 Michel Sanouillet asked, "What is your profession?" and he answered, "Why are you all for classifying people? What am I? Do I know? A man, quite simply, a 'breather.'" Marcel Duchamp interview by Michel Sanouillet in *Les Nouvelles Littéraires,* December 16, 1954, quoted in Gough-Cooper and Caumont, "Ephemerides," unpaginated [entry for December 16, 1954].

In 1957 he declared to another writer, "People always ask artists how they live. They don't have to live. They just breathe." Geoffrey Hellman, "Marcel Duchamp," *New Yorker,* April 6, 1957, 26.

And to William Seitz in 1963 he stated, with regard to the rising cost of living that had begun to make the kind of "bohemian" lifestyle of his own youth impossible: "Now the zero is too high. You can not afford to be a young man who doesn't do a thing. Who doesn't work? You can't live without working, which is a terrible thing. I remember a book called *The Right to Be Lazy:* that right doesn't exist now. You have to work to justify your breathing." William Seitz, "What's Happened to Art?," *Vogue* (February 1963), quoted in Gough-Cooper and Caumont, "Ephemerides," unpaginated [entry for February 15, 1963].

48. Duchamp described at length the function of "ventilation" in the bride, which might be understood as a mechanized form of breathing. He named it as one of four qualities of the "wasp" section of the bride and associated it with an "interior *draft*." Ibid., 45.

49. Ibid., 36.

50. Nancy Ring, *New York Dada and the Crisis of Masculinity: Man Ray, Francis Picabia, and Marcel Duchamp in the United States, 1913–1921* (Ann Arbor: UMI Research Press, 1993), 236.

51. Sanouillet and Peterson, *The Writings of Marcel Duchamp,* 30.

52. Naumann, "Affectueusement, Marcel," 17.

53. There has been a great deal of attention paid in recent years to the feminist nature of Duchamp's masquerade as Rrose Sélavy. Both Nancy Ring and Amelia Jones have argued that Duchamp's adoption of a feminine alter ego is a challenge to the stability and hegemony of masculine or patriarchal authority. While I am enthusiastically sympathetic to this point of view, I think these rather global claims on behalf of Duchamp's "feminization" have distorted the larger significance of this gesture in his work. Most importantly, a too-hasty generalization of Duchamp's masquerade tends to obscure the degree to which his "transformation" into a woman (which occurred only in photographs and text in the context of works of art, *never* as a "live performance") is part of a larger multiplication of identities characteristic of the works of the twenties (i.e., *Monte Carlo Bond* and *Wanted: $2,000 Reward*). There is also a somewhat conservative oedipal quality to Duchamp's division into male and female selves. As I have argued with regard to the *Monte Carlo Bond,* Rrose is placed in the position of mother (if also chairman of the board) within the traditional family triad. The "liberatory" notion of Rrose tends to underplay, if not completely ignore, the ways in which Duchamp's invention of a feminine alter ego allowed him to *perform* the sorts of onanistic standoffs and experiences of commodification that found more traditional iconographic expression in his cubism and *Large Glass* (see my discussion of *Fresh Widow* in chapter 3 and *Why Not Sneeze Rose Sélavy?* earlier in this chapter). By appearing as a woman, Duchamp could transpose his representations of virgin and bride into the spaces of everyday life, one of the major accomplishments of his art of the twenties. It is not clear to me that this change of site in any way releases Duchamp's art from what may be perceived as a misogynist attitude toward woman as caught within the optic

of successive forms of measurement. Both because of the recent books focusing on the Rrose Sélavy gesture and because, for my purposes, the more general function of masquerade in Duchamp's oeuvre is of greater relevance, I have omitted an extended discussion of it and instead refer the reader to Ring and Jones. See Ring, *New York Dada and the Crisis of Masculinity,* and Amelia Jones, *Postmodernism and the En-Gendering of Marcel Duchamp* (Cambridge: Cambridge University Press, 1994). See also my review of the latter, "Duchamp's Legacy," *Art in America* 82, no. 9 (September 1994): 35.

54. André Breton, *Mad Love (L'Amour fou),* trans. Mary Ann Caws (Lincoln: University of Nebraska Press, 1987), 32. Italics in original.

55. Hal Foster, *Compulsive Beauty* (Cambridge: MIT Press, 1993), 5.

56. This term is dangerous since, although Duchamp maintained a long friendship with Breton, who always supported his work, and although he collaborated frequently with surrealist exhibitions (actually designing two of them), he never was an official member of the group.

57. Sigmund Freud, *Beyond the Pleasure Principle,* trans. James Strachey (New York: W. W. Norton, 1961), 43.

58. In addition to Foster, *Compulsive Beauty,* one of the most notable of these is Leo Bersani, "Pleasures of Repetition," in *The Freudian Body: Psychoanalysis and Art* (New York: Columbia University Press, 1986), 51–78.

59. Freud, *Beyond the Pleasure Principle,* 46; italics in original.

60. Gough-Cooper and Caumont, "Ephemerides," unpaginated [entry for August 6, 1945].

61. Marcel Duchamp, interview by Richard Hamilton, *Monitor,* British Broadcasting Corporation, September 27, 1961, quoted in Gough-Cooper and Caumont, "Ephemerides," unpaginated [entry for September 27, 1961].

62. This complex edition has been exhaustively catalogued by Ecke Bonk in his book *Marcel Duchamp: The Box in a Valise.*

Between 1935 and 1940 Duchamp undertook the painstaking process of creating all of the sixty-nine reproductions for the *Boîte* edition of three hundred. Between 1941 and 1949 he produced a series of deluxe boxes, the only ones that technically carry the title *Boîte-en-valise,* versus simply *Boîte.* There were ultimately twenty-four of these deluxe works, twenty of which were numbered and four of which were *hors-série.* These deluxe works were contained in actual valises with handles (versus the boxes of later series), and each included an original work of art. In the first several this "original" was one of Duchamp's *coloriages originaux,* which served as proofs for the hand-colored reproductions of paintings and works on glass. Between 1941 and 1968 there were seven series of *Boîtes,* each slightly modified. The edition was only finished posthumously by Jacqueline Matisse Monnier, Teeny Duchamp's daughter, in 1971.

For a different account of the relationship between the *Boîtes* and the readymades, see Martha Buskirk, "Thoroughly Modern Marcel," in Martha Buskirk and Mignon Nixon, eds., *The Duchamp Effect: Essays, Interviews, Round Table* (Cambridge: MIT Press, 1996), 191–203.

63. Ibid., 154.

64. In an important article Moira Roth discusses Duchamp's various personas—ranging in her analysis from Dandy to Femme Fatale—as alternate manifestations of "a self ready-made." I have dwelled more on what I see as the readymade nature of psychic structures of selfhood, and their intersection with Duchamp's successive practices of the readymade. See Moira Roth, "Marcel Duchamp in America: A Self Ready-Made," *Arts Magazine* 51, no. 9 (May 1977): 92–96.

CONCLUSION

1. This would seem to parallel Freud's notion of the death drive, in which "*the aim of all life is death.*"

2. Peter Bürger's book *Theory of the Avant-Garde* was published in German in 1974 and translated into English in 1984. Building from Frankfurt School theorists like Theodor Adorno and Walter Benjamin, Bürger argues that the purpose of what he calls the historical avant-gardes—movements like dada and Soviet constructivism that emerge around World War I—was to challenge not simply the forms of art but the very social institutions within which art is pro-

duced and exhibited. If the art object had become no more than a specialized form of the commodity by the mid-teens and twenties, the purpose of avant-garde movements was to reveal this commodity status. Peter Bürger, *Theory of the Avant-Garde,* trans. Michael Shaw (Minneapolis: University of Minnesota Press, 1984).

3. Buchloh makes such an argument with regard to Bürger's assertion that originary avant-garde gestures are repeated in their various iterations by an inauthentic neo-avant-garde: "The word *genuinely* betrays Bürger's evaluation of the 'historical' avant-garde artists: they were original, while their postwar followers are imitators, recapitulators. The neo-avant-garde has copied and therefore falsified the original moment of rupture with the discursive practice and institutional system of modernism. While it is evident that Bürger's model of repetition is infinitely more complex than those which traditionally separate the unique, auratic original from the debased copy . . . it is also evident that Bürger's notion of the 'genuine' original versus the 'fraudulent' copy is still determined by the binary opposition ultimately deriving from the cult of the auratic original." Benjamin H. D. Buchloh, "The Primary Colors for the Second Time," *October,* no. 37 (Summer 1986): 42.

Index

Pages with figures are indicated in italics.

Made in United States
Troutdale, OR
08/19/2025

33781084R00146